THE
QUEEN'S STORY

Also by Denys Blakeway

The Falklands War
Fields of Thunder

THE
QUEEN'S STORY

MARCUS KIGGELL
AND DENYS BLAKEWAY

headline

First published in 2002
by HEADLINE BOOK PUBLISHING

10 9 8 7 6 5 4 3 2

Cataloguing in Publication Data is available from the British Library

ISBN 0 7553 1033 0

Text design by
Jane Coney

Typeset by Avon Dataset Ltd, Bidford-on-Avon, Warks

Printed and bound in Great Britain by
Mackays of Chatham plc, Chatham, Kent

HEADLINE BOOK PUBLISHING
A division of Hodder Headline
338 Euston Road
London NW1 3BH

www.headline.co.uk
www.hodderheadline.com

CONTENTS

ACNOWLEDGEMENTS

The authors are grateful to all the historians and biographers whose work has informed this book and the ITV series on which it is based. Sarah Bradford and Ben Pimlott in particular have written about the Queen with great authority and insight and *The Queen's Story* has been greatly helped both by their published works and by the interviews that the production team recorded with them. A great debt is also owed to the many friends, relations and employees of the Queen who agreed to take part in the TV series and whose testimony forms the backbone of this book as well as to the documentary-makers who carried out the interviews and assembled all the material. Leonie Jameson, as series producer, made an immense contribution, and deserves special thanks. So too do Melissa FitzGerald (assistant producer) and Tessa Reading (researcher) who assiduously trawled the many archives and provided key back-up at every stage; and Christine Carter (consultant producer) who helped arrange the interviews.

CHAPTER ONE

'It almost frightens me that the people should love
Elizabeth so much. I suppose it is a good thing and
I hope she will be worthy of it, poor little darling.'
Duchess of York to Queen Mary

On 2 June 1953, Elizabeth was quite relaxed as she made
ready at Buckingham Palace. It was the day of her
Coronation. Earlier that morning, as Prince Philip told his
friend Michael Hobbs, 'the Queen and I were lying in bed and someone
came in with a telegram – they'd climbed Everest. So the day started
well.'

Since 9am, visiting heads of state, royal relations and foreign
dignitaries had left in open coaches from the Palace courtyard, while
inside the Queen showed off her dress, stiff with jewels and the

embroidered emblems of the Crown, to her maids and ladies-in-waiting. Whatever nervousness she felt was hidden with characteristic self-discipline. 'I think the apprehension of what was happening was very disturbing to her,' says John Taylor, one of the royal footmen who later that day would walk beside the Coronation coach. 'But once the Queen gets to do anything, it just goes like clockwork. She makes up her mind that if it's going to be done then it will be done.'

At around 10.30am, she left Buckingham Palace in the Gold State Coach, Philip at her side, to ride to the Abbey. Charles and Anne, who were thought too young to sit through the whole service, watched from an upstairs window as their mother set off to be crowned. 'We walked out into this tremendous throng of people,' recalls Taylor, 'and the noise was absolutely incredible.'

Like the whole of Elizabeth's reign, her Coronation was a mixture of the sublime and the prosaic. Half a million people lined the route to the Abbey, among them the recently married Margaret Thatcher. 'Denis and I decided to splash out on buying two seats round Parliament Square,' she recalls, 'so we were in those seats and watching with great interest and talking to everyone around. And I remember the thrill as the Queen came past and you really did feel that a new era had begun. We had no doubts about it, strangely enough.' The people in the royal procession were bothered by less lofty thoughts, though. Elizabeth herself was worried that the Archbishop of Canterbury might put her crown on back-to-front, and travelling behind the Queen was Lady Rayne – one of her maids-of-honour – who was almost overcome by the clapping and cheering crowds that lined the way. 'We were quite hungry,' she remembers, 'and I said something about "Oh, it seems such a long time since breakfast," and this lovely man called Lord Tryon – he was the Keeper of the Privy Purse, and the Privy Purses were beautiful oblong-shaped velvet bags, with wonderful gold embroidery – and he sort of slipped his hand inside and brought out these wonderful toffees and sweets and all kinds of things. I couldn't believe it. I thought the Privy Purse was so sacred, but it was very, very welcome and we all gobbled them down. That kept us going for the morning.'

Given what was to follow, Elizabeth had arrived in the world in April 1926 with surprisingly little fanfare. The announcement in the *Daily Mail* took up just half a column, tucked away on an inside page dominated by the looming coalminers' strike and well below news of the civil war in China and Ramsay MacDonald's struggle for supremacy within the Labour Party. She was born at 17 Bruton Street, the London house belonging to her mother's parents, the Earl and Countess of Strathmore. Her father was the Duke of York, second son of King George V, which made Elizabeth only third in line to the throne after her father and his elder brother, the Prince of Wales.

Elizabeth's was not expected to be a particularly prominent role in the royal drama; even being third-in-line seemed like a temporary position. The Prince of Wales was still unmarried; he still had not met Wallis Simpson; he remained popular, handsome and charming; and there was little reason to think that he would not continue the dynasty with children of his own. The Abdication was still ten years away, and in 1926 nobody expected either that the Duke of York would become King, or that Elizabeth would ever succeed him as Queen. It was, as one of Elizabeth's cousins, Lady Clayton, recalls, delightful that the Yorks had had a little girl. But it was no more than that.

The family into which she was born was an odd one. At its head stood the forbidding figure of King George V. In his sixties at the time of Elizabeth's birth, the King was a man who appeared incapable of showing any form of outward affection. By 1926, he had been on the throne for sixteen years. Before that he had been in the Royal Navy and, whether on the quarterdeck or at Court, he was used to having authority and used to exercising it. From a child's point of view, the King seemed to spend most of his time telling people not to do things – not to sit on that chair, not to feed that parrot, not to run in that corridor. 'He had a very gruff manner,' remembers his eldest grandchild, the Earl of Harewood. 'I think he liked the idea that he was frightening.' Taken to visit his grandfather at Windsor one April, Harewood was unlucky enough to succumb to an early dose of hayfever and sneezed in front of the King, who immediately shouted, 'Get that bloody child out of here! He's going to give me a cold!'

The King was just as strict and domineering with adults. He conducted a long war of attrition with his eldest son, David, the Prince of Wales, over whether or not it was appropriate to wear trousers with turn-ups (the King thought not), while the Duke of York maintained cordial relations with his father only by adopting an attitude of almost complete servility. 'You have always been so sensible and easy to work with,' the King once wrote to Elizabeth's father, 'and you have always been ready to listen to any advice and to agree with my opinions about people and things, that I feel we have always got on very well together (very different to dear David).' Elizabeth's mother, the Duchess of York, once referred to the King as 'a tyrant' and being anywhere near him made everyone feel as though they had to stand to attention – which on the whole they did. Sir Owen Morshead, Royal Librarian to George V, took a dim view of the Royal Family's home life, noting that 'the House of Hanover, like ducks, produce bad parents; they trample their young'.[1]

George's wife, Queen Mary, was an equally imposing figure. 'She was a very, very regal lady,' recalls John Taylor, one of the Yorks' footmen. 'She could be quite charming, actually, but invariably she was very abrupt.' Her public image and dress reflected the formality and grandeur of a bygone age. Walking or sitting, she carried herself bolt-upright and even in the late 1920s, she wore the fashions of a decade earlier, with her trademark *toque* hat and veil, long dress, formal gloves, and glittering strands of pearls or diamonds. (She later gave her magnificent tiara and earrings to Elizabeth as a wedding gift. Elizabeth in turn presented them to Lady Diana Spencer in 1981.)

Queen Mary restricted her public utterances to naming ships or opening railway stations and heartily disapproved of the idea that members of the Royal Family should ever unbend enough to make speeches in public. 'We in our position have often to avoid answering indiscreet questions,' she once told the diarist Harold Nicolson. 'I remember that I once had a lady-in-waiting who was a fool and used to ask indiscreet questions of my husband in the motor-car. He always answered exactly what he thought. I had to get rid of the woman.'

Queen Mary did, though, have one rather odd quirk of character. When she visited friends they were expected to present her with anything around the house that she particularly admired – a habit which created understandable nervousness in her aristocratic hosts, as they wondered on which of their prized possessions the royal eye might fall next. At the age of sixteen, Lady Rayne – who would later be one of Elizabeth's maids-of-honour at her Coronation – was once taken to tea with Queen Mary at her great-aunt's and expected the house to be completely emptied of possessions by the end of the afternoon. On that occasion the Queen restrained herself, but such was the atmosphere of reverence at the Court that it does not seem to have occurred to Mary to refuse such gifts. Nor, it seems, could her friends restrain themselves from offering them.

Queen Mary may have been widely admired and respected, but the emotional temperature of the Court was icy. Her marriage to George V was an arranged one and, although they did come to love one another, they both remained unable to express their affection either in public or face to face. While they were still engaged, Mary wrote to George, 'I am very sorry that I am still so shy with you, I tried not to be so the other day but alas failed! I was angry with myself! It is stupid to be so stiff together & really there is nothing I would not tell you, except that I *love* you more than anybody in the world & this I cannot tell you myself, so I write it to relieve my feelings.' George poignantly replied in kind: 'Thank God we both understand each other & I think it really unnecessary for me to tell you how deep my love for you my darling is & I feel it growing stronger and stronger every time I see you: although I may appear shy and cold . . .'[2] Even in an age which placed more emphasis on controlling personal emotions rather than displaying them – let alone allowing oneself to be led by them – the court of King George and Queen Mary was a straitlaced, repressive environment.

It was in this environment that Elizabeth spent much of her early childhood. The Yorks themselves were overjoyed with their new baby, but Elizabeth's father was characteristically apprehensive about the reaction of the King and Queen. 'We always wanted a child to make our happiness complete,' the duke wrote to his mother. 'I do hope that you and Papa are as delighted as we are, to have a granddaughter, or would you sooner have a grandson?' The Duchess of York herself had always wanted a daughter, and any fears she may have had about the disapproval of her in-laws were laid to rest when Queen Mary came to visit. Upright, stiff and formal, the Queen declared the infant princess to be 'a little darling, with lovely complexion and pretty fair hair'. It was just as well that the King and Queen approved, for when Elizabeth was just eight months old, her parents left her behind with her grandparents in January 1927 while they went on a six-month tour of Fiji, New Zealand and Australia.

The Duchess of York was far from happy at the idea of leaving her daughter behind, confessing to Queen Mary 'that it quite broke me up'.) Such long absences were par for the royal course, however, and there was no question of either refusing to go, or of taking the infant Elizabeth with them. Not for another fifty-seven years, when the Prince and Princess of Wales insisted that Prince William accompany them to Australia in 1982, would a royal baby accompany its parents on an official tour.

For one thing, what with nursery maids, nannies, governesses and – for the Royal Family at least – nursery footmen, there existed in 1927 a vast apparatus that was specially designed to limit parents' exposure to their children and that was widely accepted as normal among the upper and middle classes. In addition, the simple act of travelling anywhere, let alone getting to Australia, was far more laborious and time-consuming than it is now. Commercial flights were still a rarity and only available on short-haul routes. It took twelve weeks at sea before the Yorks' Australian tour even started.

Nonetheless – and perhaps partly because the monarchy of George V had such a gruff and forbidding image – when the new parents *did* arrive they found that Elizabeth was the absent star of the trip. She may not have been there in person, but the mere idea of the baby princess seemed to provide a more human, sympathetic aspect of the Royal Family to which the public could relate more easily than they could to the distant King-Emperor. 'Wherever we go,' the duke wrote to his parents, 'cheers are given for her as well and the children write to us about her.' On their return to London in June the following year, they arrived with three tons of presents for Elizabeth from members of the public.

In the absence of her parents, Elizabeth had fared a lot better than might have been expected. The King and Queen had never been very accomplished at handling their own offspring and did not usually seem

keen on dealing with children of any description. Yet they took a shine
to their latest grandchild. She stayed at Buckingham Palace and every
afternoon, when she was brought down to have tea with George and
Mary, her appearance was invariably greeted by the Queen's delighted
cry, 'Here comes the Bambino!'[3] The King took an almost paternal
pride in keeping Elizabeth's real parents up to date with their daughter's
progress – 'She has four teeth now, which is quite good at eleven
months,' he wrote to the Yorks in March 1927. 'She is very happy and
drives in a carriage every afternoon, which amuses her' – and for her
part, perhaps because she was so much younger, perhaps because she
was a girl, Elizabeth found George V far less intimidating than her
cousins did.

When she was a little older, she would even prevail upon the man
who so scared the rest of his family to play with her. One day the King
was found on his hands and knees pretending to be a horse, being led
around his study by an excited Elizabeth, tugging on his beard and
urging the man she called 'Grandpa England' to go faster. Yet formality
was never completely forgotten: when it was time to say goodnight,
Elizabeth would walk backwards towards the door, before curtseying
to her grandfather and politely saying, 'I trust Your Majesty will sleep
well.'[4] But the fact that the King enjoyed her company at all was
extraordinary. That he played with her was startling.

* * *

After six months away, Elizabeth's parents returned to England in June
1927. Elizabeth's childhood home in London now became No. 145
Piccadilly, a five-storey house at the Hyde Park end of the street. Later
destroyed during the war, it had twenty-five bedrooms and a staff that
included a butler, a cook, a housekeeper and several valets. For all its
size and grandeur, it was more a family home than a palace and Percy
Benham – one of the footmen who worked there from February 1934 –

was struck by the light, cheerful atmosphere (not something that anyone was used to finding in other royal houses). The Yorks seldom entertained, but usually ate quietly in the dining room on their own, and their tranquil, happy way of life was in marked contrast to the racier, more fashionable style of the Prince of Wales and his set. While the Duke of York's elder brother was out charming his way through London society, Elizabeth's parents, once the children had been put to bed, would spend their evenings sitting on either side of the fireplace, talking or reading or, in the duke's case, relaxing with some *petit point*. It helped a great deal, and was remarked upon by those who saw them regularly, that they were very much in love.

In 1930 they had a second daughter, Margaret Rose. The care of both girls was at first entrusted to a nanny – Clara Knight. Known as 'Alla' – the childish version of her Christian name – Clara Knight had worked first for the Strathmore family (Elizabeth's maternal grandparents). As Margaret Rhodes, one of Elizabeth's cousins, recalls, she was 'quite a strong disciplinarian but wonderfully huggable and cosy and delicious'. She was assisted by the footman, Percy Benham, one of whose duties was to clean and polish the royal prams after the children had been taken out. They would be inspected every morning to make sure they were sufficiently bright and shiny.

The Duke of York – who always referred to his family as 'us four' – had long dreamed of creating a perfectly happy, enclosed world for his wife and children and, in the early years, Elizabeth's life came fairly close to this ideal. During the week, while they were in London, Elizabeth and Margaret would be taken out for walks in the park, or they would play on the grand staircase with Percy Benham, who gave them rides down the lower flights of steps on an old enamel butler's tray. At weekends, the York household would move to Royal Lodge, a house on the Windsor estate. It seemed to Elizabeth's governess, Marion

Crawford, an impressionable young Scotswoman who joined the household in 1933, as though it was always spring while the Yorks had a house of their own. This was an achievement all the more remarkable given the extraordinary economic conditions the rest of the country was suffering.

At the end of 1929 the US stockmarket had crashed. After a two-year speculative boom, 132 million shares were sold in a spiral of panic that wiped $30 billion off the value of Wall Street shares. At this time, only ten years after the end of the First World War, European industry still depended heavily on American loans. When these were called in by desperate US banks, the Great Depression spread to Europe. In Germany it created the economic conditions that helped to destroy the Weimar Republic. In Britain, as Bill Deedes, then a young journalist, remembers, 'it was the lowest period of day-to-day living that I remember in my lifetime – lower even than the second part of the war, when there was rationing and all sorts of stringency. We had three million unemployed, on a much smaller workforce than we've got today, so that now it would be nearer four or five million.' Privately, some politicians worried that the economic situation was so serious that it would lead to the breakdown of the whole democratic system.[5] In the areas of the country where people were worst affected – in the mines, the factories and the dockyards – there were families who had been out of work for two generations.

None of this touched Elizabeth. She was, of course, too young to take any real interest in the outside world, but it is a measure of the extraordinary isolation in which she was brought up that no hint of the country's troubles seems to have penetrated the walls of 145 Piccadilly. Her father, along with other senior members of the Royal Family, may have taken a keen interest in alleviating the effects of the Depression, but Elizabeth was not so much cocooned from reality as divorced from it. In 1932, when the country's mining communities were still enduring the worst deprivation and hopelessness that Britain would see for the whole of the twentieth century, Elizabeth received 'The Little House' (Y Bwthyn Bach) as a gift from 'the people of Wales' for her sixth birthday.

Two-thirds the size of a real cottage, the Little House was a perfect scale model of a working-class home and was Elizabeth's favourite toy. It was installed in the grounds of Windsor, and Margaret Rhodes, who used to play there with the two princesses, remembers it as 'a wonderful little thatched-roof two-up and two-down cottage. Everything in it was miniature. It was perfect. It had a little four-poster bed, it had a bath and it had a wonderful kitchen with a cooker and a mangle – that was before the days of clothes washers – and armchairs and sofas and everything was little-child size. You could pretend you were cooking the dinner and having people to tea. One could play in it absolutely endlessly. It was wonderful.' Hot water came out of the taps, there was a heated towel-rail in the bathroom, a working radio and even a miniature portrait of the Duchess of York over the mantelpiece.

When she was in Scotland, staying either at Balmoral with the King and Queen or at Glamis Castle with the Duchess of York's parents, Elizabeth's childhood was equally carefree. Margaret Rhodes and other childhood friends remember it as a time of unspoiled innocence. In the autumn, Elizabeth and her cousins would play Happy Days, trying to catch the leaves as they blew off the trees: every leaf they caught meant an extra day of happiness later in life. At other times, one of the nursery maids might teach them Highland dancing on the lawns of Balmoral, take them on picnics or let them ride the pony that a doting George V had given Elizabeth for her fourth birthday.

Between teatime and bedtime there would be games of Kick the Tin involving both princesses, their parents and any visiting dignitaries who could be roped in, as well as the Strathmore cousins. 'You had to kick the tin as far away as you could,' Margaret Rhodes recalls, 'and in the interim you had to rush and hide and then, when you had hidden, the person who was It had to find you and then you had to race back. I wish you could have seen the rather grand visiting people who were made to tear round the rhododendron bushes chasing very small girls. It must have surprised them enormously.'

It was a happy childhood, but also an extremely protected one. Although Elizabeth's parents wanted her to enjoy a normal childhood, life at 145 Piccadilly was both socially privileged and emotionally isolated. The Duke of York was a shy man who was not particularly sociable, and he saw his family as something to be carefully tucked away. The world outside – even the upper-class world of Britain in the 1930s – was to be resisted rather than embraced. Elizabeth's mother had a more outward-looking, relaxed approach to life, but it was her father's reserved seriousness that Elizabeth inherited.

Even without her father's emotional influence – both sustaining and limiting – the constraint and deference surrounding the Royal Family at every turn inevitably had its effect. After all, not many children were brought up in a house with twenty-five bedrooms. And the royal nanny, Clara Knight – who was, in the opinion of Elizabeth's governess Marion Crawford, a good deal more regal than either of her employers – had decided opinions about how princesses should act. When Elizabeth and Margaret were taken out for walks in London by Mrs Knight, they would notice other children playing on swings and wonder why they were not allowed to do the same. 'Other children,' remembered Crawford, 'had an enormous fascination, like mystic beings from a different world and the little girls used to smile shyly at those they liked the look of. They would so have loved to speak to them and make friends, but this was never encouraged.' Driving or walking sedately through the London parks, members of the public would wave to the royal children, but their nanny instructed Elizabeth not to wave back. The reason for all these restrictions, Elizabeth was told, was simple: 'Because you are a Royal Highness.'

In a way that is almost impossible to imagine now, royalty were a class apart, and the few children Elizabeth did play with, like Margaret Rhodes and Mary Clayton, were usually aristocratic cousins. Accord/ing to Marion Crawford's account, Elizabeth had not even been allowed to get dirty until the arrival of the new governess and her more relaxed regime in 1933, and by then it was almost too late. By the time Elizabeth did get to play Red Indians in the shrubbery of nearby Hamilton Gardens, she was so used to her special status and so caught up in her own world of make/believe that she did not even notice the lines of curious faces peering in at her from the public side of the railings.

Make/believe is part of most childhoods, but Elizabeth's fantasy world was particularly elaborate and characteristically disciplined. The idea of having something of her own to look after struck a particular chord, and Elizabeth took great pleasure in doing her own cleaning and dusting in the Little House. Whenever the York household moved back to London, Elizabeth would copy what the adults were doing, putting away all the blankets and linen, covering the furniture in dust sheets and even wrapping the silver up in newspapers – 'to prevent it from getting tarnished', as she explained to her governess. Above all, Elizabeth's childish world of make/believe centred on horses, of which there were thirty toy ones, each about a foot high and mounted on wheels. They were kept on the top floor of 145 Piccadilly and had their own saddles and bridles, which the princesses carefully kept in immacu/late condition. Every night, Elizabeth would unsaddle each one and then pretend to feed and water it from tiny buckets.

Real horses were, of course, objects of intense interest to both children. A pair of brewer's drayhorses would regularly pull up at the traffic lights just below the nursery window overlooking Piccadilly and every night Elizabeth and Margaret would watch for them, their faces pressed up against the window, growing anxious if they were late. Marion Crawford records that, while watching the riding school horses turn and turn wearily about along Rotten Row, Elizabeth made an early resolution that 'if ever I am Queen, I shall make a law that there must be no riding on Sundays. Horses should have a rest too. And I shan't let anyone dock their pony's tail.'

In the absence of real horses or her toys, humans had to do. Margaret Rhodes, who often found herself roped into her cousin's games, recalls that 'horses came into it a great deal and one played at being a circus horse, or being a horse in a stable being looked after by someone else. I can remember having to prance around being a circus horse. I wasn't that keen on horses myself, but they figured large in the enjoyment of life.' One of Elizabeth's favourite games with her governess was to harness her with a pair of red reins and pretend to go off delivering groceries. 'Sometimes,' Crawford wrote, 'she would whisper to me, "Crawfie, you must pretend to be impatient. Paw the ground a bit." So I would paw. Frosty mornings were wonderful, for then my breath came in clouds, "just like a proper horse," said Lilibet contentedly. Or she herself would be the horse, prancing around, sidling up to me, nosing in my pockets for sugar, making convincing little whinnying noises.'

Horses aside, it was Margaret who was the more high-spirited of the sisters – and the one most able to charm her way out of trouble. As Margaret Rhodes noticed, 'The Queen was always the more serious of the two. Princess Margaret could always manage to make her parents laugh, especially if she was in the smallest danger of being reprimanded. She would make wonderful jokes and everybody would then forget about the reprimand.'

Elizabeth was much graver, and even when she did misbehave she did so with a peculiar mixture of childish candour and adult gravitas. On one occasion, when one of the royal chaplains came to tea with her mother, he asked Elizabeth whether he could go and see Margaret, still a baby. 'No,' Elizabeth replied, 'because I think she'll be frightened of your teeth.' Another time, when the Archbishop of Canterbury asked her if she would like to walk with him in the garden at Sandringham, Elizabeth answered, 'Yes, very much. But please do not tell me anything more about God. I know all about him already.'[6] Once, during a French lesson, she picked up a big inkpot that stood in the schoolroom and emptied it over her head. But this one example of childish misbehaviour seems more indicative of speechless boredom than the tomboyish love of fooling around to which her sister was prone.

Above all, Elizabeth preferred to avoid trouble – either with her parents or with her sister. In a saccharine biography, *The Story of Princess Elizabeth and Princess Margaret*, written by Anne Ring in 1930 – and reprinted four times within two years – she was portrayed as supernaturally well-behaved. When Elizabeth had to go to bed, readers learned, 'there are no poutings or protests, just a few joyous skips and impromptu dance steps, a few last-minute laughs at Mummy's delicious bedtime jokes and then Princess Elizabeth's hand slips into her nurse's hand and the two go off gaily together across the deep chestnut pile of the hall carpet to the accommodating lift, which in two seconds has whisked them off to the familiar dear domain, which is theirs to hold and share'.

This book was an obvious piece of propaganda intended to boost the homely, wholesome image of the Royal Family (Wallis Simpson, Elizabeth's aunt-by-marriage, sourly observed that the young princess was becoming a bigger star than Shirley Temple). But the picture it painted of Elizabeth the Good had more than a kernel of truth. She never liked arguments, never liked rows and hated noise: if ever there was a dispute with Margaret, Elizabeth would give in just to keep the peace. One of her earliest characteristics was a desire to keep things on an even keel and she approached all of life's problems like a particularly serious head prefect – a trait that would remain deeply ingrained for the rest of her life. Her governess recalled how 'Sometimes she would say to me, in her funny responsible manner, "I really don't know what we are going to do with Margaret, Crawfie," and go on to tell me of something she had been up to.' Going down to a garden party at Buckingham Palace, Marion Crawford overheard Elizabeth telling her sister, 'If you see someone with a funny hat, Margaret, you must *not* point at it and laugh and you must *not* be in too much of a hurry to get through the crowds to the tea table. That's not polite either.'

Elizabeth's isolation was increased by the plans her parents had for her education. Twenty years earlier, at the turn of the century, it had been the normal destiny of upper-class girls to be educated at home by a governess – often not particularly well – before being launched into Society, marrying early and subjecting their own daughters to the same limiting round. By the 1920s and 1930s the pattern was beginning to change. Women had been granted the vote in 1918 and there was a growing realisation at every level of society (though perhaps more so for the middle classes, and less so for the very rich or very poor) that women's horizons could and should be expanded. Many aristocratic girls were still educated at home, but more and more were being sent to boarding school where they could get a decent education. Elizabeth, however, was not one of them.

The Duchess of York took an old-fashioned view of girls' upbringing and Marion Crawford remembers her explaining simply that 'we want our children to have a happy childhood which they can always look back on'. She and the Duke were not overly concerned about higher education, nor about the benefits that mixing regularly with her contemporaries might offer Elizabeth. Considering the miserable time the duke had as a child at naval college (like his own father and grandfather), it was perhaps in royal terms a humane and rather revolutionary approach: better to run about catching leaves and playing Happy Days than be terrorised by your parents and private tutors and still not come out of it all that well educated anyway. It was not, on the other hand, an approach designed to help a naturally shy and withdrawn child to come out of her shell. Even though nobody at first expected Elizabeth to become Queen, this almost complete exclusion of the outside world was a strange preparation for any child's life.

Luckily for Elizabeth, her grandparents and governess all agreed that she must have a more rigorous education than that envisaged by her parents. George V, meeting Marion Crawford for the first time, boomed, 'For goodness' sake, teach Margaret and Lilibet to write a decent hand, that's all I ask you. Not one of my children can write properly. They all do it exactly the same way. I like a hand with a bit of character in it.' Queen Mary, on the other hand, was not impressed by the narrowness of the princesses' education, nor by its lack of depth. She demanded that Elizabeth read 'the best type of children's books' and dreamed up instructive excursions for her that would at least get her out of the schoolroom.

When the children's governess went on holiday the Queen sternly told her, 'What a waste of time when you go away for holidays and the French lessons have to stop. They have the whole holidays and no language study at all. When I was a child I kept up my French and German and had a certain amount of holiday work to do.' The daughter of Queen Mary's own French teacher, Georgina Guérin, was accordingly drafted in to maintain momentum over the summer break.

Mary's influence even extended to the drafting of Elizabeth's school timetable. After tactfully complimenting the governess on the ingenuity of the original curriculum and on how many subjects were covered, Marion Crawford recounts how the Queen gave her a series of 'suggestions' on how it might be tightened up and improved. There was, for instance, not nearly enough history and Bible reading, while some arithmetic, she argued, could surely be sacrificed, given that Elizabeth was never going to have to do her own household accounts. Old-fashioned geography, the Queen agreed, was 'hopelessly out of date', but that should not preclude a detailed knowledge of the physical geography of the British Dominions and of India. As for poetry – did the princesses ever learn it by heart? It was, perhaps, rather an old-fashioned practice and was, in the Queen's opinion, often overdone. 'But was not a little of it rather wonderful memory training, and would it not help "get through" a good deal of first-rate interesting stuff which otherwise they might never read?' In addition, 'Her Majesty felt that genealogies, historical and dynastic, were very interesting to children and, for these children, really important.'

Marion Crawford adjusted the timetable accordingly: each week, in the mornings, Elizabeth would spend two and a half hours on poetry, literature and grammar, half an hour on the Bible, two hours each on history and arithmetic and half an hour on geography. At lunchtime, she would spend an hour reading and in the afternoons there would be dancing, drawing and music lessons. With just over twelve hours classroom teaching each week, it was not an exacting regime but it was considerably more tuition than the princess would have got without the intervention of the Queen and the arrival of Marion Crawford.

Aware of the children's extraordinary isolation, Crawford's other achievement – in which she was also supported by Queen Mary – was to bring Elizabeth and Margaret into greater contact with the outside world. To members of the public, then as now, life behind palace doors seemed endlessly fascinating, but for the young princesses, their lives a careful round of royal residences from London to Windsor to Balmoral, it was other people who appeared strange and intriguing. As she walked past Hyde Park Corner one day, Elizabeth said wistfully, 'Oh dear, what fun it must be to ride in those trains.'

Crawford accordingly got permission from the Duke of York to take the princesses on the Underground and it was a trip which seemed to the children like a visit to another world. They were able to buy their own tickets and collect their own change, which they did very slowly and very solemnly. On an earlier expedition, Crawford had taken them to Woolworths and had had to explain what the various coin denominations were and how they were used. Crawford's niece, Linda Cunniffe, remembers her aunt telling her, 'They were really fascinated by money. They didn't know what it was. They didn't know pennies and half-a-crown and a florin, they didn't know that at all.' Slightly apprehensive, they travelled on the escalators for the first time. Once they had got to Tottenham Court Road and sat down in a café, they were even able to buy their own tea and get shouted at by the waitress for leaving the teapot behind at the counter.

Crawford also took the princesses on buses, to art galleries and the Serpentine and, wherever possible, to places of historical interest that they were covering in the schoolroom. Above all, she encouraged independence of mind. As her niece, Linda Cunniffe recalls, if you were wondering what to do about anything, she would not tell you the answer. Instead, she would present various options and leave you to make up your own mind.

The closer you were to the throne, though, the less room there was for independence of mind or action. The arrival of Marion Crawford and the intervention of Queen Mary may have broadened Elizabeth's horizons somewhat, but the Queen's interest in Elizabeth stemmed not just from kindness; there were dynastic and political reasons as well. As long as Elizabeth's uncle, the Prince of Wales, remained in play as the King's heir, Elizabeth was relatively safe from the royal juggernaut. But by the mid-1930s, as Elizabeth was approaching her tenth birthday, the situation became confused.

George V was ill and the Prince of Wales was turning out to be something of a liability. There were increasing doubts in royal circles about his suitability as King and even greater worries about how long – if he ever got there – he might remain on the throne. If Elizabeth's uncle – who was still unmarried – did take himself out of the running, then Elizabeth's father would become King and Elizabeth would be next in line. As long as Elizabeth was in a position similar to that of the present Duke of York's children (which she was at birth and for most of her first ten years), nobody at Court or in the Government minded terribly what happened to her. Once she became the next heir-but-one, as Prince William is today, her private life and upbringing became everyone's concern.

The heart of the problem was that Elizabeth's uncle, the Prince of Wales, did not particularly want to be King. Indeed, he was thoroughly bored by the rituals and duties of kingship. 'I want no more of this Princing!' he once exclaimed. 'I want to be an ordinary person. I must have a life of my own . . . What does it take to be a good King? You must be a figurehead, a wooden man! Do nothing to upset the Prime Minister or the Court or the Archbishop of Canterbury! Show yourself to the people! Mind your manners! Go to church! What modern man wants that kind of life?'[7] The obvious answer was that nobody did, least of all his brother and his niece, who had the most to lose from his truculence. With his impatience of duty and his insistence on personal happiness, the Prince of Wales was the antithesis of all that Elizabeth was and would be. His horror of the royal straitjacket is, to modern eyes, more than understandable; but his refusal to wear it only ensured that it fitted all the more snugly around Elizabeth when her turn came.

The prince had, at first, looked rather a promising heir. He had great star quality, and when he was sent off on a royal tour of Canada and the United States he performed to sensational effect. He liked the limelight, he had a great ability to deal with crowds and he was equally charming face-to-face. Unlike his father – and his stammering brother – he was good at making off-the-cuff speeches. But he also had a taste for enjoying life that was quite at odds with the severe ethos of George V and Queen Mary. While the prince was in the United States, one of his entourage wrote to the King, telling him that 'I'm also to arrange one or two dances. This is really very important in its way, for it'll enable HRH to meet official Washington with its wives and daughters in a less formal way. The prince very strongly holds that he can influence American feeling even better by dancing with senators' daughters than by talking to senators. And I'm sure he's right.'

The Court was less sure. Its unease was heightened by the fact that, within his own circles, the Prince of Wales made no secret of his weakness for attractive women or of the fact that he often slept with them. If that had been the whole extent of the problem then perhaps the prince and the Court might have been able to reach an accommodation: Edward VII, after all, had kept a mistress (Alice Keppel, the great-grandmother of the current Prince of Wales's friend, Camilla Parker Bowles) and as long as matters were conducted discreetly then there could be some leeway for royal bad behaviour. The Prince of Wales, however, was not especially discreet as a young man and when he did set his heart on one woman in particular, he made a catastrophic choice.

Elizabeth's uncle met Wallis Simpson in March 1934. She was a clever, sharp-witted American which did not endear her to George V or his courtiers. She also had the Prince of Wales entirely under her thumb. He showered her with presents (after her death, Wallis Simpson's personal jewellery, nearly all of which had been given to her by the prince, was auctioned for over £31 million) and was happy to display his slavish devotion to her for all to see. Worst of all, Mrs Simpson was married to one man and had already divorced a previous husband. It was this last fact which put her beyond the pale: while adultery could be winked at in the 1920s, divorce was utterly unacceptable. In George V's view, the main role of the Royal Family was to provide a moral example for the rest of the nation, and the notion that his eldest son might be infatuated with an American divorcée was anathema to him. As long as George was alive, the Prince of Wales claimed that his relationship with Mrs Simpson was simply one of friendship. It was a lie that could just about be sustained as long as the prince remained a prince. Once he became King, it could not.

George V died on 20 January 1936. The day before, at 9.25pm, the Palace had issued a warning bulletin – 'The King's life is moving peacefully towards its close' – and both the Duke of York and the Prince of Wales had immediately flown to Sandringham to be with their father at the end. Elizabeth, nearly ten years old, had stayed in London. She took the news in her stride and with a telling concern for the correct forms. According to Marion Crawford, 'Lilibet in her sensitive fashion felt it all deeply. It was very touching to see how hard she tried to do what she felt was expected of her. I remember her pausing doubtfully as she groomed one of the toy horses and looking up at me for a moment. "Oh, Crawfie . . . ought we to play?" ' The grooming of the toy horses went on, though in rather muted fashion. While her parents were out preparing for the funeral, Elizabeth and Margaret stayed at home, playing endless games of noughts and crosses. When Elizabeth was eventually taken to see the King's lying-in-state, she seemed as much struck by the spectacle as by its meaning. 'Uncle David was there,' she told her governess, 'and he never moved at all. Not even an eyelid. It was wonderful. And everyone was so quiet. As if the King were asleep.'

At the funeral itself, Elizabeth played more noughts and crosses as she waited in the stationmaster's office at Paddington for the cortège to arrive (the King's body was to be buried at Windsor) and there was a moment, as her grandfather's coffin wheeled into sight, when it seemed as though Elizabeth might lose control, her face quivering with emotion. But she was distracted by a sailor who fainted in the procession below but who was nonetheless kept upright by the other men marching on either side of him. It was a demonstration of strength overcoming weakness that entranced the young princess and enabled her to get through her own moment of sadness.

The new King, Edward VIII, was not long on the throne. To the dismay of all around him, Edward continued his liaison with Wallis Simpson, who seemed to revel in the power of her new position. She behaved as if she were already married to Edward, and airily announced her plans to redecorate Balmoral Castle, whose tartan furnishings had remained untouched since the time of Queen Victoria. She was loathed by the royal servants, among them Percy Benham, Elizabeth's nursery footman. He recalls: 'The boys at the Palace called her "the Cobra". I only saw her once, and, from what I saw, it was like an oil painting, dubbed over with all different exotic colours. In other words, it was something we were not used to. I didn't understand what make-up was, but I knew it was sickening to look at and that's why I think she was detested by many. She was a scrawny, painted thing. She should have been put in Madame Tussaud's.'

The contrast between the exotic Mrs Simpson and the homely Duchess of York was particularly noted, even in such small things as drinks. 'Mrs Simpson was kind of domineering. Drink-wise, everything had to be American cocktails. Not like the present Queen today or, bless her, Queen Elizabeth the Queen Mother, who would have a little martini.' Under the new regime, 'exotic' drinks were the order of the day.

Wallis Simpson's real faults, of course, lay not in her make-up or her taste in *aperitifs*. Rather, they lay in the fact that she represented modernity and change. The footmen and the rest of the staff hated her because they thought, probably correctly, that they would all be sacked once she became Queen. Edward's relatives hated her for similar reasons: not having jobs to start with, they had no fear of the sack, but they did fear change and they knew that Wallis was pushy and wanted to refashion the Court in her own image. She was not dutiful and her influence on Edward VIII, it was feared, would make him even less biddable. Then as now, a willingness to knuckle under was one of the main characteristics the Court and Government looked for in the sovereign.

More important than all these reservations, however, was the moral objection to letting the King marry a divorced woman. Britain's Government would not stand for it and neither would the Dominion Governments of Canada, Australia and South Africa. It was not a subject on which the majority of the British population had any say but one which was hotly debated behind the closed doors of the Establish-ment. While ministers, bishops, civil servants and the leading lights of London society argued about what was best for the country's morals, the British press actually conspired to keep any mention of Mrs Simpson out of the newspapers. It was not until Edward himself forced the issue that most British people learned what was going on. Forced to choose between keeping Wallis or the Crown, Edward chose Wallis: 'I am going to marry Mrs Simpson,' he told the Prime Minister, 'and I am prepared to go.'[8]

The Earl of Harewood was at Eton during the crisis and was kept up to date by his mother, the Princess Royal (sister of Edward VIII):

> My mother wrote to me to say that he was intending to abdicate and that nothing would persuade him to avoid that and that this was a step they were all extremely sad about but that that was the position and she wanted me to know and not read about it in the newspapers. Of course, the newspapers had been speculating and I was enjoined in the letter to say absolutely nothing to anyone, including all the people I was at school with. They constantly asked, 'When is your uncle going to abdicate?' and I always said I hadn't the faintest idea . . .'

On 11 December 1936, the news did become public, as the Prime Minister announced that 'King Edward VIII has abdicated the throne and will leave the country tonight'. Later that day, witnessed by his three brothers, Edward VIII signed the Instrument of Abdication at Fort Belvedere, his Windsor home, and, at a stroke, became a free man. That evening he broadcast his decision by radio. 'I have,' he told the country, 'found it impossible to carry the heavy burden of responsibility and to discharge my duties as King as I would have wished to do without the help and support of the woman I love.' After paying tribute to the family that he would leave behind, he concluded with the promise that 'it may be some time before I return to my native land, but I shall always follow the fortunes of the British race and Empire with profound interest, and if at any time in the future I can be found of service to His Majesty in a private station, I shall not fail. And now we all have a new King. I wish him, and you, his people, happiness and prosperity with all my heart. God bless you all! God Save the King!'

The accession of Elizabeth's father brought about a general name change and shuffling of ranks. Edward VIII became the Duke of Windsor and Elizabeth's cousins, who had previously addressed the new King in private as 'Uncle Bertie' now had to call him 'Sir'. In public, his style changed from Duke of York to King George VI and the Duchess became Queen Elizabeth. Their daughters – who had known nothing about the Abdication until the announcement became public – were utterly dismayed at the upheaval. As Lady Glenconner, one of Princess Margaret's ladies-in-waiting, recalls, 'the whole of their life fell apart when it happened and everything changed tremendously'. When their governess, Crawfie, told them that they would have to move into Buckingham Palace, Elizabeth stared at her in horror. 'What?' she said. 'You mean for ever?'

As their father left home on 12 December to attend his Accession Council at the Palace, Elizabeth and Margaret ran to hug him goodbye. While he was away, Marion Crawford reminded the children that they would always have to curtsey to the new King and Queen, just as they had to Edward VIII and George V. 'You mean,' asked Elizabeth, 'we must do it to Papa and Mummy?' Yes, she was told, 'and try not to topple over'. Accordingly, when George VI returned home, both his children made him a deep curtsey.

The move to Buckingham Palace was shocking for everyone. No. 145 Piccadilly had been a large house, but it was a comfortable size for the Yorks and it did at least exist in the real world of neighbours, busy normal streets outside, and the occasional friend or relative coming over for tea. Buckingham Palace, by contrast, was isolated, impersonal, surrounded by curious tourists and visited mainly by politicians or foreign diplomats. Percy Benham, who had worked as the nursery footman in the relative intimacy of the Yorks' old home at 145 Piccadilly, thought it was 'so vast and with so many tradesmen's rooms and workshops, it was more like a village or a small town. I was flabber-gasted. You walked a mile before you got anywhere near where you expected to be. It was so strange and so different. We were used to Piccadilly where it was a cosy, warm atmosphere.'

In the Piccadilly house, there had been a handful of servants; in the Buckingham Palace silver pantry alone there were four under-butlers and four assistants under the Chief Yeoman of the Silver Pantry, as well as a silversmith. The silver pantry itself was at one end of the Palace and the dining room at the other, making it almost impossible to get the food upstairs and on the table before it went cold.

As her father gloomily practised his new signature (he had been known as Albert but now officially had to sign himself George RI), Elizabeth adapted to her new life. She still had a peculiar and isolated existence, but on a larger and grander scale. Like Percy Benham, she was struck by the size of the Palace and the length of the corridors. While that was a nightmare for the servants, for the two children there were, as Lady Glenconner remembers, quite a lot of pluses: 'I think that they rather enjoyed it. They raced around the corridors – I think they had tricycles – and they had their dogs and a big garden.' The garden, of course, was not open to the public and there were other external signs of the princesses' new status – Elizabeth was delighted at the way the Palace guards would snap to attention as she walked past, and, at the Queen's suggestion, the children now had their nursery meals served by two footmen in scarlet livery.[9] But Elizabeth, still only ten years old, quickly got used to it. Her bedroom looked out over the Mall, where large crowds gathered every day in case something else new and exciting happened to the Royal Family. And Elizabeth, hiding behind the curtains, would peer back at the mass of people, equally curious.

Otherwise, the daily routine established at 145 Piccadilly went on. Outside her bedroom, along one of the endless corridors, she lined up her thirty toy horses, which had all been carefully groomed and packed for the move. 'It took quite a time to walk down all the passages to get to the rooms they were using,' remembers Lady Mountbatten, one of Elizabeth's cousins, 'but once you arrived in their own nurseries or apartments, it was the same cosy, warm atmosphere that any children's rooms would have.' The old Palace schoolroom, where George VI had spent many unhappy days as a boy, was in the centre of the top floor, also facing the Mall. It was gloomy and dark, the heavy balustrades resembling bars outside the windows. Peering into it once again from the doorway, the King was not impressed and ordered a move to a smaller, brighter room that overlooked the gardens.

In the mornings, lessons with Marion Crawford continued. If Elizabeth did feel any deep concern about the changes which had overtaken her family, she kept her thoughts entirely to herself. As Lady Mountbatten observes, 'I really don't believe the Queen would have felt greatly worried by her destiny. I think she would have accepted it rather like, you know, if somebody feels they have a career ahead of them in art or dancing or whatever it is. This is going to be your career and you prepare yourself for it as best you can.'

CHAPTER TWO

In the spring of 1937, Elizabeth had a foretaste of the first and most impressive event that lay in wait for her as Queen: her father's Coronation. For her, as for her father, it was not just an event which confirmed the monarch's social and constitutional pre-eminence. It was also a mystical religious event – an extra sacrament that was only available to kings and queens. Elizabeth was not the sort to let such thoughts go to her head, though, and alongside her awareness of the exalted nature of kingship went a prosaic concern to do the right thing. She felt especially responsible for the good behaviour of her younger sister during the Coronation. 'I do hope,' Marion Crawford remembers the eleven-year-old Elizabeth saying, 'she won't disgrace us all by falling asleep in the middle. After all, she is *very* young for a Coronation, isn't she?'

On the morning of the service, 12 May, the two sisters woke up early and went to see their parents arrayed in all the splendour of their Coronation robes. They themselves were dressed in ermine cloaks and child-sized coronets that their father had had specially made. They drove to Westminster Abbey with Queen Mary and sat next to her in the royal box, only a few yards from where their mother and father sat in state. It was a grand, mysterious and awe-inspiring event, and it moved Elizabeth profoundly. She later wrote her own account of the ceremony:

> I thought it all *very, very* wonderful and I expect the Abbey did, too. The arches and beams at the top were covered with a sort of haze of wonder as Papa was crowned, at least I thought so. When Mummy was crowned and all the peeresses put on their coronets it looked wonderful to see arms and coronets hovering in the air and then the arms disappear as if by magic. Also the music was lovely and the band, the orchestra and the new organ all played beautifully.
>
> What struck me as being rather odd was that Grannie did not remember much of her own Coronation. I should have thought that it would have stayed in her mind for ever. At the end the service got rather boring as it was all prayers. Grannie and I were looking to see how many more pages to the end and we turned one more and then I pointed to the word at the bottom of the page and it said 'Finis'. We both smiled at each other and turned back to the service.

Margaret's good behaviour had surpassed all her sister's expectations. As Elizabeth proudly told Marion Crawford, 'she was wonderful. I only had to nudge her once or twice when she played with the prayer books too loudly.' But it was an exhausting experience for all the members of the Royal Family. The King himself took his consecration extremely seriously and had been in something of a religious daze throughout the service. He later told the former Labour Prime Minister, Ramsay MacDonald, that there were long periods in the Abbey when he was not completely aware of what was going on,[10] and just as Elizabeth had been struck by the 'haze of wonder' that hung about the rafters, so her father (according to the Archbishop of Canterbury) had felt that God was especially near as he was crowned.[11]

Back at the Palace, the crowds and the photographers provided little relief. 'We aren't supposed to be human,' Elizabeth's mother observed as the family prepared for yet another appearance. 'We all went on to the Balcony where *millions* of people were waiting below,' Elizabeth wrote in her own account. 'After that we all went to be photographed in front of those awful lights.'[12] When Elizabeth finally got to bed at 8pm, she fell asleep as soon as her head hit the pillow and did not wake up until 8 the next morning.

Now that he was King, George VI did all that he could to prevent his new status from affecting his family, in particular the two princesses. Lady Mountbatten, two years older than Elizabeth, observed that 'his wife and his daughters were the centre of his world. He always referred to "us four" and, from that point of view, they had a very loving and unrestricted childhood. I think they were very, very happy in their family.' Another of Elizabeth's cousins, Margaret Rhodes, notes that 'the clever thing was that they didn't let the fact that Princess Elizabeth was now heir to the throne change the way they led their lives. They still kept themselves very much as a happy family unit with, in that day and age, as little publicity as possible.'

If anything, the pressures of his new job and the intense scrutiny with which his life was observed only made the King more determined to draw a distinction between his public duties and his private affairs. When she stayed with the Royal Family at Balmoral, Margaret Rhodes was struck by how 'every single night, the King and Queen would come up to the nursery to say goodnight to the children and laugh with them and perhaps read them a story and kiss them goodnight and tuck them up. Every night.' The pattern established at 145 Piccadilly continued, and it was a childhood which apparently had no room for unpleasantness of any kind and which involved the adults just as much as the children:

> There were a lot of little jokes and laughs – but of such a gentle and uncomplicated nature that they hardly seem funny now. Like at Balmoral, there was a lift that went up to the Queen's bedroom, so at night, when they went to bed, the King and Queen would get into the lift and go up. But, being them, they'd get halfway up so that one could just see the tops of their legs and then they'd press the button and come down again and so the lift used to sort of yo-yo up and down. Which sounds feeble, but it was funny.

Unfortunately for Elizabeth and her family, there was only so much relief to be had from playing around in lifts at Balmoral. George VI was certainly a doting father – 'my mother wanted to call me Isabel,' one of his god-daughters ruefully comments, 'but he wanted everyone to be called Elizabeth'[13] – but he also used his family to protect himself. He found the strains of his job and the duties that it imposed occasionally unbearable. 'How I hate being King!' he once shouted. 'Sometimes at ceremonies I want to stand up and scream and scream!'[14] So Elizabeth's childhood had to be protected not only for her sake, but also to provide a refuge in which the new King could take shelter.

Overshadowing everything was the treachery (as the new Royal Family saw it) of the last King. Edward VIII – now known as the Duke of Windsor – had married Mrs Simpson in June 1937 and was living very comfortably in France. For all the fuss that had been made at the time, with the future of the Empire and the monarchy itself supposedly at stake, the Abdication slid out of public consciousness surprisingly quickly. But it was something that Elizabeth and her parents found harder to forget. As Michael Mann, Dean of Windsor and family friend, comments, 'the one effect that the Abdication did have was to remove the King as a father to the young princesses. They'd been a very close-knit family indeed and suddenly he was pitchforked into a position where he could no longer give that time and attention because of his public duties and who he was'. When the family was in Scotland Elizabeth's parents may have had time to play with her and say goodnight, but when they were back in London there was a marked change. According to Marion Crawford's niece, Linda Cunniffe, 'Sometimes they didn't see them for days on end really, and on those occasions, Aunt May [Marion Crawford] would take over the role of a mother, and say their prayers with them at night and get them into bed and have little conversations.'

Above all, the Abdication increased the stranglehold of Duty over the Royal Family. Duty and conformity had been the watchwords of George V's reign and, to that extent, George VI modelled himself on his father. When she became Queen, Elizabeth would continue the pattern. According to Martin Charteris (private secretary to Elizabeth both when she was princess and Queen), 'She's got a great sense of duty. I imagine that she inherited this from her father or inherited it from her family. It's quite true that the Duke of Windsor was an exception to this rule, but on the whole all our Royal Family have a great sense of duty. Certainly those who sit on the throne have. And I think it's simply born into the Queen. It's just her nature.'[15]

The Abdication, in the words of Michael Mann, 'is almost like something burning there the whole time. It's remembered, that must never happen again.' Rather like a disgraced Cabinet minister trying to salvage his reputation, the monarchy under George VI and Elizabeth

II tried to whitewash the racy excitements and disgraces of the past with endless good works, royal visits and dogged attention to the details of royal paperwork. It was only after another forty or fifty years, when Elizabeth's own children came of age, that the ghost of Edward put on flesh again and the public were reminded that members of the Royal Family were capable of behaving badly.

In the late 1930s, the young Elizabeth, now heir to the throne, did not provide the slightest hint of bad behaviour. 'I think the Queen is highly phlegmatic,' Michael Shea, her former press secretary, explains. 'She is not a fusser. She is very calm when others around her are flapping. She doesn't ever get furious. She gets upset by people being rude about things but she is somebody who is really quite settled and doesn't show her emotions terribly easily. That is in the nature of the lady.' Her parents were under added stress and she saw less of them, but, for all the demands that shoring up the monarchy made on her, Elizabeth remained apparently unmoved. Not yet thirteen, she seemed to accept without question that her private life was becoming public property and, in 1939, she dealt unfazed with what must have been the distinctly unnerving experience of being taken to visit her old home at 145 Piccadilly.

Now that the family had moved into the monarchy's official residences, the Yorks' old house had been turned into a museum housing what were referred to as 'royal and historic treasures'. Filmed by Pathé News, Elizabeth's visit was presented less as a trip down memory lane than a pilgrimage to the shrine of her childhood. With her sister at her side, but otherwise entirely surrounded by adults, the young Elizabeth was shown moving gravely through rooms now cordoned off with red rope while the newsreel commentary solemnly intoned that the young princesses 'take a special interest in an exhibition of jewellery once worn by Queen Victoria'. Only a few years earlier, Elizabeth had played happily with her toy horses in the rooms of 145 Piccadilly. Now, when she and her sister came to a room full of toys, it was only to discover that they were special 'exhibits' made by 'crippled children of the Heritage Craft School'. Both princesses were urged to take one of the toys as a gift. Margaret picked a doll; Elizabeth, slipping easily into her role as a living royal and historic treasure, took a tiny carved gilt model of the Coronation coach.

Dutiful, and with a sense of decorum inherited from her grand-mother, Queen Mary, her new position cannot have come as that much of a shock to Elizabeth. Even if she still had no idea that she might one day be Queen, she had spent her first ten years of life within royal circles, often staying at Balmoral, Windsor and Sandringham. When they were in the country, her family took their duties as local squires just as seriously as their royal responsibilities, and in many ways the two aspects of royal life complemented each other. Margaret Rhodes, who had a similar upbringing, thinks that 'that generation was brought up with an immense sense of what you owed to other people. It wasn't a "let's enjoy ourselves and not think of anybody else" kind of society. From childhood, you visited people on your estate to see if they were well or if the children were all right'.

One aspect of her upbringing which had not prepared Elizabeth very well for her future role was her education. Despite the stiffening influence of Queen Mary and Marion Crawford, her early years in the schoolroom were not, by today's standards, much of a grounding for normal adult life, let alone being Head of State. Forty years on, during a conversation about whether Prince Charles would get into Cambridge, Elizabeth turned to her sister and ruefully commented, 'You and I would never have got into university.'[16]

This judgement has been echoed by others. Journalist Bill Deedes believes that 'they have to work quite hard to keep up and fulfil their duties. There's no discredit attached to that, but there are people who can get through a day's work without feeling the weight on their shoulders. I think the recent Windsors have all had to apply themselves very solidly to the job, and the Queen herself is no exception.' Barbara Castle, a former Labour Cabinet minister, similarly found her personal liking for Elizabeth tempered by indignation at the poor preparation she had received for the role. 'The wickedness of isolating princesses of the realm, of educating them in isolation from the rest of their peer group, I think it's really outrageous.'

Elizabeth's parents, perhaps rather late in the day, also felt the lack. From 1937, they made arrangements both to broaden and deepen their elder daughter's knowledge of the world (although the need for extra royal cramming was not thought to extend to their younger daughter, Margaret). The man enlisted for the purpose was Sir Henry Marten, Vice-Provost of Eton College. Elizabeth would go and see him twice a week in his study for a private tutorial on the British Constitution. ('Crawfie,' she gasped when she first saw the books that lined and littered Marten's rooms. 'Do you mean to tell me he has read them *all*?')

While Miss Crawford leafed through the latest P.G. Wodehouse, Elizabeth was drilled on the rights and duties of the sovereign, on how the monarchy had evolved since Anglo-Saxon times and on the all-important relationship with Parliament. Sir Henry Marten, as one of the Queen's recent biographers describes, also 'taught her what he considered the two great events affecting the monarchy in their own time, the 1931 Statute of Westminster and the advent of broadcasting. The Statute . . . had founded the modern British Commonwealth by making a common allegiance to the Crown the sole surviving link between Great Britain and the Dominions; while broadcasting enabled the Royal Family, by talking personally on the air, to sustain that link.'[17]

Marten was a good teacher. On constitutional matters, Sir Michael Oswald, one of her courtiers, reckons, Elizabeth 'knows her position backwards', and she has made her devotion to the Commonwealth one of the defining characteristics of her reign. Neither she nor her teacher, though, could have foreseen just how important a role broadcasting would play in her life. By 1937, most households had a radio, but the BBC had been established a mere ten years earlier and television had only just been invented (there were only a few hundred, very expensive, television sets in the whole country). Of the two great influences that Marten identified, Elizabeth unfortunately maintained a life-long affection for the one that was doomed to slow decline and an equally lasting dislike for the fast-rising new power of television.

The broadening of Elizabeth's education proceeded rather more unevenly. Educated alone, mixing with a very limited number of friends, she had enjoyed an extremely isolated and protected childhood, and the line between being well-behaved and good-natured and being almost compulsively rigid and correct sometimes seemed a narrow one. On one occasion, her governess recounts that she 'got quite anxious about Lilibet and her fads. She became almost too methodical and tidy. She would hop out of bed several times a night to get her shoes quite straight, her clothes arranged just so.' Perhaps fortunately, there were no child psychologists around to tackle the problem, and Marion Crawford 'soon laughed her out' of the night-time drill. At the same time, though, Crawford, Queen Mary and Elizabeth's parents recognised the need to widen Elizabeth's horizons socially as well as academically.

Crawfie's contribution was to start a Girl Guide company at the Palace. Besides keeping Elizabeth and Margaret in touch with what children of their own ages were doing, she 'knew it would bring them into contact with others of their own ages and of all kinds and conditions'. In the end, though, the social mix did not represent as full a cross-section of the British public as Crawford had hoped. Although some of the other Guides were the children of Palace officials and employees, most of them were aristocratic or royal daughters of Elizabeth's age and would at first turn up wearing party frocks and white gloves with a detachment of nannies and governesses in tow. But it did at least offer the princess an opportunity to mix with others on roughly equal terms, without being singled out for special treatment. Patricia Mountbatten was one of those who took part, and recalls: 'She and I were in the same patrol, the Kingfisher patrol. I was a couple of years older and had been a Guide before, and so I was made a Patrol Leader and she was my Patrol Second. I remember at the time thinking that she was an excellent Patrol Second, very efficient and very reliable. It's hardly surprising now, looking back, but that was definitely my impression even in those days.'

Elizabeth had another opportunity to show her sterling qualities when her parents left for a tour of Canada and the United States in May 1939. As with their visit to France in July the preceding year, the King and Queen were despatched by the Government with the explicit aim of strengthening Britain's foreign alliances. The political situation in Europe was growing more worrying by the day, and it was increasingly clear that Britain would need all the friends she could get.

November 1938 had seen the first Nazi-led pogroms in Berlin. By the time Elizabeth's parents sailed for North America, Austria and parts of Czechoslovakia were already under German rule, while Italy had successfully invaded Albania and Ethiopia. The King did not want to leave the country – or his two daughters – at such a time, but, as he told his mother, he felt it was impossible to avoid his duty. 'We must start for Canada on Saturday,' he wrote to Queen Mary, 'unless there is any really good reason as to why we should not. I hate leaving here with the situation as it is, but one must carry on with one's plans as they are all settled, & Canada will be so disappointed.'[18]

Canada's gain was the Royal Family's loss, but when Queen Mary, Elizabeth and Margaret went down to Portsmouth to say goodbye Elizabeth kept her emotions under typically strict control. As Queen Mary recorded in her diary, 'the ship left punctually at 3 – it was a fine sight from the jetty – & we waved handkerchiefs. Margaret said, "I have my handkerchief" & Lilibet answered, "To wave, not to cry" – which I thought charming.'[19]

With the newspapers full of worsening reports from Germany, Elizabeth saw her parents again six weeks later in June, when she sailed out aboard a Royal Navy destroyer to meet them off Southampton. Just as the staff were doing at the Palace, she and Margaret had prepared for the reunion by spring-cleaning the Little House that had been given to her for her sixth birthday – brushing the carpets, sweeping the mats and tidying it from top to bottom. But, while their leave-taking had been notably restrained, their private reunion was openly affectionate. As Marion Crawford remembered, 'The little girls could hardly rush up the ladder quickly enough, for climbing was very awkward, but when they reached the top they rushed to Mummy and Papa. They kissed them and hugged them again and again.' On board the ship, 'the King could not take his eyes off Lilibet'.

He had missed both children enormously, but was already beginning to treat Elizabeth in particular as if she were much older than she was. Around the time that Elizabeth's constitutional lessons began with Henry Marten, the King had started talking to his daughter much more seriously – almost as though she were his equal. Perhaps it was partly an attempt to give Elizabeth the extra breadth of outlook that her earlier education had failed to provide – but there were more personal reasons, too. 'He must,' Patricia Mountbatten thinks, 'have felt very close to his elder daughter, in the sense that she was going to literally inherit his crown. Probably he felt some sympathy, knowing the problems that she would encounter only too well, and wanting, as far as he could, to try and explain matters to her and make life a little easier.'

By the late summer of 1939 the King must also have known that, despite his Government's policy of appeasing Germany, war was unavoidable. On 3 September 1939, the day the Prime Minister broadcast Britain's declaration of war on Germany to the nation, the King and Queen were in London. Elizabeth stayed on the Balmoral estate with her sister and her cousin, Margaret Rhodes, who recalls:

> We all went to church, as one always does up there, and there was a very dear old minister called Dr Lamb and he made a very impassioned sermon. And suddenly there we were, from 11 o'clock in the morning we were at war, and at that age one didn't really know what that involved or what it meant. In a funny way it just seemed awfully exciting. I suppose one had visions of knights in armour. But it was a moment that made a deep impact on the three of us.

Inevitably, the war made for greater informality at Court. Elizabeth's parents rejected suggestions that the children should be sent to Canada, so Elizabeth and Margaret lived in Windsor for most of the war, staying either in the castle or at Royal Lodge, one of the houses on the estate. Their parents lived in London during the week, and came down to join the family at weekends, when the evening routine was regularly disturbed by German air-raids. Margaret Rhodes remembers that 'there was a wonderfully formal, grand butler at Royal Lodge, and they had a series of different coloured warnings as to when the German aeroplanes were getting closer. Purple was the nearest and most dramatic and I can remember him coming in and saying in a voice of doom, "Purple warning, Your Majesty," upon which one expected the next bomb to drop on the garden.'

The bomb shelters were in the cellars of Windsor Castle but were not, in the end, used very much. According to Margaret Rhodes, the journey to whatever safety the shelters offered involved endless passageways. The staff 'would try to hurry the Royal Family . . . and that made Queen Elizabeth [the Queen Mother] walk slower and slower, in a more and more dignified way, refusing to be hurried'. Eventually, Elizabeth's mother decided that the fuss of getting down to the cellars was hardly worth it and that the family might as well take their chances staying in their usual bedrooms.

For security reasons, Elizabeth rarely appeared in public in the early years of the war. Even the fact that she was living at Windsor was kept secret – as far as the public knew, Elizabeth and her sister were simply living at 'a house in the country' – but she was not altogether shut away. Anne Glenconner – later one of Princess Margaret's ladiesinwaiting – thought that 'she enjoyed a lot of it very much, because they had a lot of young officers billeted at Windsor to look after them and they used to get up a pantomime and musicals and I think they actually had rather a jolly time'.

The pantomimes and musicals began in Christmas 1940 and continued, becoming more and more elaborate, every year until 1944. In the King's eyes, they were an opportunity not just to have fun and meet people, but also a means of giving Elizabeth the extra poise she would need when she assumed her role as Queen. Elizabeth and Margaret invariably got the star parts, and the rest of the cast was made up of children from Royal School at Windsor Great Park, among them thirteenyearold Cyril Woods, who noticed that 'Princess Margaret had a certain natural ability in holding an audience. Princess

Elizabeth was a more reserved and shyer sort of person, but I think she built in confidence in appearing in front of people.'

The first year, they put on a short Nativity play called *The Christmas Child* and followed it up in 1941 with a more ambitious production of *Cinderella*, with Margaret in the title part and Elizabeth playing the Prince. Cyril Woods remembers that the humour was often simple slapstick – 'Have you got frogs' legs?' the diner asks the waiter in one scene. 'No sir,' replies the waiter, 'I always walk like this' – but there were proper programmes and tickets, the Guards' band played the music, the costumes were run up by one of the Palace dressmakers and Elizabeth's mother lent the cast her tiaras to go with them. In the first year, the production was staged in front of 100 people in a hall on the Windsor estate. It proved so popular that in later years it was moved to the Waterloo Chamber at Windsor Castle, where an invited audience of royal relations, army officers and estate workers could buy tickets that ranged from seven shillings and sixpence for the best seats, down to one shilling for those with a restricted view.

In 1940, Elizabeth made her first radio broadcast. Aged only thirteen at the outbreak of the war, there was not much she could do to help Britain's military effort herself, and the Palace had initially been strongly opposed to the idea of using her for wartime propaganda. But by the end of the first year of war, any chance of boosting American public support for Britain seemed worth taking. All the country's European allies had surrendered, and German bombing raids had just begun on the British mainland. There seemed a real danger that Britain was staggering towards defeat and that the United States would stay out of the fighting altogether.

At the BBC's suggestion, Elizabeth introduced a series of programmes called 'Children in Wartime', supposedly addressed to the thousands of British children who had been evacuated overseas.

Broadcast live to the United States and Canada, its real purpose was to stimulate the sympathy of adult Americans, as Elizabeth reminded their children in her high, piping voice of how 'thousands of you in this country have had to leave your homes and be separated from your father and mother. My sister Margaret Rose and I feel so much for you, as we know from experience what it means to be away from those we love most of all.' The broadcast ended with a piece of scripted dialogue with Princess Margaret: 'My sister is by my side and we are both going to say goodnight to you. Come on, Margaret.' 'Good night.' 'Good night and good luck to you all.'

It was not much to keep Elizabeth occupied, though, and she felt keenly the lack of anything worthwhile to do. Idleness did not suit her and especially not at a time when the rest of the country was being urged on to greater efforts of industry and sacrifice. 'Oh, Crawfie,' she once asked her governess, 'do you think we are being too happy?' As she grew older, though, her parents did give her one or two outlets for her energies. In 1942, she was made Colonel of the Grenadier Guards – an honorary position which mainly involved inspecting lines of soldiers drawn up on ceremonial parade. With her eye for detail, it was a job (though not an over-demanding one) to which she was perfectly suited and she leaped into it with all the energy of one who had been long confined. On one occasion, the sixteen-year-old Elizabeth carried out an inspection with such seriousness and made so many ringing and rather pointed criticisms that one of the officers there suggested quietly that she should tone things down a bit in the future.

Much more fun for Elizabeth (and those around her) was the Auxiliary Territorial Service (ATS). Since she had turned sixteen, Elizabeth had been pestering her parents for a proper wartime job, arguing that she ought to do as other girls of her age did. It was an argument she had pursued throughout her life – ever since her nanny had stopped her playing on the swings with the other children – but it took her nearly until the end of the war to get her way. In February 1945 she registered as Second Subaltern Elizabeth Alexandra Mary Windsor and started on a driving and vehicle-maintenance course at Aldershot.

'The princess is to be treated in exactly the same way as any other officer learning at the driving training centre,' *The Times* reported.[20] However, as with the Girl Guides, it was by no means a completely natural experience. The other officers on her course were carefully vetted, while Elizabeth herself was photographed constantly. She was nearly nineteen when she joined the ATS, yet those around her conspired to treat her as though she were five years younger. Marion Crawford was still a dominant influence in her life, and every morning the ATS commandant would come and ask the governess, 'Do you think the princess will be able to do this or that?' Elizabeth herself may have been desperate to live like other girls of her age, but it seems unlikely that, when other eighteen-year-old girls caught a cold, it required a three-way discussion between their nanny, their governess and their military commander before deciding that they had better stay in bed for the day.

For all that, Elizabeth's time in the ATS was an eye-opener. When her aunt, the Princess Royal, came down for an inspection, Elizabeth, like everyone else, had to spend days beforehand in a frenzy of polishing and cleaning. 'Now I realise,' she told Marion Crawford, 'what must happen when Papa and Mummy go anywhere. That's something I shall never forget.' She was more closely monitored than any other young officer, but she did enjoy the unique experience of taking exams and passing tests on a more-or-less equal footing with everybody else. Decades later, talking to Barbara Castle, one of her Cabinet ministers, Elizabeth observed that 'the only collective contact she'd had was in the ATS and she said she loved it, "because, you see, we have no means of knowing how we really rank in relation to other people". And so, to enter into any kind of competitive sport or anything would be a revelation. And she loved it.'

In 1945, as Londoners were celebrating VE Day, Elizabeth was also able to use her ATS uniform as a disguise when she slipped out of Buckingham Palace to join the masses in the streets, lit up for the first time since the start of the war. 'I remember the thrill and relief after the previous days waiting for the Prime Minister's announcement for the end of the war in Europe,' she later said in a rare interview. 'I think we went on the balcony nearly every hour, six times, and then, when the excitement of the floodlights being switched on got through to us, my sister and I realised we couldn't see what the crowds were enjoying. My mother had put her tiara on for the occasion so we asked our parents if we could go out and see for ourselves.' With her cap pulled well down over her eyes, she and Princess Margaret and six or eight friends joined the crowds and walked up to Trafalgar Square. Margaret Rhodes remembers, 'It was so wonderful to see the lights on again, and everybody was drinking champagne and kissing everybody in sight and shouting'.

After all the close supervision that had hemmed her in, it seems extraordinary that Elizabeth was allowed to join the crowds on the streets – all the more extraordinary for the princess who, safe in the anonymity of her uniform, for once found herself standing by the Victoria Memorial shouting 'We want the King! We want the King!' and watching her parents appear on the balcony to acknowledge the cheers of the crowd. Elizabeth herself describes it as 'one of the most memorable nights of my life'. It had taken the end of almost six years of war to get there, but for once Elizabeth was on the other side of the Palace windows, standing unrecognised among the people whose lives she had so often wondered about.

CHAPTER THREE

For all the special protection that surrounded her, Elizabeth did have one important thing in common with other women in the country – a forces sweetheart. She had met Philip a month before the outbreak of war, in August 1939, when she went with her parents to visit Dartmouth Royal Naval College. Philip, one of the naval cadets at Dartmouth, was eighteen at the time and Elizabeth only thirteen, but from the moment she set eyes on him, Elizabeth was smitten. 'He was frightfully good-looking,' Margaret Rhodes recalls. 'He looked rather like a young Viking. Very, very blond and tall and with piercing blue eyes.' Philip was one of the cadets deputised to show the royal party around Dartmouth and afterwards he was invited to play with the princesses and have lunch with them. 'How good he is, Crawfie!' Elizabeth told her governess after watching Philip leaping over a tennis net. 'How high he can jump!' All the time Philip was with them, Elizabeth could not take her eyes off him.

When Elizabeth left with her parents aboard the King's yacht, *Victoria and Albert*, Philip rowed after them so long that the King at last exclaimed, 'The young fool! He must go back, otherwise we will have to heave to and send him back.' Elizabeth, all the while, was studying Philip through a pair of binoculars. She next saw him in London, as she told Margaret Rhodes by letter:

We went up to London today with Mummy and Papa. Then Philip came to lunch to say goodbye. He is sailing tomorrow as a Midshipman. It was so sad saying goodbye to him. I sat next to him. He is as nice as ever, perhaps even better looking, because he is very pleased and excited that he is going. Mummy says he can come to lunch with us again when he gets his leave. I also am going to try and get her to let him come and stay with us. I am hoping his leave will come quite soon again.

When Philip did get leave, he began to come to Windsor regularly to see Elizabeth, and was there, sitting in the front row, to watch one of the royal Christmas pantomimes. ('Who *do* you think is coming to see us act, Crawfie?' a rather flustered Elizabeth asked her governess when she heard.) When he had to return to his ship, Elizabeth wrote to him regularly and she had a sparkle about her that many of the courtiers had not noticed before. Later on, after Philip had taken her to see the musical *Oklahoma!*, Marion Crawford noticed that Elizabeth took to playing one of the show's songs constantly: it was 'People Will Say We're in Love'.

The man on whom Elizabeth had set her heart was no stranger to royal circles, but Philip's upbringing had been the complete opposite of the intimate, slightly claustrophobic world of Elizabeth's childhood. His mother, Princess Alice, was the great-granddaughter of Queen Victoria and his father, Prince Andrew, was the younger brother of the King of Greece. As one of his Navy friends, Michael Parker, remembers, 'It was quite funny, really, because when we first met, he was always known as Philip. He didn't have a surname and that was fairly unique. You would say, Philip who? He'd say he was Philip of Greece.'

In fact, the Greek Royal Family had been deposed in 1923 and Philip had been driven into exile with his parents, neither of whom reacted very well to the shock of leaving home. His mother became very religious and sometimes mentally unstable: at one time she spent two and a half years in a psychiatric clinic outside Berlin. She later recovered and founded her own order of Greek nuns, but Philip's father, whom Greek republicans had wanted to execute as a scapegoat for their recent military defeats, ended up leaving his wife in 1930. He took refuge in Monte Carlo and the arms of his mistress.

This left Philip to be brought up mainly by his extended family. 'He had four sisters, who were very good in giving him homes,' one of his cousins, Countess Mountbatten, remembers, 'and he had a couple of uncles, so he wasn't somebody who had no relations at all. But he did not have what every child would want, which was a close and loving relationship with his parents.' He was, in the words of Elizabeth's governess, 'a prince without a home or a kingdom', and it was his uncles – George and Louis Mountbatten – who encouraged him to join the Navy and whose surname he eventually adopted, becoming Lieutenant Philip Mountbatten, RN. At the time he met Elizabeth, Patricia Mountbatten recalls, he 'was living basically on a young naval officer's pay. I think he had a small income otherwise, a very small income, so he was far from well-off. His own background was a royal background, so he was perfectly used to visiting and living in castles and palaces and going about visiting royal relations. But, as far as his own income was concerned, it was very small.'

Even as a young man, Philip had a brisk, no-nonsense manner but for Louis Mountbatten's two daughters, he was 'a very glamorous cousin to have'. According to one of them, Pamela Hicks, 'he looked fabulous and was great fun. He would often stay in our parents' small house in London and the entire place sort of rocked and exploded when he was there.' On top of that, close friends of Philip maintain that he is much more compassionate than people realise. Lord Brabourne, Louis Mountbatten's son-in-law, says, 'He's got a really good heart. If somebody is in trouble, I know no better person to go and talk to. He doesn't wear his heart on his sleeve, so to speak, but he is a very caring person in many, many ways.' Looked at objectively, it seems likely that Philip's good nature was an added bonus rather than his primary attraction — but Elizabeth was not disposed to consider the matter objectively at all. High-spirited, irreverent and forceful, Philip was her complete opposite and he brought out a streak of stubbornness in Elizabeth that, until now, had been hidden in her loyalty to her parents and the quiet certainties of home life.

Until she met Philip, Elizabeth had appeared fairly happy to knuckle under and do as she was told. She may have gazed out of the windows wistfully from time to time, wondering what life was like on the other side, but she had little of her sister's wilfulness or her uncle's enthusiasm for the grand gesture. Throughout her childhood, she and Margaret had been treated the same way and even dressed the same, despite the fact that there were four years between them. Their parents wanted to continue the happy world of 'us four' for as long as possible. But although treating the two sisters as though they were the same age may have been good news for Margaret (who got to be treated as though she were more grown up than she was), it was bad news for Elizabeth, who was held back in the fantasy childhood which her parents had constructed, even as she was approaching her twentieth birthday. Falling in love with Philip gave Elizabeth her first opportunity to test her mettle and fight for something she really wanted for herself – for, if she was devoted to him, there were many at Court who were not.

For all his royal connections, Philip was not cast from a traditional mould ('There was nothing of the polished courtier about him,' according to Marion Crawford) and he was not prepared to trim his sails to suit the more lethargic and deferential climate of the British Court. With some understatement, Pamela Hicks acknowledges this: 'I think there were several people who were more than slightly nervous or strongly disapproved. An old-established concern that seems to be running quite well is always very wary of a newcomer who appears very brash.'

Elizabeth may have been charmed to see Philip wandering around the Palace in his shirt-sleeves, but the more old-fashioned members of the King's staff were certainly not. Edward Ford, then assistant private secretary to George VI, thought that 'he never showed the respect that an English boy would have had for the older people around. He had no retiring graces and wasn't in the least afraid to tell the King's friend, Lord Salisbury, what he felt. Everybody thought, "This rough diamond – will he treat the princess with the sensitivity she deserves?" '[21] Peter Ashmore, one of the King's equerries, was also struck by the way 'the Eldons and the Salisburys, who were close friends of the King and Queen, ganged up against him and made it plain that they hoped they were not going to let their daughter marry this chap. None of the aristocrats and Old Etonians were in favour of him.'[22] As her niece, Linda Cunniffe, reveals, even Marion Crawford, who was polite about Philip in public, in private 'certainly did not like him. She thought he was too arrogant and she hoped that this was puppy love.'

Philip's uncle, Louis Mountbatten, was another black mark against him. A romantic and glittering figure – he was a cousin of George VI, had been promoted Supreme Allied Commander in South-east Asia during the war, and in 1946 had been appointed the last Viceroy of India – he also had a talent for self-promotion that put a number of courtly backs up. William Heseltine, who was Elizabeth's press secretary in the 1960s, notes that 'it was a rather endearing quality in him but Lord Mountbatten always seemed to attach enormous importance to the fact that he was a member of the Royal Family and in somebody who had such other achievements to his credit this was perhaps a little surprising'.

Mountbatten was a keen match-maker between Elizabeth and his nephew and on at least one occasion Philip had to write to his uncle and politely warn him to back off: 'Please, I beg of you, not too much advice in an affair of the heart, or I shall be forced to do the wooing by proxy . . .'[23] Mountbatten's great desire was to graft his own family onto ever grander and more royal stock and, in the event, his involvement probably did his nephew more harm than good. In the eyes of many courtiers, Philip was already 'a foreign interloper out for the goodies',[24] and the fact that Louis Mountbatten was his main sponsor only made things worse – particularly in the eyes of Elizabeth's mother.

Elizabeth's father took a more measured view. Rather than actively opposing the match, he simply preferred to avoid encouraging it. 'I like Philip,' he wrote to Queen Mary. 'He is intelligent, has a good sense of humour and thinks about things in the right way.'[24] Like many parents, though, he was still partly reluctant to acknowledge that his daughter really had grown up and was ready to leave his family and start one of her own. Another part, less selfishly, recognised that Elizabeth was young for her age. She had had a particularly protected childhood in which she had not met very many friends and Philip – with whom she had, after all, fallen in love when she was only thirteen – was practically the first eligible bachelor she had clapped eyes on. The King, therefore, added his weight to the already considerable forces ranged against the match. In 1944, when Philip's uncle (now restored to the throne of Greece) wrote to George VI, asking about the possibility of an engage-ment between Elizabeth and Philip, George wrote back, telling the Greek king 'that P. had better not think any more about it for the present'.

Elizabeth herself never showed the slightest doubts about Philip, but she was inevitably affected by the general air of disapproval and uncertainty that hung over their romance. As one courtier observed to her governess, 'if there is not to be an engagement, the boy ought not to be around so much. There is too much talk and speculation already.' Although the newspapers were much more restrained in the late 1940s than they are now, the public was just as prurient, shouting out 'Where's Philip?' when Elizabeth was on a public visit to a factory in 1946 – an experience which the shy princess described as 'horrible'. 'Poor Lil,' her sister sympathised. 'Nothing of your own, not even your love affair.' Elizabeth not only had all the private agonies and joys of a first romance to deal with, but intense interest centring on the fact that, as heir to the throne, her private life was fair game for general discussion. In fact, as an heir to the throne who wanted to marry someone she loved, Elizabeth was in the middle of a completely new game. Her parents had married for love, but at a time when her father was Duke of York and was not expected to become King. Her grandparents and great-grandparents had had arranged marriages and, before that, every one of her pre-decessors had either married for political reasons or they had married once they were already on the throne, which at least gave them some extra leeway. None of them had had to undergo Elizabeth's particular form of trial by endurance. She was the first heir to the throne to fall in love and then want to get married: usually, in royal circles, things happened the other way around.

At the end of 1946, after a rather doleful holiday at Balmoral which left Elizabeth noticeably subdued – Philip was one of the guests, but he and Elizabeth were never left alone – the Palace officially denied that there was any engagement planned. At the same time, it was announced that Elizabeth would be joining her family for a four-month state visit to South Africa in the New Year. 'It was clear,' Marion Crawford wrote, that 'she was not happy about the South African trip. She would have liked to have matters fixed and to be properly engaged before she went away, I know. Four months is a long, long time to a girl in love. Prince Philip was not in London at this time, but he rang her up every evening. She would grow restless as the hour arranged came near. Then she would say to me, "Someone is going to phone me, Crawfie. I must go." '

In fact, Elizabeth's persistence had nearly paid off and her agreement to come to South Africa was by way of a bargain with her father. According to her cousin, Margaret Rhodes, 'Obviously they had a trip planned, but I think it was to give her a little leeway, to have time to think about whether she was absolutely sure about her wish to get married.' Elizabeth's mother, explaining to Marion Crawford why she wanted Margaret to come with them too, seemed to acknowledge that the game was up, telling her, 'I think we both realise that this break in routine is perhaps a pity. But it seemed too bad to separate the family just now.' If, after four months away, Elizabeth still wanted to marry Philip on her return, the King would give his consent.

The King and Queen and the two princesses left Portsmouth aboard HMS *Vanguard*, the largest battleship in the Royal Navy and one which Elizabeth herself had launched in 1944. There were tears in Elizabeth's eyes as she said goodbye to the Palace staff at Buckingham Palace and there were mountainous seas in the Bay of Biscay, which made everyone apart from the Queen seasick, but after the first few days the voyage became almost light-hearted. It was the first holiday the Royal Family had enjoyed together since before the war and it was the first time either Elizabeth or Margaret had ever been abroad. As Edmund Grove (who worked in the office of the Privy Purse and made up one of the party) puts it, this was, 'really a golden time for the princesses because they were very, very close to their father. They'd been with the King and Queen throughout the war and the South African tour was the first opportunity that they'd had really to go outside the country and see something of the world.'

While they were at sea, there were deck-games and sing-songs in the wardroom. There was rifle-shooting on deck and a treasure hunt organised by one of the King's equerries with simple clues that reflected the innocent, child-like atmosphere still surrounding the twenty-year-old Elizabeth. 'Use Mr Bell's invention to call the royal room. When a male voice answers, mention this word, "silk cocoon",' went one of the coded instructions, remembers Sir Peter Ashmore, equerry to the King, prompting the treasure hunters to telephone the private secretaries' office in order to get to the next clue. The atmosphere of harmless fun continued when the ship crossed the Line of the Equator, as the traditional pranks were played on anyone who had not voyaged into the Southern Hemisphere before. Edmund Grove recalls: 'When we came to the crossing of the Line, we had quite a big ceremony and they had a ducking pool and you had to be very careful to avoid being ducked. And nearly everyone in the royal party got ducked, except the ladies. When it came to the royal princesses, they weren't ducked, they were given very large pills and then they were dusted with a powder puff and that was them done. They got their certificate.'

It was a good time to be away. The winter of 1946–7 was the worst of the century, with floods across the whole of southern England and snow that continued into May. The Thames froze and roads everywhere were blocked by snow and ice. Electricity was rationed, with power cuts of up to five hours a day imposed across the country and supplies of coal – on which most people depended at that time for heat – began to run out. They were months of material hardship greater than any the country had had to endure during the war and the King, stuck on the tour of South Africa, felt terrible about his absence. Edmund Grove was one day chatting to some of his colleagues in the office of the Privy Purse when the King suddenly 'came in with a look of thunder. He had a newspaper in his hand and steam was coming out of his ears and he threw the newspaper down on to the table and said, "Look at that, look at that!" And we looked at it – I was terrorised – and it said, "Floods in Windsor, hundreds homeless." And he said, "Why is it that nobody tells me about the suffering that my people are undergoing in Windsor? Nobody tells me. Get on to them at once. I want to know." '

Worrying about conditions back home set the undertone for what, on the face of it, was a successful trip. The British Government had been concerned that republican demonstrations would spoil the effect of the tour. But the Afrikaner press on the whole ignored the royal visit, and while the teams of South African secret policemen who followed the King about everywhere annoyed him inordinately ('Well, Mother,' he remarked to his wife while out for a private walk one day, 'we've shaken off the Gestapo at last.'[25]) in the event, the King and his family were greeted with enormous enthusiasm wherever they went. The ANC officially voted to boycott the royal visit but that did not, as Nelson Mandela recalls, prevent thousands of members – including the ANC president – ignoring the ban.

Behind the scenes, though, all was not so well. The main problem was the exhaustion of the King, who lost a stone in weight during the tour. He had come out of the war tired and frail, and he was now on

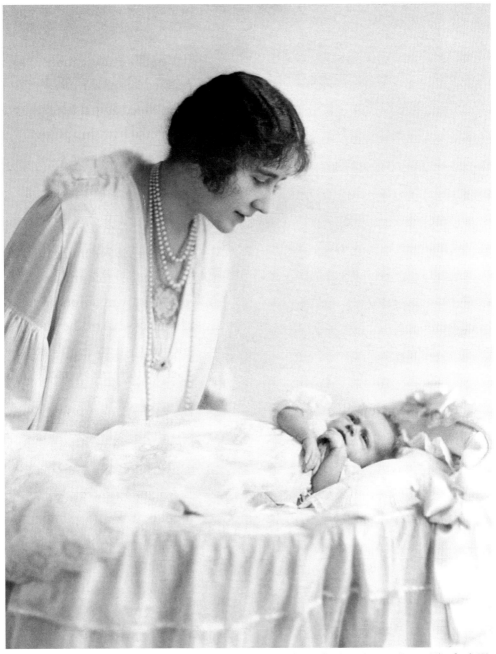

The new-born Elizabeth and her mother in 1926 (*Royal Archives © Her Majesty Queen Elizabeth II*)

'A little darling with a lovely complexion and pretty fair hair,' according to Queen Mary (*Camera Press Ltd*)

Elizabeth leading two-year-old Margaret on one of her favourite ponies (*Royal Archives © Her Majesty Queen Elizabeth II*)

George V and Queen Mary with Elizabeth at Bognor, 1929 (*Royal Archives © Her Majesty Queen Elizabeth II*)

Elizabeth and the man she called 'Grandpa England', June 1929 (*Royal Archives © Her Majesty Queen Elizabeth II*)

'Us Four' (*Camera Press Ltd*)

On an outing with governess
Marion Crawford, May 1939
(*Hulton Getty*)

Rehearsing *Cinderella* (with
Elizabeth as Prince Charming) at
Windsor, 1941 (*Hulton Archive*)

Marion Crawford

WATERLOO CHAMBER
WINDSOR CASTLE

•

A Christmas Pantomime

"Old Mother
Red Riding Boots"

December 21st, 22nd and 23rd, 1944

DEVISED BY

*Princess Elizabeth, Princess Margaret
and Hubert Tannar*

THE "SALON ORCHESTRA" OF
THE ROYAL HORSE GUARDS (THE BLUES)
(By permission of Col. R. E. S. Gooch)

Under the Direction of Capt. A. J. Thornburrow

Stage Manager : Stanley A. Williams

Price 1/-

The 1944 Windsor pantomime *Old Mother Red Riding Boots* (above: *Hulton Archive*; left: *Royal Archives © Her Majesty Queen Elizabeth II*)

Elizabeth wearing her mother's tiara (*Hulton Archive*)

Aboard HMS *Vanguard* on the way to South Africa, 1947 (*Royal Archives © Her Majesty Queen Elizabeth II*)

A wistful Elizabeth during target practice on the deck of *Vanguard* (*Royal Archives © Her Majesty Queen Elizabeth II*)

constant public show. He found the endless hours of smalltalk with mayors and local politicians, followed by public speeches and celebratory fêtes that required unfalteringly genial approval, rather hard to bear. Travelling and sleeping on the White Train – usually reserved for the Governor-General – the King covered 6000 miles and was on constant call. On one occasion, Edmund Grove received a message that the train was approaching a country town and that 'literally thousands of people were waiting to greet the King'. He remembers:

> It was about 11 o'clock at night and the King had gone to bed, but we were advised by the tour organisers that the King ought to get up and meet these people . . . So we had to get the King out of bed, and he walked along the train being rather cross, with the Queen walking behind him, calming him down, saying, "Well, you must go out and we'll get you back as soon as possible." And he was fuming. But when he got out of the train, he was all smiles, with the Queen behind him, smoothing the path, so to speak. And we met all the various townspeople, and when we got the King back on the train again he went back to bed, cursing all the way.

Seeing the strain that her father was under cannot have made the monarch's job look that appealing to Elizabeth; yet, once more, it was his dutiful example which influenced her own character. One of the royal chaplains, Michael Mann, remembers her saying, 'I have never forgotten what my father told me: remember that when anyone meets you they will remember that point all their lives, therefore the way in which you behave to them is absolutely vital.' It is a lesson the Queen has never forgotten.

It was against this background that Elizabeth made one of the most important speeches of her life. Given at Cape Town on her twenty-first birthday, her words summed up her personal philosophy and provided a yardstick against which to measure her own time on the throne. Speaking, as Lady Glenconner recalls, 'in that very, very high voice', Elizabeth told the world:

> There is a motto which has been borne by many of my ancestors — a noble motto, 'I swear'. Those words were an inspiration to many bygone heirs to the throne when they made their knightly dedication as they came to manhood. I cannot do quite as they did, but through the inventions of science I can do what was not possible for any of them. I can make my solemn act of dedication with a whole Empire listening. I should like to make that dedication now. It is very simple. I declare before you all that my whole life, whether it be long or short, shall be devoted to your service and the service of our great Imperial family to which we all belong. But I shall not have the strength to carry out this resolution alone unless you join in with me, as I now invite you to do. I know that your support will be unfailingly given. God help me to make good my vow and God bless all of you who are willing to share in it.

Like all royal speeches, Elizabeth's words had been shaped by suggestions from her family and, in particular, from her father's private secretary. Edmund Grove, who prepared the final version, nonetheless insists that 'it was the princess herself who drew the thing together and she wrote it out in her own hand. She might have had several crossings-out beforehand, but the draft I had at the end was one which was completely one hundred per cent in her own pencilled handwriting. This was the draft I had and I typed it from her own draft. So it is essentially her own speech.'

Listening to Elizabeth back in England, even those who knew her well were surprised at its lofty tone. Lady Penn, one of her friends, remembers thinking, 'When she said, "I cannot face this task on my own," that she was going to say that she needed the support of a husband. But she didn't.' Another friend, Lady Glenconner, recalls her grandmother 'saying what a fine example she was giving us all and we were very impressed and thought that she was amazing, you know, to say at such a young age that her whole life was going to be devoted to her country'. Even in 1947, only two years after a war in which men and women the same age or even younger had actually given their lives for their country, Elizabeth's dedication seemed remarkable. It was almost as though she was saying goodbye, before embarking upon some chivalrous and perilous quest. Even if the dangers of the quest were, in fact, no more than the mundane, tedious routines of the monarchy, it was still, as Elizabeth acknowledged herself, a quest that would end only in death and one that she took utterly seriously. Whether deliberate or not, it was a striking echo of Queen Victoria's promise when she became Queen just over a century earlier: 'I will be good.'

Her engagement to Philip remained the only matter on which Elizabeth was determined to get her own way. She had kept his photograph on her dressing table throughout her time away and they wrote to each other regularly. Philip would mark his letters with a special sign on the bottom left-hand corner of the envelope so that the royal staff would know to pass them on to Elizabeth without delay. And as HMS *Vanguard* finally steamed home in May 1947, Elizabeth danced with joy at the sight of land. When the Royal Family got back to Buckingham Palace, Marion Crawford was struck by how tired and ill they all looked – apart from Elizabeth, who knew she was finally reaching the romantic home straight.

The reservations of many courtiers and the Queen's friends remained, but the King finally bowed to his daughter's wishes and allowed Philip to resume his courtship. After seven years of waiting, events moved quickly. Philip's black sportscar was once again to be seen tearing into the courtyard of Buckingham Palace and he was allowed to take Elizabeth out on the royal equivalent of dates. His style of driving – like his personal manner, reckless and occasionally ill-judged – raised courtly eyebrows. He once overturned his car (when driving alone) and another time, when out with Elizabeth, hit a taxi. ('Oh, Crawfie,' Elizabeth complained, 'how am I to make Mummy and Papa realise that this time it *really* wasn't Philip's fault? It was the taxi. They will never believe it.') But unlike the previous summer at Balmoral, nobody intervened to keep the two apart. 'They seemed so happy together,' remembers Prudence Penn. 'They used to giggle a lot together and she was quite clearly very much in love. I think they both were, but it was very obvious she was – she looked so happy.'

On 8 July, Philip was invited to dinner and Elizabeth rushed upstairs to tell her governess, 'Something is going to happen at last . . . He's coming tonight!' The next morning, she was wearing an engage-ment ring and on 10 July, 'after seven years of thinking about Philip and not anybody else', as she told Margaret Rhodes, the engagement was officially announced.

The wedding was set for 20 November 1947 and was treated as a national celebration as much as a private one. As Lord Brabourne points out, 'Everybody remembers now those tremendous scenes for Prince Charles and Princess Diana when they married, but it was something very similar, you know. Here was this young princess, very, very beautiful she was at that time, and there's no doubt about it, the public were absolutely entranced by them.' Economically, the country was still in one of its darkest hours: food and clothes were still strictly rationed, while the fuel crisis that had so upset the King during his time in South Africa was barely over. Yet, as Lord Harewood remembers, Elizabeth's wedding 'was one of the big excitements. It was a time for letting your hair down, for forgetting the rationing and the restrictions and things of that kind.'

'Everybody,' Margaret Rhodes explains, 'was so frightfully pleased and happy to be able to splurge a bit. All through the war we'd had clothing coupons and miserable beastly clothes. One had to cut up one's sister's old dresses and never had enough coupons to buy new ones. We'd worn very short straight skirts – and then suddenly the new look came in and one wore much longer skirts and felt actually quite feminine after people had been in uniform. And so it was a moment of expansion and just enjoying life so much.'

There were over 2,000 wedding presents, including a racehorse, a gold tiara and a piece of cloth woven by Gandhi which Queen Mary disgustedly mistook for his loincloth. ('Such an indelicate gift,' she remarked.[26]) Every country in the Commonwealth sent some official gift, and there were countless jumpers and tea-cosies from members of the public – all of which, in a break with tradition, Elizabeth was allowed to keep.

Only two years after the war, the most unmistakably German of the Royal Family's relatives were kept tactfully off the invitation list (including Prince Philip's sisters, who were all married to Germans). For a host of other royal relatives, though, the wedding was a chance to relive the happy days they had enjoyed before six years of fighting had destroyed their homes and, in some cases, their thrones. In 1947, much of Europe still lay in ruins, but at Buckingham Palace, as Princess Margaret recalled in an interview with Ben Pimlott for his biography

The Queen, 'people who had been starving in little garrets all over Europe suddenly reappeared'. There was a ball before the wedding which one of the bridesmaids, Pamela Hicks, found overwhelming – 'Suddenly to see all the royal relations wearing fabulous jewellery and tiaras and the men in white tie and tails and decorations. I was eighteen, but of course an austerity child with the war, so it was marvellous to see it all.'

After the party at Buckingham Palace on the evening of 19 November, Elizabeth went to bed singing. She woke up early the next day and spent the first few hours of the morning – in a position that must by now have become familiar to her – peering down at the crowds and saying, 'I can't believe it's really happening. I have to keep pinching myself.' At 11.15am, she rode with her father in the Irish State Coach to Westminster Abbey. Her wedding dress was designed by Norman Hartnell, for which Elizabeth had received a special allowance of 100 clothing coupons (the usual wartime allowance for a family of four was 48 coupons a year; the bridesmaids were allowed 23 coupons each). Meanwhile, Philip himself had designed presents for each of the bridesmaids – small gold powder compacts, initialled with the royal couple's monograms 'E' and 'P' and picked out with jewels.

During the service, the Archbishop of Canterbury, overflowing with romantic licence, proclaimed that 'this service is in all essentials the same as it would be for any cottager who might be married this afternoon in some small country church', while afterwards Elizabeth's father told her how 'I was so proud of & thrilled at having you so close to me on our long walk in Westminster Abbey, but when I handed your hand to the Archbishop I felt that I had lost something very precious. You were so calm and composed during the Service & said your words with such conviction, that I knew everything was all right.'[27] Later on, as the bride and groom left Buckingham Palace for their honeymoon (with Elizabeth's favourite corgi tucked under the travelling rugs), Pamela Hicks remembers that 'the entire Royal Family ran, picking up their long skirts, into the forecourt to throw the confetti and rose petals'.

In later years, Elizabeth seems to have forgotten what a bold step she took in marrying Philip. As Pamela Hicks recalls, 'I was quite surprised because my eldest daughter is her god-daughter, and when I said to the Queen, would it be all right if she announced her engagement to be married, the Queen was quite surprised that she was marrying so young and I said, "But she's exactly the same age as you were." ' In 1947, the country had no such doubts. Elizabeth's youth and beauty, and the unswerving single-mindedness with which she pursued her romance, coupled with Philip's own apparent charms, turned the royal couple into objects of public adulation that was for the time being every bit as frenzied as that which greeted the marriage of Charles and Diana. A crowd of 50,000 gathered outside Buckingham Palace to cheer them after the wedding. During the first part of their honeymoon (which was spent at the Mountbattens' country house in Hampshire), when Elizabeth and Philip tried to go to church at Romsey Abbey, they found themselves besieged by thousands more royal-watchers as well as the press. During the service, the crowd outside climbed onto tombstones and put ladders up against the church windows to peer in at the newly-weds. After Elizabeth and Philip had left, the public queued to sit in the pews where they had sat.

All through her childhood, Elizabeth had been devoted to her parents. They had an enormous influence over her even after her marriage and long into adult life. On her honeymoon, she wrote to her mother, reassuring her that the long wait before the engagement and wedding

had been worth it and received in reply a letter from her father which
ended:

> Our family, us four, the 'Royal Family' must remain together
> with additions of course at suitable moments!! I have watched
> you grow up all these years under the skilful direction of
> Mummy, who as you know is the most marvellous person in
> the World in my eyes, & I can, I know, always count on you, &
> now Philip, to help us in our work. Your leaving has left a
> great blank in our lives but do remember that your old home is
> still yours & do come back to it as much & as often as possible.
> I can see that you are sublimely happy with Philip which is
> right, but don't forget us is the wish of your ever loving and
> devoted Papa.[28]

Throughout his life, Elizabeth's father – who had broken down and
sobbed when told that he had to be King – had tried to compensate for
the demanding dullness of the job by wrapping his family in a protective
cocoon. As much for his sake as for theirs, 'us four' provided a separate,
emotionally intense world into which any of them could retreat when
the outside world of ceremonial and smalltalk got too much. It was a
world which perhaps meant most to him and to Elizabeth – the two
shyest and most reserved members of the family – and he under-
estimated his daughter if he thought that her marriage meant that she
was going to leave it. The world of 'us four' would always define the
way she looked at life and she could no more leave it than her father
could.

For a start, she and Philip found themselves back at the 'old home'
much sooner than either of them had anticipated. The house in which
they had intended to live – Sunninghill Park, near Ascot – burned

down while they were on their honeymoon. So, for the first year of her married life, Elizabeth was back at Buckingham Palace, almost as if nothing in her life had changed. She had no household of her own to run and, according to Marion Crawford, 'Lilibet continued her childhood's habit and always went down to the Queen to ask, "Shall I do this?" or "Do you approve of that?" '[29] Philip was, of course, living with her, but during the day he was at work in the Admiralty. With a disregard for security and public curiosity that now seems remarkable, he used to walk to work along the Mall each day and every afternoon, at 4.30pm, Elizabeth would look out of the Palace window to see him come back through the gates. She did not get a chance to look out of her own windows until July 1949, when she moved into Clarence House – the London palace currently occupied by the Queen Mother.

In Clarence House, at last, Elizabeth had a chance to spread her wings. As Mike Parker, Philip's equerry, recalls, 'it was wedding presents, their own wedding presents, that were put into the house, so they had this feeling of establishing their own house and their own home. It was absolute magic right from the word go. That place really clicked. The princess was enormously happy there. Prince Philip couldn't wait to get there whenever he could.' In public, Elizabeth took precedence over her husband, but in private, according to Lord Brabourne, 'he was very much the husband and that's how she wanted it to be'. She took a traditional view of marriage and, although she was quite used to being the focus of public attention, she did not have an active or domineering personality and she found in Philip the perfect foil. On one occasion, as Lord Brabourne recalls, 'they were driving up to Windsor and Princess Elizabeth felt that Prince Philip was driving too fast, so she started making comments and he stopped the car and said, "Look, only one person can drive. If you'd like to get out, I'll leave you." And she knew perfectly well that he would, so that was the end of the argument.'

As long as the King was alive and well, it was also Philip's job, not Elizabeth's, that dictated the couple's movements – an experience which, Margaret Rhodes says, was 'rather a lovely eye-opener for her'. There were some royal duties that she had to perform – openings, ceremonies, Court events – but they were not very onerous and certainly not enough for Philip to give up his career. In October that year, he was posted to Malta, and Elizabeth would stay in the Mountbattens' house when he was on leave. It was true that while he was at sea – which was most of the time – Elizabeth would go back to London alone, but according to Louis Mountbatten's daughter, 'because the King was still on the throne, largely they were able to get on with their own private life and so that was lovely for her. As a naval officer's wife, she was able to come out to Malta and they stayed with us. And another time they actually took our house over from us when we weren't out there. And really and truly, 90 per cent of the time she was like an ordinary naval officer's wife in Malta, which for her was marvellous.'

Her eldest son, Charles, was born on 14 November 1948, almost a year after the wedding. Anne followed on 15 August 1950, and initially Elizabeth was able to spend as much time with her children as she wanted. They were both christened, as Elizabeth had been, in the Music Room at Buckingham Palace. Queen Mary, with a keen eye for strengthening royal traditions, noted in her diary after Charles's christening, 'I am delighted at being a great grandmother! I gave the baby a silver gilt cup & cover which George III had given to a godson in 1780, so that I gave a present from my gt grandfather, to my great grandson 168 years later.'[30]

Later on, when her children were grown up, Elizabeth would face criticism for being a distant, 'hands-off' mother, but, in the early years at least, her friends are keen to argue the opposite. Michael Parker, who became Prince Philip's private secretary and spent nearly all his time in Elizabeth's household, recalls that 'there was a time after 5 o'clock, for the evening meal, when they had it in the nursery with the children and that was sacrosanct. And even Churchill and everybody else had to come after that time. I mean, the devotion to the children, to see that they were regularly there, was terrific.' It was, admittedly, devotion by the upper-class standards of half a century before: the children had only two daily encounters with their parents, first thing in the morning and last thing at night, and the rest of the time they were looked after by nannies. Even so, it was a routine which meant that they saw almost as much of their parents as children of working parents today. Whenever she stayed with one of her friends, as Lady Rupert Nevill remembers, Elizabeth would always go and read Charles and Anne a bedtime story. Prudence Penn, meanwhile, recalls 'her coming to tea with me with the children when they were tiny and we'd sit on the floor and make castles with cards and things together and she spent as much time as she could with them. But she was a hard-working mother and obviously she had to do both. And that's why I get cross when people accuse her of having neglected her children, because it isn't true at all.'

Elizabeth may have spent time with her children in the first few years after her marriage but she saw progressively less of them as her father's health deteriorated. By the end of 1948, after months of painful cramp, George VI was diagnosed with arteriosclerosis – a disease which had hardened and thickened his arteries, cutting off the flow of blood to his legs. It was an illness which could lead to gangrene, the only cure for which would be to amputate the affected limbs. Or, by allowing blood clots to form within the body, it could cause a heart attack.

Elizabeth was not told about the threat to her father's life until after the birth of Prince Charles; by early 1949 she was informed that her father had been successfully operated on to restore some of the blood circulation to his legs. Even so, the King was urged to rest and especially to avoid long royal ceremonies – such as investitures, military parades and overseas visits – which would involve long periods of standing. Inevitably, this meant that Elizabeth had to deputise for him and by 1951 her father's health had became much worse. To add to his poor circulation, he had had a very bad cough for some months: X-rays revealed a patch on his left lung which he believed was an infection. In fact it was cancer and the lung was cut out in September. With a high-handedness that perhaps went with the job (George V's doctor, after all, had hastened the death of his patient with a lethal injection so that his demise could be reported in time for the next morning's edition of *The Times* rather than the less reputable evening papers) his doctors did not tell him that it was cancer, referring only to a blockage of one of the bronchial tubes. But even if the King did not know exactly what was wrong with him, it was quite clear to his family that he was not well, and it meant that his daughter's relatively carefree days were coming to an end.

'They're putting the bird back into its cage,'[31] Lady Mountbatten's mother observed in 1951, and in October that year Elizabeth and Philip left for an official visit to Canada and the United States. Rather than the usual long sea-crossing, they travelled by aeroplane – an innovation that required the Prime Minister's approval on grounds of safety – but the tour itself was overshadowed by the King's illness. Elizabeth's private secretary, Martin Charteris, later admitted that he was so worried about her father's health that 'I had with me the necessary papers to hold an accession council in Canada should the King die while Princess Elizabeth was on tour. And I had them under my bed whenever and wherever I slept. And so you can imagine what kind of feeling that was.' During the same trip, Elizabeth was for the first time criticised in the American press, which drew unfavourable comparisons between her own crowd-pleasing abilities and those of her mother. Her private secretary later explained:

> The Queen is not quite as easy at dealing with large crowds and she's also got a square face, where her mother's got a round face and it's easier to look smiley with a round face than it is with a square face. They suddenly said, 'Why doesn't she smile?' And so I said, 'Well, I don't know, I'd better talk to her about this.' And so I went, and said, 'Ma'am, I suppose you've read all the press. I wonder if you could perhaps smile a bit more.' She said, 'Martin, my cheeks are aching with smiling, I cannot smile any more.' You know, she was quite firm about that.

The Canadian trip also meant that Elizabeth missed her son's third birthday – something which was remarked upon, with a loyal spin, by the press back home. Charles' parents had left special presents behind, newspaper readers learned, while cinema-goers were shown newsreel footage of a forlorn-looking Charles being wheeled about by his nanny, offset by a jauntily upbeat commentary – 'Here's wishing a very important young gentleman many happy returns of the day on his third birthday. It's unfortunate that Mother and Father are not here to share it with him, but what a party they'll have when they do get back!'

In fact, when they did get back and Charles was taken to meet his parents at the railway station, he barely seemed to recognise his mother and had to have his attention drawn to her before he would step forward for the reunion. Elizabeth for her part seemed just as awkward when she leaned forward to pat him on the head. For his first five birthdays, Charles saw his father for only one and became particularly close to his grandmother while his parents were so often away.

In the 1950s, as Margaret Rhodes points out, Elizabeth genuinely must have felt that she had no choice but to leave her children in London during her prolonged foreign tours: 'That was the duty part of life. I don't think it would have occurred to anybody to have lugged a poor child around on some foreign trip. You know, it stands to reason that the child would be happier in his nursery with his nanny in a stable place, rather than having to take him on aeroplanes and to stay in strange houses and I think she was actually very sensible.'

There was nothing in Elizabeth's upbringing to make her think that one should ever choose personal satisfaction over the demands of the job and Edward VIII was, in the minds of the Royal Family at least, an ever-present reminder of what happened to princes who did. But this did not mean that there was any difference between Elizabeth-the-adult and Elizabeth-the-child, who had wondered why she was not allowed to play on the swings with the other children. Eileen Parker, whose husband worked for Prince Philip, thinks that 'the Queen as Princess Elizabeth really did envy our life, because I remember once her saying – I think we were talking about children and various everyday things – and she said, "I wish I could be more like you, Eileen." And I think that she really meant it.'

Whether hidden in the crowds at VE Day, training with the ATS or simply talking to her tenants at Balmoral or Sandringham, Elizabeth always seemed most at ease when she was inconspicuously off-duty. Her character, though, was to take such times as unlooked-for treats, rather than to seek them out, and she adopted the same slightly austere approach with her children. Even when Elizabeth was older, and more able to make her own choices, many of those close to her noticed that family always came second to work. 'When there was a choice between helping little Charles with his homework or signing state papers, she always chose the duty bit,'[32] says one of her courtiers.

It was a strange reversal of the way her father had approached life. He was just as hard-working a sovereign as his daughter would be. But, whereas George VI had drawn his emotional sustenance from his tight-knit family, it is hard not to conclude that Elizabeth did just the opposite. However much she loved her children and enjoyed being with them, it was the endless stream of royal paperwork that always seemed the real heart of her life. Another courtier relates the story, possibly apocryphal, that many years later, when the divorced Princess Anne wanted to get married for the second time, it was to Elizabeth's private secretary that she first turned for advice. When the private secretary told her to bring the matter up herself with the Queen, it still took three weekends before Anne managed to get hold of her mother for a private conversation.[33]

Elizabeth left her family behind again at the beginning of 1952, when she and Philip left on another official tour. It was a visit originally designed for George VI, centring on Australia and New Zealand, and was meant to last six months. The King had been forced to pull out after his lung operation and so Elizabeth was sent in his place. A few days' holiday in East Africa were added at the start of the voyage. There were, ironically, fewer worries about the King's health for this tour than there had been for the Canadian trip. Martin Charteris did not bother to pack the official papers he would need if Elizabeth became Queen while she was away and the King came himself with the Queen and Princess Margaret to wave Elizabeth off at the airport. Photographs show him looking gaunt and strained, staring keenly through the biting January wind as his daughter's plane taxied down the runway, but those who were with him had no sense of foreboding.

Newspaper articles devoted more space to the dresses that Elizabeth's ladies-in-waiting would be wearing than to the health of her father and Mike Parker, who travelled with Philip as his equerry, remembers that 'we were all relieved that this marvellous man was looking better than we'd seen him look for a while'. Pamela Hicks – whose clothes had been the subject of the newspapers' speculation – notes that 'often one's asked, "Did she know how ill he was?" But I'm sure the answer is no, because although he had been so terribly ill, I'm sure we would never have left on that trip if they'd thought that he was at death's door.' Winston Churchill, who had joined the King at the airport, described him as 'gay and even jaunty, and drank a glass of champagne', although he added, 'I think he knew he had not long to live.'[34]

As she left London, Elizabeth had no such intimations of her father's mortality. Her first stop was Kenya where, after a few days of official engagements, she and Philip went for a break at Sagana Lodge which they had been given by the Kenyan colonial government as a wedding present. There, as Pamela Hicks recalls, 'We had a lovely few days. We went riding, Prince Philip went fishing – which was quite difficult because to ensure that he caught a fish the pool had been stocked to such a degree that it wasn't all that fun. He couldn't avoid catching too many fish. But it was a real time of relaxation.'

The high point of their break was a visit to the Treetops Hotel – a small wooden construction built in the boughs of an enormous fig tree that overlooked a watering hole and salt lick where wild animals would come. There were three small bedrooms, a tiny dining room and a large viewing platform, all accessed by a precarious rope ladder. There were no tourists and no press and the only problem on Elizabeth's arrival was caused by the animals, as Pamela Hicks discovered: 'There was, of course, a new beautiful roll of loo paper, but unfortunately the baboons had got there first and they'd thrust their arms in and seized this roll of loo paper and thrown it around to each other, so the whole hotel was festooned in lovely white bands.'

For Elizabeth, she says, 'it was wonderful, because the princess had her movie camera, which in those days was an enormous great thing, but she loved it because she spent the next few hours filming. The elephants were all milling around the salt lick and I remember they were taking dust up in their trunks and blowing it over each other and particularly blowing it over pigeons that were annoying them.' At night-time, 'They had a way of lighting it as though it was moonlight – it was floodlighting but it looked like moonlight – and in a way I think the animals were almost encouraged to come and lick the salt.' That night, Elizabeth and her party had a couple of hours' sleep before dawn, when a huge rhino turned up along with various other animals. 'It was such a highlight of her life,' Hicks remembers. 'It really, really was. But of course, the terrible thing was that she went up that ladder as a princess and she came down as a queen.'

The King's death took everyone by surprise. He died during the small hours of the morning of 6 February and Mike Parker was with Elizabeth at the time, standing on the platform at Treetops. 'We saw this incredible iridescent light that comes with sunrise over the jungle, which I'm sure she'll never forget. And then we had this eerie experience of an eagle flying right over the top of our heads and very close – a big fish-eagle, immense bird – and my hackles were standing up because I thought, if that bird dives, I've got to go into action. It didn't. It flew away and I never thought about it until later, but that was roughly the time when the King died.'

It was a blood clot which killed him in the end, not cancer, and only the day before he had been out shooting. At dinner on the night of his death, 'There were jolly jokes,' Princess Margaret said,[35] 'and he went to bed early because he was convalescing. Then he wasn't there any more. He died just as he was getting better.' On his bedside table, Edmund Grove recalls, there was a note to remind him to give a pair of cufflinks to a member of the Sandringham staff. Edward Ford, one of the assistant private secretaries, was sent to tell Winston Churchill. He arrived at Downing Street and was led up to Churchill's bedroom, where he found the Prime Minister, 'lying in bed, smoking a cigar in his boiler suit with a little green candle on the side, which they always put by his bedside because he was such a bad smoker, and his bed was covered in papers. He was working on a speech. And I told him that I had bad news for him, that the King was dead. "Bad news?" he said. "The worst." '

Ford then had to go to Marlborough House to inform Queen Mary that her son had died. In fact, one of her ladies-in-waiting had already broken the news, and Ford found her 'sitting very upright in a chair' saying repeatedly and distractedly, 'What a shock! What a shock!'

Elizabeth herself was the last in her immediate family to hear. The bird that Michael Parker saw hovering over her seemed ominous only in hindsight, and there was no way of getting a message to her while she was at Treetops. Even when she got back to Sagana Lodge on 6 February the information took time to get through. Buckingham Palace was supposed to send a coded telegram to Elizabeth's – now the Queen's – party but if it was sent, it never arrived. Edward Ford's belief is that somewhere along the line the code word itself – 'Hyde Park Corner' – was mistaken for the address.[36]

In the end, Martin Charteris, who was staying in an hotel near Sagana Lodge, heard about it from a journalist and telephoned ahead to warn Mike Parker. Parker wanted to double-check the facts and found a radio in the study at Sagana. He switched it on, keeping the volume very low so as not to alert Elizabeth or Philip until he found the BBC overseas wavelength and heard the bells tolling and the announcer's voice confirming that the King was indeed dead. Then he went to tell Philip: 'Imagine being woken up and told that news. He was shattered. He was shocked and shattered. All he could say was, "This will be a terrible blow." '

Pamela Hicks, who had known Philip ever since he had come to stay with her family as a child, describes his reaction:

> It was as though the world had fallen on him. I mean, he put a newspaper over his face and just remained like that for about five minutes. And then he pulled himself together and said he must go and find the princess . . . she was having a rest in her bedroom . . . and so they went for a walk in the garden and you could tell, walking up and down, up and down, that he was telling her. And then she came back into the Lodge – and one just thought, this poor girl who really adored her father, they were very close. And I think I gave her a hug and said how sorry I was. And then suddenly, I thought, my God, but she's Queen!

It was a double blow. Elizabeth had to bear not only the grief that anyone might have felt but also the realisation that she was now in the position that her father had never wanted and that her uncle had refused. Nonetheless, it seemed to affect those around her more obviously than Elizabeth herself. Mike Parker noticed how 'they just went on doing what they were doing, but the whole pressure of the day was there and you could see it in their eyes. That was the most telling part, their eyes, especially with the Queen. I didn't want to look at her too much because, if I did, I'd just burst into tears.'

It was a still self-contained and emotionally controlled Elizabeth that Martin Charteris found later that day, when he finally reached Sagana. As he describes it, he walked into the drawing room:

And there across the room, seated very upright, high colour, was the Queen. And so I did my usual bow and said, 'I'm so sorry, Ma'am.' And she said, 'Well there you are and I think we ought to send off these telegrams.' And so I went and took the telegrams for her and then I did what I had to do, which was to say, 'Now, the only question I have to ask at this stage is what do you wish to be called when you're on the throne?' And she said, 'Oh, my own name, of course. Elizabeth.' So I said, 'Right, Elizabeth II.'

The Queen's *sangfroid* did not desert her when the party immediately had to leave for London. She remembered all the small details and courtesies of departure, made sure that all the staff were given presents and even apologised for the enforced change of plans. She looked strained[37] when she got to the airport at Entebbe, but her flight was delayed by driving rain and thunder and she had to spend three hours making smalltalk with the Governor of Uganda and his wife, 'which must,' Pamela Hicks observes, 'have been quite a trial'. Once they were on the flight home, though, she stayed in her cabin with Philip for the whole journey. It was the only moment since she had heard the news when she was unobserved by her staff and the only chance, if she took it, to express her feelings in private.

As the plane was about to land, Pamela Hicks had a sudden realisation:

We were stooping down, looking through the porthole, and we could see Churchill and the Duke of Gloucester and my father and the Cabinet all drawn up on the runway. And she looked out and said, 'Oh, they've sent the hearses,' meaning that her own car wasn't there and that it was one of those big black royal limousines. And one suddenly thought, this is the end of her private life. She's twenty-five, with a young husband and two tiny children, and from now on until the end of her life, it's public life and public duty.

CHAPTER FOUR

The death of the King left a gaping hole at the heart of
Elizabeth's family and, it seemed to many, of the whole nation.
Patricia Mountbatten found the country's reaction 'really quite
surprising and very touching, because here was a man who had done
his level best to fill a role that he'd never wanted and never felt himself
cut out to do, but somehow it had got over to people what a tremendous
effort he'd made and how supportive he'd been during the war. You
could feel an absolute sense of genuine mourning, of the passing of a
good man as well as a good King.'

National mourning was ordered by the office of the Earl Marshal –
the Court official responsible for all royal ceremonial – which put out
a general request that 'everybody should try and dress as soberly as
possible. Anyone who does possess black clothes should wear them.'[38]
Race meetings were cancelled, cinemas, theatres and dance-halls were
shut, and along the route of the funeral procession shops were closed,
their blinds drawn. The King's body lay in state for three days in
Westminster Hall, where 300,000 people – some of them in tears –

queued through bitter winds and showers of sleet to pay their last respects. The present Duke of Wellington was one of the honour guard around the coffin and remembers how it was possible to stand there for only 20 minutes at a time: standing at attention, staring stock-still at the floor, 'all you could see was feet going past and it made you feel giddy after a while'.

Elizabeth's mother told a friend of the days 'when one felt engulfed by great black clouds of unhappiness and misery' and for months isolated herself at the Castle of Mey in Scotland, trying to come to terms with her grief. To this day, according to Edmund Grove, 'the Queen Mother always likes the opportunity to speak to somebody who was with the King and served with him and sometimes, when I see her, we still talk about the old days'. Elizabeth's sister, still used to the very protected childhood that her father had always tried to maintain, was equally inconsolable. 'I think it was particularly hard for her, in a way,' notes Margaret Rhodes. 'Her father doted on her, you know. Partly because she could do this wonderful thing of making him laugh all the time and I think she missed him quite, quite dreadfully.' For Elizabeth, the plight of her mother and sister seemed almost more pathetic than her own situation. 'Mummy and Margaret have the biggest grief to bear,' she told one friend, 'for their future must seem very blank, while I have a job and family to think of.'[39] To Margaret Rhodes she wrote, 'You struck the nail on the head when you said that it was agony to have been away when Papa died. It really was ghastly, the feeling that you were unable to help or comfort Mummy or Margaret and that there was nothing one could do at all.'

It was, her friends thought, typical of Elizabeth to worry about others rather than herself but her generosity of spirit was combined with emotional level-headedness and a pragmatic approach to life that left little room for self-pity or hesitation. 'My father died much too young,' Elizabeth said many years later, 'and so it was all a very sudden kind of *taking on* and making the best job you can . . . and accepting the fact that it's your fate.'[40] She was undoubtedly helped by the fact that fate held plenty of things to keep her occupied while she tried to reconcile herself to the loss of her father, for her duties as Queen began almost as soon as she arrived back in Britain. Her father had died on 6 February, she arrived at Heathrow the next day, and as soon as she got home to Clarence House she was met by Sir Alan Lascelles, her father's private secretary, who had papers for her to sign concerning an army man who had been court-martialled for homosexuality. Any doubts she may have had about her change in status were further allayed that day by Queen Mary – always a stickler for royal protocol – who had come from Marlborough House to curtsey to her granddaughter, explaining that 'her old Grannie and subject must be the first to kiss her hand'.[41]

In fact, the loss of her father left just as big a scar upon Elizabeth as on those close to her. On 8 February she was formally proclaimed Queen at St James's Palace, where she told her Privy Council, 'My heart is too full for me to say more to you today than that I shall always work as my father did.'[42] She has since built the anniversary of his death into her annual routine, always keeping the Court at Sandringham until 6 February before the move back to London, and always attending a memorial service for him at the Sandringham chapel. Rather as though she had stopped all the clocks at the moment of his death, she has done all she can to keep his memory – and his way of doing things – fresh. On the royal estates, according to one of her courtiers, 'She likes to keep things the way they were in her father's time. If anyone changes anything in her garden or on the estates without asking, she wants to know why.'[43] Her attitude to anything, says another of her friends, is 'if it was good enough for Papa, it's good enough for me'.[44]

Churchill had been concerned that the new reign would mean a change of style. 'There he was,' his daughter, Mary Soames, explains, 'with all the post-war problems still, and this very young sovereign who he didn't really know at all. And I think that he was quite unsettled at first. He'd just lost this King, with whom he had a sort of relationship and bond with the war, and of course he admired and was enthralled by the youth and attractiveness of the Queen and her husband, but I think he was abashed at first.'

'She's a child,' he once complained to Edward Ford. 'I don't really know her.' However, the Prime Minister need not have worried. Elizabeth's desire to follow in her father's footsteps at home applied equally to the way in which she approached the business of being Queen. Continuity was her style, not change. And, just as George VI had done all he could to copy the domestic, rather-dull-but-decent style of George V, so Elizabeth wanted – and was well-suited – to carry on the family tradition.

'She is,' one of her private secretaries thinks, 'absolutely marvellous at knowing when not to do things. And I think, with great respect, she's rather better at that than she is in knowing what to do. She has superb, faultless negative judgement and while her positive judgement's also good, she's not by nature a great initiator.'

Edward Ford, who had been a member of George VI's private office, remembers that 'there was no guarantee that that the Queen was going to carry on with her father's staff'. Within a week, though, Elizabeth had told all her father's courtiers that she wanted them to carry on in their positions. 'There was virtually no change in the way in which the official work of the sovereign went on,' says Ford. 'She was just as conscientious and regular in sending for her secretaries, sending for the papers, making plans for visits and audiences and so on. She did continue the way her father had done. Very much so.'

Philip was less able to take their change of circumstances in his stride. As long as Elizabeth was still a princess, Philip was relatively free to pursue his naval career – for which he was showing some aptitude – and to run his family's affairs without too much outside interference.

His father-in-law was only fifty-six when he died so Philip might reasonably have expected this comparatively normal way of life to continue for several more years. As it was, Elizabeth became Queen when she was twenty-five and Philip was only thirty.

'You must remember,' his friend Mike Parker points out, 'that Prince Philip's whole life had been geared to being in the Navy and he was going to be a damn good naval officer and he was well on the way when he was married. It's very hard for a man who's set off in that direction, and set so well, to change course so utterly. It was like stepping off a cliff into the unknown. He was not going to be the King or the Queen or anything. He was going to be, really, nothing.'

Whereas Elizabeth was used to having her life mapped out for her, Philip was not. They were both very happy with their own household at Clarence House, and hated the idea of moving back to Buckingham Palace. It was, Mike Parker thought, 'the coldest, most unfriendly and unsatisfying place in the world for any family to live in' and he hatched a plan with Philip for the family to stay in Clarence House – which was, after all, only a few hundred yards down the Mall. The Queen was delighted with the idea. To this day, Sir Kenneth Scott, a member of her staff, says, 'she thinks of Buckingham Palace really as the office. It's where she goes on a Monday to do her job, to meet the people she ought to meet, to talk to the people she ought to talk to, deal with the questions she ought to deal with and then she takes off on Friday for the country. So she's really a weekend commuter.' The Government, however, was firmly opposed to shifting the base of operations. 'Churchill was not having it,' Parker recalls. 'Buckingham Palace was the centre of the Empire, where the Royal Standard flew. It came down heavy from the Government that we had to move there. The Queen asked us to go with her for the short ride from Clarence House, and I can tell you there was not a dry eye in the car.'[45]

It could scarcely have caused a constitutional crisis if the Queen had refused to move. George V had kept his own royal time-zone when the Court was at Sandringham (all the clocks ran half an hour early so that he could squeeze some extra hours out of the day for shooting) and to this day nobody has ever successfully suggested that the Court should alter its annual migrations between London, Windsor, Sandringham and Balmoral in order to spare Government ministers a trip to Scotland when they need to see the sovereign. Even though the Government, in the end, held the purse strings and manned all the heavy guns, wanting to live in Clarence House was hardly the same as marrying Mrs Simpson. It was not in Elizabeth's character to argue, however. Leaving aside her desire to follow in her father's footsteps, she also had a deep reverence for tradition – and even if she had not, her youth and inexperience scarcely equipped her to face down someone of Churchill's reputation and standing.

Elizabeth's unwillingness to assert herself caused even sharper anguish for Philip over the issue of the family name. Elizabeth's surname, were she ever to have cause to use it, would be Windsor. Philip, who had taken out British citizenship when he joined the Navy, had adopted his uncle's name, Mountbatten. At the time they were married the issue had been skated over – perhaps because, as prince and princess, there was no need to put a surname when they signed the marriage register. Twelve days after the death of George VI, though, Philip's uncle forced the issue when he unwisely boasted at a dinner party 'that the House of Mountbatten now reigned'. It was a goal which he had long pursued. 'He had,' remembers William Heseltine, former press secretary to the Queen, 'an enormous capacity for pursuing an idea to its eventual adoption, very reluctant to admit that any of his ideas should not be adopted . . . He would work away at it, like water dripping on a stone, until he'd finally achieve what it was he wanted.'

But now, when it seemed that Mountbatten had finally achieved his dynastic ambitions, his words found their way back to Queen Mary and from her to Churchill. Queen Mary and the older generation of the Royal Family had a strong sense of propriety and had no intention of seeing the House of Windsor superseded by what they saw as an upstart line. Churchill, who had the same reservations as well as some political distrust of Louis Mountbatten, quickly advised the Queen that it was the Government's view that 'the family name of Windsor should be retained'.[46] According to Martin Charteris, 'The opposition to the use of the name Mountbatten on behalf of the Government was partly due to a suspicion that Admiral Mountbatten might be too keen on influencing the Queen in his own ideas.'

Faced with this formal 'advice' from her Government, Elizabeth felt she had little choice but to agree, and issued a proclamation along the lines suggested. The decision infuriated Philip, though. His occupation already gone, he now found that his name was being taken away as well. 'I'm nothing but a bloody amoeba,' Pamela Hicks remembers him exploding, and the precedents were on Philip's side. After all, when Queen Victoria had married Prince Albert she had taken his name and the House of Hanover had become the House of Saxe-Coburg-Gotha. George V had only changed the family name to Windsor during the First World War because it sounded more English. As with the move to Buckingham Palace, however, Elizabeth was unable to stand her ground. 'Of course the Queen was young and felt that she couldn't argue with this world-famous statesman,' Pamela Hicks explains. It would not be until the 1960s that a more confident Elizabeth would have the opportunity to tackle the issue again.

The Queen's conservative nature showed itself once again on the question of whether or not to allow television cameras into the

Coronation. John Grigg, a journalist who later made a name for himself criticising the old-fashioned stuffiness of Elizabeth's Court, points out that 'it's often thought that she insisted on the Coronation being televised, which would be an unusual sign of pro-activity and making a suggestion against the established custom, but actually it's not true. I wish one could claim on her behalf that she insisted on it, but that is a myth.' In fact, Elizabeth, like her father, disliked making broadcasts of any sort and particularly on television. Until 1957 she insisted on transmitting her Christmas message (a royal tradition started by her grandfather) by radio, and for the television version the BBC had to make do with a sort of royal test-card – a still photograph showing the Queen sitting in front of a microphone, underneath which her words were played.[47] Her objections did not extend to film cameras – parts of her father's Coronation had been shown in newsreels – but television seemed threateningly new. According to Edward Ford, 'It was thought of as selling your soul, so to speak,' and there were worries that the most sacred ritual of the monarchy might be watched 'in the pubs when people are sitting around in their cloth caps and drinking beer'. As research by the historian Ben Pimlott has shown, the initial advice of the Palace to the Government was to keep the cameras out and it was only after a sustained campaign from the BBC and members of parliament that Elizabeth changed her mind.

It was the Court and the Government that caught the flak over the issue of television cameras, though, not Elizabeth herself. In the run-up to the Coronation, the Queen's person was beyond reproach. 'People felt that this extremely young Queen, called rather suddenly to the throne and with the name of a famous forebear, was just what was needed at that particular time,' says Bill Deedes. 'The years after the war were not only austere but there hadn't been many of them and I think it was felt that this young Queen would add a bit of life.'

Martin Charteris, with a courtier's *tendresse* for his employer, adds that 'everybody had been starved not only of bread and meat and butter but of light and colour and excitement. And there came to the throne this dazzling creature. I mean, you can't believe what she looked like, particularly when she put her tiara on, she really looked marvellous. Wonderful eyes and a lovely, lovely smile. And a gallant, handsome consort. What more could you want?'

In case anyone did want more, the Government did what it could to encourage a mood of national celebration. Food-rationing was still in force, but for the national holiday of Coronation Day, everyone was allowed an extra 1lb of sugar, while eggs and sweets were taken off the ration list altogether. Over a million people came to London just to see the decorations and Churchill added to the atmosphere of over-excited optimism by heralding the Queen's reign as 'the Dawn of a New Elizabethan Age'.

Harold Nicolson noted in his diary on 7 February 1952, 'how furious the great Elizabeth would be to know that she has been succeeded by this sweet girl'. But Gerald Lascelles, the new Queen's cousin, thinks that 'huge numbers of people really did believe that a new era had started. I certainly did. I was just thirty and it seemed that we were going to just steam ahead.' Elizabeth's official status may have diminished – her father had been hailed, among his other titles, as Emperor of India but his daughter would have to sign herself plain 'Elizabeth R' – and Britain's position as a Great Power was increasingly a matter of fiction rather than fact. Nevertheless, the pomp and display of the Coronation surpassed anything Britain had seen since the Diamond Jubilee of Queen Victoria in 1897. It was a display of imperial majesty that combined, as future EU Commissioner Chris Patten remembers, 'all the razzmatazz of Hollywood with all the dignity of the Church of England'.

'The war had changed an awful lot of things,' says Elizabeth's friend, Lady Glenconner, 'but for the Coronation, we really went back to before the war, you know. Everything started again as though the war hadn't been.' To John Grigg's more critical eye, it was more simply 'a compensation to us for diminished power' and one that placed a hopelessly unrealistic burden of expectation on the central figure. As one of Elizabeth's ladies-in-waiting, Lady Rayne, admits, 'it was all the hopes and aspirations of what people had been yearning for for years and all of a sudden they saw it was a possibility. All our hopes rested with this young woman and how she was going to change everything and there was just such jubilation and such excitement. It was extraordinary.'

The preparations for the Coronation ceremony were minutely planned. Eileen Parker, whose husband was Philip's private secretary, recalls that 'we had instructions as to what we had to wear. If it was a long dress you had to have either a tiara, which I didn't possess, or something on your head. You had to have your shoulders covered. Your dress couldn't be wider than a certain width because of the width of the chair, so that all had to be measured. And you couldn't wear dark colours – it had to be light.'

Under the direction of the Duke of Norfolk, whose family traditionally organised great state events, there were several rehearsals at the Abbey, with the Duchess of Norfolk standing in for the Queen. Elizabeth herself had practised wearing her crown off-duty and even had two silver stars sewn onto the front so that the Archbishop would know how to put it on the right way round. One of her attendants, Lady Glenconner, recalls that there were two velvet trains: 'She had one train going up and then there was a different train coming down.' They required six maids-of-honour to carry them and had special handles sewn to the underside to help the maids keep hold of the heavy cloth. The Queen herself did not attend rehearsals at the Abbey, but did practise her manoeuvres at Buckingham Palace, wearing a sheet instead of the official robes. Her maids-of-honour, whether by accident or design, were paired together by matching height and, according to Lady Glenconner, 'we knew that we had to be a daughter of an earl, a duke or a marquess'. Even allowing for the fact that coronations, by their very nature, confer the ultimate class distinction, it was an aristocratic line-up that would be almost unthinkable today. But Britain in the 1950s was a totally different place. Anne Glenconner recalls:

> It then became very exciting because we were treated rather like the Spice Girls. In those days you didn't have pop groups but we were the maids-of-honour and we were photographed and our clothes were discussed and, looking back, it was extraordinary. Wherever, whatever we did, somebody was asking us questions. I got lots of letters, and I think the others did too, from people not being jealous of us, but just saying how wonderful it was that we'd been chosen and how lucky we were.

The Coronation was held on 2 June 1953. In Westminster Abbey, the congregation – largely made up of peers – had started to assemble from 9am. Among them was Patricia Mountbatten, whose day had not started so well: 'Personally, I had a terrible moment when I discovered my coronet had not been sent back by the jewellers as they had been supposed to do and we had to get the poor man back from the suburbs somewhere in the wee hours to get hold of it.' Once she got to the Abbey, she found that waiting would be the first order of the day. Many of the assembled noblemen had brought sandwiches with them, concealed in their coronets, and took to munching them surreptitiously when nothing seemed to be happening. At one moment, says Lady Mountbatten, 'There was a sort of hush and one felt that the main star was about to arrive and three little ladies in bright blue overalls appeared with hoovers, which they plugged in somewhere and proceeded to hoover the blue carpet all the way down, which was so unexpected that it almost made one giggle.'

Most of the maids-of-honour were also sent ahead to the Abbey, all of them very heavily made up with super-dark eyebrows and unnaturally bright red lips 'because it was the first time that it was going to be televised and filmed in colour', Lady Glenconner explains. They were meant to have somewhere to sit, 'but there were so many very ancient old men standing around that we had to say, "Do have our seats," so we were fairly tired out by the time the Queen arrived.'

Keeping up the physical stamina of the key players seems to have been a major part of the behind-the-scenes plans. There had been suggestions beforehand that the crown itself should be made lighter so as not to tire the Queen – although Elizabeth typically rejected the suggestion on the grounds that if her father could stand it, so could she. All the maids-of-honour had been given smelling-salts to conceal in their gloves in case of sudden faintness (one of them ended up contin-ually braced against such an eventuality when her vial broke as she shook someone's hand). And Lady Glenconner says that when the Coronation ritual reached a point of such solemnity that it had to be carried out behind a screen, the Archbishop of Canterbury produced a flask of brandy and asked 'Is there anybody who wants a sip?' (Some of the attendants accepted, but the Queen refused.) Despite all these precautions, however, Anne Glenconner came very close to passing out during the service:

> I had my back against the wall, standing next to Black Rod, and I suddenly realised I was feeling terribly faint, I think because my dress was too tight. We'd been told to wiggle our

toes and that helped, but nothing made very much difference. Black Rod realised because I was starting to sweat and so he just put out his arm and pinioned me to the pillar, thank goodness. The Queen, I think, realised that I wasn't well, because I did get a message that if I really wasn't feeling well, to go out, but I was determined not to miss it.

Elizabeth herself performed almost flawlessly, forgetting only once to curtsey in the right direction as her titles were proclaimed to each point of the compass. She had signalled the start of the proceedings in an almost off-hand manner – 'She just turned round,' Lady Glenconner says, 'and she said, "Ready, girls?" And we said, "Yes, we're ready," and off we went' – but they were of the deepest possible significance to her.

The solemnity of the occasion was almost overwhelming. Elizabeth entered the Abbey to a fanfare of trumpets, wearing a robe of crimson velvet trimmed with ermine and bordered with gold lace, and with her six maids-of-honour carrying her train. Before her went all the emblems of the country's power – the standards of the British Dominions carried by their High Commissioners and the Royal Standard borne by Field Marshal Montgomery, all the Commonwealth prime ministers followed by Winston Churchill wearing his Garter robes, the Archbishops of Canterbury and York with their crosses carried in front and the Duke of Edinburgh with his coronet carried behind. Behind them came another group of peers in crimson robes carrying the royal regalia – the four Swords of State, the Orb, the Sceptre, the Rod, the Staff and the Crown of St Edward. 'The ceremonies you have seen today are ancient and some of their origins are lost in the mists of time,'[48] observed Elizabeth in a radio broadcast later that day. But it was not the splendour of her Coronation that affected the Queen most deeply but its religious significance.

'The Coronation was a deeply moving spiritual experience for her,' says Elizabeth's cousin, Margaret Rhodes. At the heart of the ceremony – which was thought to be too intimate and holy to be filmed – Elizabeth stood bareheaded, wearing only a white linen shift, as the Archbishop of Canterbury marked the sign of the Cross on her with the words 'As Solomon was anointed by Zadok the priest, so be thou anointed, blessed and consecrated as Queen over the peoples whom the Lord thy God hath given thee to govern.' It was a point at which, Anne Glenconner thought, 'she looked like a nun being married to the Church. It was a very, very moving moment.' Afterwards another lady-in-waiting, Lady Longford, heard the Queen Mother say that, during the whole service, Elizabeth had thought of nothing but what her vows meant.

When she was only twenty-one, Elizabeth had publicly told the world that she viewed her life as one of service and, while some of her predecessors had shown varying degrees of willingness to see the job through, the new Queen seemed almost to welcome it as a confirmation of her life's purpose. 'The Queen is a person of very deep faith,' says Michael Mann, a former Dean of Windsor, 'and she looked on the Coronation in the way in which the Coronation is intended. It is a sacrament. She believes that when she was crowned, she was set aside, consecrated for a particular purpose. When I retired, I had to go and see her and say that I was going to retire and the only comment I got was "Huh, it's all right for you. I can't." And this feeling of being set aside to a particular task for the whole of her life was something that the Coronation set upon her like a seal.'

Watching the ceremony at home was the future Prime Minister, John Major. 'I was just ten years old,' he recalls, 'but one suddenly had a new Queen, a young Queen. Everything seemed very glamorous and there were celebrations everywhere. Our neighbours didn't have a television, so people crowded in and we had a tremendous party. I spent most of the day serving tea and watching in the distance the flickering black-and-white pictures on the television screen. It was a tremendous occasion.'

Back at the Abbey, there was profound relief when the ceremony was over. 'The Queen was very happy,' Lady Glenconner remembers, 'and said, "Well done," and everyone was saying how beautifully it had all gone.' There was only one hitch during the procession back, when one of the attendants walking by the Queen's coach started to head off in the wrong direction through Hyde Park. John Taylor, one of the footmen walking next to him, was more alert: 'The Queen noticed and told the duke, who yelled out of the window to me, "Where does that man think he's going? Get him back!" So I had to shout at him not to turn left.'

Safely back at Buckingham Palace, Elizabeth was almost carefree and light-hearted. The rooms were packed with her relatives. All the women wore tiaras and their long trains were carried by pages or maids-of-honour – which tended to enforce a one-way system of movement, as reversing or turning around became a major exercise in crowd control. For a while, Elizabeth simply sat down, her crown off, while Prince Charles played hide-and-seek under the Queen Mother's robes. At one stage, Lady Rayne remembers, Charles 'picked up the crown, which was just lying on a coffee table and put it on his head. I don't think, as he picked it up, that he could see how heavy it was and he sort of staggered to put it on his head and he couldn't even walk with it, it was so heavy. But he did look rather sweet and everybody laughed. It broke the tension.'

There were long sessions of official photographs at which Prince Philip tried to help, although his efforts went unappreciated. 'He told me to smile at one point,' Anne Glenconner recalls, 'and I could see that Cecil Beaton was getting very, very irritated because he is a professional photographer and the Duke of Edinburgh was telling him what to do.' When the photographs were at last finished, Elizabeth clapped her hands in relief. Then there were the balcony appearances, which went on all afternoon. Lady Rayne, tucked in at the back, found them an extraordinary experience:

> The noise was welling up to this roar. I've never heard a noise like that before and it wasn't just the crowds in the courtyard or even outside the gates of the Palace, it was all the way up the Mall. As far as you could see, there were I don't know how many thousands upon thousands of people and, even from where I was standing, you could see people were crying, they were waving. And if I'd been the Queen, I would have been in tears to think that all that was for her. It was deeply moving. It was moving for me and it wasn't all for me, it was for her, and it was incredible. I'm sure she remembers it to this day. I don't know how you could not.

Images of the Coronation, of the young Queen dedicating herself to her country, and of the massed pomp and pageantry, had a deep effect on the image of the Crown and on what was expected of Elizabeth. The next day *The Times* described how at the end of the service the Queen's expression was one of 'exaltation, of high dedication', adding that 'she did not smile now, nor was she solemn. She seemed unwearied. Her bearing was magnificent in its dignity and she was wholly regal.' Winston Churchill's daughter, Lady Soames, was struck by how, during the Coronation, 'the whole congregation joined in singing the two verses of "God Save the Queen" both as a prayer and as a hymn'.

However, the combination of patriotic fervour and moral enthusi‑ asm did not appeal to everyone. For John Grigg:

The mood in Britain at the time of the Coronation was a very unhealthy one and it became progressively worse over the next two years. I don't think the monarchy should ever become a quasi-religious cult. It shouldn't become a kind of Shinto. Well, it was becoming like that at the time of the Coronation and the feeling that the Queen was a kind of priestess was really very widely shared. It's very hard for younger people now to grasp what it was like at that time, to imagine that it would have been like that, but it was.

Perhaps because of the strength of public acclamation, behind the scenes Elizabeth often felt overshadowed by the memory of her parents' reign. She did, as Michael Oswald, one of her staff members, stresses, take her role very seriously ('Nothing is more important. She lives by the Coronation Oath.') But, whereas her parents had divided the business of the monarchy between them (her father starring as the hard-working, dedicated Father of the Nation and her mother supplying the glamour and the charm), Elizabeth took it all upon herself. It was perhaps partly because she was a woman and therefore had no choice. Kings at least usually had their wives to smile at the crowds and to provide a softer focus for the monarchy, whereas Elizabeth had Philip, who was never going to replace the Queen Mother in the public's affections even if he had wanted to.

She was also naturally conservative, not seeing the need to change anything and apparently never even considering whether to make the reign of Elizabeth II different in style from that of George VI. As Barbara Castle, a former Cabinet minister, puts it, 'I think she was cautious because she was never brought up to trust her own judgement. She was brought up to do her duty – which she did, with great selflessness and some efficiency – but she had to be cautious because she had never been encouraged to trust her own human reactions. She wasn't supposed to be a human being.' Even though Elizabeth was the only sovereign since Queen Victoria to reign under her own name (all the others, from Edward VII to George VI, had used a different name in private) she would show a marked unwillingness throughout her life to project her own vision of the monarchy.

More like her father in her serious-mindedness and dogged attention to detail, Elizabeth also found her mother's act hard to follow. In the opinion of some Palace officials, the Queen Mother had provided the real steel and backbone to George VI's reign, yet in public she had a natural performer's ability to engage with the crowds. Like the late Princess of Wales, she was also able to give the impression both of liking the people she met and of forming some sort of emotional bond with them. These were not the talents of her shy and withdrawn elder daughter. As Lady Soames explains, 'The Queen was brought up in an entirely different atmosphere and era, when the Royal Family never offered their views on anything except the weather.' And whereas the Queen Mother had the star-quality to make her views on the weather sound gracious, warm and intimate, Elizabeth did not.

Martin Charteris thinks that 'the Queen is a lady of very strong emotions and I've seen her very moved. I've never seen her moved to tears, but I've seen her in crowds, I remember, when I could just see a little vein beating there and I knew that she was moved by it. But she had herself under great control. Very, very distant in everything she does.' Elizabeth took more after her grandmother, Queen Mary, than her mother. And to those who were unskilled at detecting the tell-tale pulse of royal emotion, Elizabeth could indeed appear cold – as she herself realised. Her problem was that she was not only naturally reserved but also keenly aware of her status and concerned not to betray the dignity of her position. Greater confidence or swagger might have enabled her to unbend more in public but, as it was, she felt she could only show emotions behind closed doors. Barbara Castle would often wonder, 'Why does she have to stand and glower? Because when you got her on her own, talking about something she really cared about, like the children, her face would light up, she'd relax and her very lovely smile would come.'

At the end of 1953, Elizabeth resumed the Commonwealth tour that her father's death had interrupted a year earlier. It was accompanied – as was usual throughout the early years of her reign – by enormous public interest, with thousands of people waiting outside Buckingham Palace to wave her off, and excited newspaper articles pointing out that Elizabeth was not only the first reigning sovereign to circumnavigate the globe but that she would do so without ever setting foot on ground that was not governed in her name.[49]

She was greeted by enormous crowds wherever she went and Pamela Hicks, who travelled with her, retains a vivid impression of the young Queen's first tour:

> It was such an example of how to suppress your own natural inclinations and to perform in the way that is your job, in that, unlike Queen Elizabeth the Queen Mother, who is naturally gregarious and marvellous with people, the Queen is a basically rather shy and very private person really. We would travel by train a lot and there would be people all along the line so that she could never relax because going through a town there would be enormous crowds. In the countryside there would be perhaps only six or twelve people but they had probably driven hundreds of miles to see her – and if she wasn't there when they waved it would be a great sadness. And so she was always having to be ready and the train would be halted and she'd talk and I

remember her so well saying, 'Oh, Mummy would be so good at this, she loves doing it, she'd do it so beautifully.' And she herself was obviously having to rather force herself to do it in those early days.

Philip, too, felt the strain and certainly could not make up for his wife's PR deficiencies. 'Here he was,' Pamela Hicks observes, 'still very young, a very active naval officer who'd been in command of destroyers and suddenly there he is, put into a car and waved at hour after hour. And, you know, to smile and to wave is not the natural job of a young man of twenty-nine or thirty and he found it difficult.' His response, 'when we were driving back from some function and it was the pubs' closing time and hordes of people would be tumbling out, very much the worse for wear and clinging to lamp-posts', was to spot a few obviously drunk targets and 'make a great point of waving at them, whereupon they got very over-excited and waved back, thereby releasing the lamp-post and crashing to the ground'. Years later, this same sense of frustration at the emptiness of his official life would spill over into Philip's famously ill-judged asides and often embarrassing jokes.

Elizabeth's own, more measured, reaction to the demands of her position was to separate each of its different aspects. As one of her staff notes, 'She is two people. She would discuss anything with me and I would tell the ordinary viewpoint. One moment we would be talking on the grouse moor and the next she was arriving somewhere and I would open the car door and I didn't exist.'[50] But it was more than just relaxing in private and being formal in public. Michael Mann thinks that 'she has in a sense almost compartmentalised her life. There is the state side, there is the private side, and there is the public image side, but they're all three different things and it's as if when she walks out of one she closes the door before she goes into the other one. In order to maintain her integrity she has to have these compartments.'

While this may have helped maintain her integrity, it increased Elizabeth's remoteness, almost as though she had elevated the art of smalltalk into a philosophy of life. 'I think people flatter themselves that they get on well with the Queen,' one of her courtiers, Shane Blewitt, observes. 'I remember once saying to the Queen about a certain member of staff – I think from the Prince of Wales's office – who had just left, "I think the chemistry wasn't quite right," and she gave me an old-fashioned look. She said, "Chemistry? What do you mean? You employ people to do a job. Chemistry is nothing to do with it." And that put me in my place and that is, I think, how she's got on so well with all sorts of people.'

The success of Elizabeth's approach depended on always being able to ignore 'chemistry' as a complicating factor and on keeping all her compartments watertight – on the belief that there would never be any irresolvable conflict between her positions as head of the Windsor clan, Head of State and a private individual with a husband and two children. Where there had been conflicts so far – as over the family name, or where they should live – Elizabeth had solved them by putting her duty to the State before herself and her family. During the 1953–4 tour of the Commonwealth, for instance, Charles and Anne did not see their parents for nearly six months.

If the trade-off between family life and royal duty sometimes seemed a harsh one, it was accepted at the start of Elizabeth's reign that sacrifice and setting a selfless example was what the monarchy was all about. But as it turned out, Elizabeth's approach was only storing up problems both for herself and for the monarchy. She encouraged the idea that the Royal Family should be held up as an example to the nation of how family life ought to be. But there was inevitable conflict between the twin ideals of public service and domestic harmony, and Elizabeth's strategy of separating things into compartments would not help her deal with family crises when they did emerge. Her vision of the monarchy depended for its success on the notion that public opinion would always put duty high up on the list of desirable virtues, and also on the belief that members of her family would always be happy to live as she did. While both seemed very likely at the start of her reign, neither of them could be guaranteed to last.

CHAPTER FIVE

Elizabeth's first real test as Queen centred on her sister Margaret, whose character and temperament were quite different from her own. Sitting next to Margaret at lunch one day, Prime Minister Edward Heath was unfortunate enough to ask her whether she had been busy lately. In reply, Margaret 'looked at me with something of a sad look and said, "That's the sort of question which mayors always ask me." So the only thing I could think of saying then was "And what do you reply?" and she said, "Well, for the first three months that they're mayor they can't really carry on a conversation and for the last three months that they're mayor I'm too bored with them and for the middle three months that they're mayor, I'm away on holiday in Scotland." '

This was characteristic of an ill-mannered approach to officials that Margaret at times extended to her sister as well. Barbara Castle, when she was a Labour Cabinet minister, remembers one state reception at Buckingham Palace when 'I said to the Queen what a lovely dress she was wearing. It really was the loveliest I'd ever seen her in. And she flushed with pleasure and Princess Margaret, who was standing by, said "Yes, but darling, the *Order*" – she had a ribbon, some sort of Order and it was of course across her shoulder and bosom – she said, "Darling, it does rather stick out, you know." And there was this contrast between this brash, vigorous Margaret and the very shy and professional Queen.' It was a contrast which had always been there.

As children, Patricia Mountbatten recalls, 'Elizabeth was always the more serious-minded, and growing up she retained that character-istic. Princess Margaret was tremendously full of life and fun and I think took life more easily and didn't have the realisation that one day heavy responsibilities would fall on her shoulders.' According to Michael Mann, it was Margaret who had always made George VI laugh and who amused him and whereas Elizabeth was shy and withdrawn, Margaret was by far 'the chirpier of the two'. While Elizabeth had eyes for only one man, Margaret revelled in being the centre of male attention. Sailing on *HMS Vanguard* to South Africa in 1947, it was the sixteen-year-old Margaret who took the lead, chatting to the officers in the wardroom, not her twenty-year-old sister. By the age of twenty-two, at the time of the Coronation, as Lady Penn, one of her ladies-in-waiting, describes, 'she was very beautiful to look at and had a wonderful sense of fun and she enjoyed life so much. Wherever she went she was the centre of attention. She was rather like the Princess of Wales later – the cameras were always there and she always looked stunning.'

If, as Martin Charteris thought, the principal role of the Royal Family was to provide 'love affairs, nowadays divorce, marriage, all these exciting things that stimulate people in their imagination', then Margaret played a key part: 'In any archetypal situation there is always the wicked fairy. Or the dark princess, if you like. I mean, the archetypal picture is of the princess with lovely golden hair, but her sister has black hair, doesn't she? And she is the subject of the moon, not the sun. And so I think that, in order to give a bit of spice, there always has to be something going slightly wrong.'

What was going wrong was that Margaret was in love with one of her father's equerries – Group Captain Peter Townsend. Townsend was a decorated RAF pilot who had fought in the Battle of Britain and later commanded a fighter base. The stress of the war left him, in his words, 'absolutely pooped out' and he was removed from the active list in the final years of the war. He joined the Palace staff in 1944 after the King decided that he ought to honour the contribution the RAF had made to the war by appointing one of its officers to his personal staff. Townsend's background, however, was not the usual upper-class, Eton-and-the-Guards training that most of the courtiers at the time had been through. He was from a middle-class family and the idea of meeting George VI initially terrified him, as he later admitted. 'I'm going to collapse in front of him,' he thought before his first presentation.

In fact, Townsend and the King got on well together. At their first meeting they 'talked very naturally, even laughed when we managed to find a joke' and Townsend remained one of George VI's closest aides until his death in 1952. He described Elizabeth's father as 'one of the few men one could really call lovable' and would spend long hours at the King's side, striding across the heather or stalking deer in Scotland. Like the King, he had suffered from a stammer as a youth and from his nerves when he was older, so he was fitted – both in experience and temperament – to deal with the King's occasionally agonising hesitancy and frustration. He was also the only member of the Royal Household who was able to calm the highly strung King when he became agitated or cross.

Beyond his individual sympathy with George VI, Townsend possessed great personal magnetism that struck all those around him. 'He was an enchanting person, he really was. Very gentle, very kind, very good-looking,' recalls Lady Penn. According to Lady Grove, 'When I had children and I used to take the afternoon walk that one always did in those days with children, with the baby in the pram, if you met Group Captain Townsend, he would always stop and talk to you as though he really was interested in you and what you said. It was natural charm. He wasn't ostentatious at all, but he was charming. It's something I don't think you can learn or maybe it's something you're born with, but he certainly had it.' Edward Ford remembers him as a slightly fey character, but 'very good-looking, rather soft-spoken and a delightful companion. It was very difficult to evade his charm.'

Margaret was thirteen years old when she first came into contact with the Townsend charm – the same age Elizabeth was when she met Philip. 'Bad luck,' Elizabeth is supposed to have said to her sister after they had both waited to see Townsend for the first time, 'he's married.'[51] Not only married, Townsend was also sixteen years older than Margaret but, as she grew older and the relative distance in their ages diminished, what might have begun as a teenage crush blossomed into a full-blown romance.

'Well, they were very much thrown together,' says Lady Penn, 'and he was always around, and I think when they went off to South Africa in 1947, I mean, he was there then and it was just a natural progress, I think, of two people who fell in love.' They shared a similar sense of humour, according to Edward Ford, and in his memoirs, Townsend wrote of Margaret that 'she was a girl of unusual, intense beauty, confined as it was to her short, slender figure and centred about large, purple-blue eyes, generous sensitive lips and a complexion as smooth as a peach. She was capable, in her face and in her whole being, of an astonishing power of expression. It could change in an instant from saintly, almost melancholic composure to hilarious, uncontrollable joy.'

Their romantic feelings for each other reached critical mass the year of the King's death. As Elizabeth had feared, Margaret took the loss of her father particularly hard: it was a sudden and shocking end to her childhood and 'it must,' her cousin, Lady Clayton, thinks, 'have been devastating because she in a sense had more time to mourn'. With her mother plunging into ever blacker pits of despair and her sister preoccupied with her new job, it was Townsend to whom Margaret turned for comfort and support. Townsend, who was in the process of divorcing his own wife for adultery, was only too happy to respond, and at the beginning of 1953 the two of them went to Elizabeth and told her that they were in love. If the rest of the Royal Family 'were disconcerted as they had every reason to be', Townsend later wrote, 'they did not flinch but faced it with perfect calm and, it must be said, considerable charity'. The Queen's response, however, was to play for time. 'Under the circumstances,' she told them, no doubt mindful that her Coronation was only months away, 'it isn't unreasonable for me to ask you to wait a year.'[52]

There were two problems with Townsend. One was that, for all his military rank and decorations, many of the Palace officials thought that he was getting above himself. 'If you probe underneath it all,' Edward Ford thinks, 'you are their servants and servants ought not to marry their masters.'[53] When the Queen's private secretary, Sir Alan Lascelles, heard about the love affair, he confronted Townsend with the words, 'You must be either mad or bad.' Almost certainly, this aspect of things mattered less to Elizabeth – who in later years raised no objections when Princess Anne married Commander Tim Lawrence, another military man on secondment as a Palace equerry. What did concern her was that Townsend was divorced. The Church of

England, of which Elizabeth was Supreme Governor, refused to allow divorce and the whole attitude in the country towards divorce was entirely different from that which exists today. As Lady Penn puts it:

> A divorced person in those days was a rarity in a way. I mean, there were all sorts of things that you couldn't do if you were divorced . . . You couldn't go into the Royal Enclosure at Ascot for a start. People didn't serve in the Royal Household if they were divorced. There were all sorts of things that made it obvious that to be divorced was not a very acceptable thing. Everybody saw what happened when King Edward VIII married a lady who was divorced. It just wasn't the right thing to do.

The fact that her sister had fallen in love with such an unsuitable man put Elizabeth in an invidious position, and her habit of carefully separating her life into supposedly watertight compartments was no help. She now found herself in three conflicting positions – as sister, Head of State and Head of the Church. As Head of the Church she felt bound to give a moral lead to the country; as Head of State it was her duty to take whatever advice the Government might offer her; as a sister, she was simply concerned for Margaret's happiness. There was no way of reconciling the three, unless Elizabeth was prepared to take control and try to shape the course of events, but that sort of leadership was not in her nature. George V might have sharply whipped any straying members of the family back into line; George VI might just conceivably have taken his daughter's side and defended her right to marry whomever she chose in a civil ceremony; Elizabeth took the line of least resistance and interfered as little as possible.

'It must,' says Lady Mountbatten, 'have been a very, very difficult moment for the Queen, who would obviously want her sister to do as she wanted to do and marry the man she loved – and yet to feel that this was going to be such an impossible move for the Commonwealth to accept.' Yet even though it was well meant, Elizabeth's policy of masterful inactivity only ensured that the drama was played out for as long as possible and caused maximum damage. It was a pattern that would repeat itself in years to come.

Elizabeth had asked Margaret and Townsend to keep things secret until after she had been crowned but rumours had already started to fly before 1953 and were, ironically, confirmed at the Coronation itself. At the end of the service, as Margaret was waiting for her carriage outside the Abbey, Audrey Whiting, a sharp-eyed journalist, says she noticed her 'going up to a man in RAF uniform. And she put her hands on his chest, and then, it was as though there was . . . well it might have been a bit of fluff or a bit of anything on his jacket, and she just lifted it off. And then they looked at one another. And do you know I'm not exaggerating, you couldn't have mistaken it. It was the most intimate moment in this vast crowd.' Small though the incident was, Margaret's brief moment of intimacy was enough to spark off a run of newspaper stories that forced the secret out into the open.

Under an Act of Parliament that George III had signed more than 150 years before, in the hope of keeping his children in line, no member of the Royal Family could marry without the permission of the King or Queen until they were twenty-five. By 1953, the permission of the Queen in effect meant the permission of the Government, and Prime Minister Winston Churchill agreed with the more old-fashioned Court officials, insisting that the Queen's sister could not marry a divorcé. Bill Deedes thinks Elizabeth agreed with this view:

Don't forget, all that was taken much more seriously, not simply by the Queen but by a great, great number of the public in those days. And attitudes today are no guide as to whether that decision was right or wrong. I suspect the Queen suffered great hurt over the whole thing, but again we see this concept of what is right by way of duty to the fore and, in a sense, the family affection element to the rear. It's one of those situations which, if you judge it today, you'll take a certain view. But it's not fair to judge it today because you have to judge it by the standards, the morals, the thinking, the outlook of the time in which that decision was taken. It was harsh, but not half as harsh as it appears in the light of today's thinking.

What made the judgement harder, though, was the manner of its execution. Margaret and Townsend did not see each other for two years after the Coronation. While she was away with her mother on a tour of Rhodesia at the end of June 1953, he was removed from his job at Court and posted to the British Embassy in Brussels as air attaché. Margaret was distraught when she heard the news: while her mother continued her Rhodesian engagements alone, it was officially put out that Margaret was unwell. The day Margaret and Townsend were holding out for was 21 August 1955 – Margaret's twenty-fifth birthday – after which she would be able to marry without the approval of Parliament. But all that meant was that she was legally free to marry whom she chose. Nobody seems to have told Margaret that even after she was twenty-five she would still need the support of the Government if she was to keep her title, her privileges and her Civil List income – or that that support was extremely unlikely ever to materialise. Even in 1955, with a new Prime Minister – Anthony Eden – who was himself divorced, there was no question of Margaret marrying Townsend and remaining a princess. The Archbishop of Canterbury was firmly opposed; a Cabinet minister threatened to resign if the marriage went ahead; and *The Times* declared that 'if the marriage which is now being discussed comes to pass, it is inevitable that . . . the princess will be entering into a union which vast numbers of her sister's people, all sincerely anxious for her lifelong happiness, cannot in conscience regard as marriage'.[54]

If anybody had told Margaret how much opposition she would face even after she was twenty-five, it might at least have saved her the two years of heartache and separation that she had to endure after the Coronation. Margaret herself blamed Alan Lascelles, the Queen's private secretary, who certainly disapproved of the whole affair and whose job it was to liaise between the Queen and the Government. 'I shall curse him to the grave,' Margaret is later reported to have said.[55]

'There's no doubt that Princess Margaret felt betrayed particularly by Sir Alan Lascelles,' says Martin Charteris. 'I think she believed that he had somehow indicated to her that her relationship with Peter was all right. And then turned round. I think that's right, but there's no doubt that Princess Margaret felt and does feel that she was betrayed. Not betrayed – that wasn't quite the word – but let down, you know, led astray. Given the wrong impression.' The least Lascelles could have done, Margaret thought, was to have given a frank assessment of the situation. But so might her sister, and Elizabeth's own decision to do all she could to remove herself from the fray scarcely helped matters. In 1955, when Margaret was about to leave Balmoral to see Townsend for the first time after his exile in Brussels, Elizabeth went out for a walk just before her sister left, whether by accident or design, and so avoided talking to her about it.[56] 'She would certainly have allowed her sister to come to her own conclusion,' says Lady Clayton. 'She wouldn't have pushed her in any way.' Yet, by trying to avoid playing the heavy-handed Head of the Family, Elizabeth also simply prolonged and magnified the crisis.

The choice which Margaret eventually faced in 1955 was between continuing to inhabit the royal world in which she had been brought up and living her future life more simply as Mrs Peter Townsend. It was not a congenial one. 'The point,' says Edward Ford, 'was that in order to marry him she would have had to give up her other role and it's like quandaries that other people face in life. You've got to give one thing up in order to get another. You've got to choose.'

One of Princess Margaret's close friends at the time was Billy Wallace, who told journalist Audrey Whiting what he thought would happen: 'I had lunch with him,' she says, 'and he said, "Nothing will come of it." And when I asked him the reason, he replied in a rather odd way. He said, "She's not ready for it," and when I said, "Ready for what?" he said, "Giving up, giving up – she won't give up the royal perks." ' Another of Margaret's friends, Lady Penn, also has her doubts about whether a Margaret–Townsend union would ever have worked. 'I'm not entirely sure that it would have been a happy marriage,' she says. 'Peter Townsend was a great deal older than Princess Margaret – twenty years. There was a very big gap and I've always felt that perhaps it would not have been the happiest of marriages.'

On 22 October 1955, Margaret and Townsend met at Clarence House. According to Townsend's account, 'We were both exhausted, mentally, emotionally, physically. We felt mute and numbed at the centre of this maelstrom.' The next day, Sunday, they spoke on the phone – Margaret in great distress – and on Monday they together decided to abandon their romance. The difference in their ages certainly bothered neither of them at the time, but both must have known how difficult it would be to live together on the pay of an RAF Group Captain, and both were also genuinely religious.

Even though Townsend was himself divorced, he had been the innocent party in the break-up and he, along with Margaret, took very seriously the moral lead that the monarchy was supposed to give the nation. It was a moral lead that could only be weakened if they got married and when Margaret next met the Archbishop of Canterbury, who had prepared for the encounter with a number of Christian texts at the ready, she told him, 'You can put your books away. I've made up my mind.'[57] On 31 October Margaret released a statement that Townsend had helped her to write:

> I would like it to be known that I have decided not to marry Group Captain Peter Townsend. I have been aware that, subject to my renouncing my rights of succession, it might have been possible for me to contract a civil marriage. But, mindful of the Church's teaching that Christian marriage is indissoluble and conscious of my duty to the Commonwealth, I have resolved to put these considerations before any others. I have reached this decision entirely alone and in doing so I have been strengthened by the unfailing support and devotion of Group Captain Townsend. I am deeply grateful for the concern of all those who have constantly prayed for my happiness.

In one sense, Margaret's behaviour and the way in which Elizabeth tacitly allowed her sister to come to her own decision showed the monarchy working in its best, most old-fashioned way. Margaret was not, as Bill Deedes points out, 'the only person who had one love in her life and failing that one love in her life could never really find another the same', and it was, after all, the self-appointed business of the Royal Family to provide a moral lead to the nation. Elizabeth may have done little actively to help her sister, but Martin Charteris does not think it is quite fair to say that she was sacrificed. 'She may have sacrificed herself. But that's not quite the same thing.'

The question which was beginning to be asked in the 1950s, though, and one which has a particular poignancy fifty years on is, sacrificed for what? A report for the *Daily Mirror* in 1953 showed that, in a poll of over 70,000 readers, over 95 per cent thought that Margaret and Townsend should have been allowed to marry.[58] And there was not much point even fifty years ago in the Royal Family providing a moral lead to the nation if most of the country did not want to follow it. Elizabeth was Queen, after all, not State Nanny and, in addition to the dangers of appearing aloof and high-minded, there were the perils of hypocrisy. Every senior member of the Royal Family, apart from the Queen and her mother (and Prince Edward), has since divorced, often in a manner that more than satisfied the public's desire to know every last detail of the break-up.

Michael Mann argues that 'in a period when change is enormous and some of us who are a bit older are sometimes baffled by the speed of change that is taking place and everything seems to be falling apart then the one thing that people can look at and know is stable and can still hold on to is the monarchy.' However, it was exactly the overlap between Elizabeth's role as the country's constitutional leader and the less defined way in which she was also supposed to embody the moral values of the nation that had made the Townsend affair into a royal crisis. And if, in the future, the home life of the Royal Family did not itself seem to be that stable, then what was the point of the monarchy anyway?

It was Elizabeth's fate to become Queen at a moment in history when the relationship between the monarchy and the public was changing more dramatically than at any time for over two centuries. If she had been born and reigned half a century earlier, she would have been amply equipped to do the job. As it was, the press was growing

less deferential and increasingly inquisitive, encouraged by an increasingly voracious and hypocritical public demand for royal titbits. It would
not be storms of bad publicity that would be the most fundamental
problem of Elizabeth's reign, but a sea-change in society's expectations.

A less traumatic but longer-running issue for Elizabeth was how to
keep her husband happy. Philip was an active, independent man used
to having his own command in the Navy, and his translation to the
shadowy role of consort was not an easy one. The last husband of
a reigning Queen, Prince Albert, had been given the official title
of Prince Consort; he was allowed to see state papers and was consulted
widely by Queen Victoria on every aspect of the monarchy's business.
Among other achievements, he was the guiding light behind the Great
Exhibition of 1851, a keen sponsor of science and the arts and took a
keen and active interest in foreign policy. He and the Queen not only
occupied the same study, they had a special desk at which they could sit
together and share whatever tasks Victoria had been sent. None of this
applied to Philip.

As a matter of personal inclination, Elizabeth may have preferred
her husband to wear the trousers and privately she saw him as the head
of the family, but on everything that touched her official duties as
sovereign Philip was sidelined. 'He would,' according to Martin
Charteris, 'very likely have said, "Look, I really don't think we ought
to go on with these presentation parties." Or he would have said, "Can't
we have a more interesting or a more cosmopolitan selection of guests
for the garden parties?" ' But he was, on Government orders, not allowed
to see state papers. And he found that the internal apparatus of the
monarchy itself – the private secretaries, the other Court officials and
staff, even the footmen – was programmed to accept orders from only
one source. 'Remember,' says Bill Deedes, 'that the Royal Household

sees only one figure that matters and that is the sovereign. That's the set-up we have. Very much, I suppose, as if we had a president it would be the president and not his children or his relations who would be seen as supreme. The Queen is the supreme figure. Everything, in a sense, is subsidiary to that. Now that makes a very difficult atmosphere in which to have a close family.'

The atmosphere was made more difficult by the fact that, while Philip accepted his exclusion from the constitutional side of the monarchy, he did want to put his stamp on the Court. His cousin, Patricia Mountbatten, remembers that 'he certainly did see that it was a useful thing for him to do, to be able to try and reorganise a bit the antiquated ways, let's say, of many of the things that happened in the Palace, which tended to go on from reign to reign. And I think that he felt that he would be able to improve matters – which he did. But not always to everyone's pleasure.'

Philip's ideas were not revolutionary. He simply, as Edward Ford recalls, 'wanted things to be done in a rational way. He's very practical and pragmatic in his approach.' But there was a sense, in the stultified atmosphere of the Court, nearly all of whose members had been working for years already under George VI, that ideas in themselves were not necessarily a good thing. According to one former courtier, 'In the old days, you used to assemble before lunch and have a drink, rather like in an officers' mess, and all that's gone out of the window. People are working far too hard now, there isn't time to have anything. If they drink anything they'll drink a tomato juice.'[59]

Philip's equerry, Mike Parker, remembers 'the attitude of those who were at Buckingham Palace towards me, coming from way out there in Australia and so on – the first one that had ever appeared from that direction – they must have been far more terrified of me than I was of them. They must have wondered from under what stone I'd crawled.'

Martin Charteris confirms that his impression was accurate: 'The fact that he was an Australian and was not particularly keen on protocol and that sort of thing meant he was looked on with considerable suspicion – not in Clarence House but over in Buckingham Palace. I think people were not quite sure, you know, that this man, this Australian, was quite like everybody else.'

The enforced move of Elizabeth's family to Buckingham Palace was not without its compensations – 'We were fascinated by the wine cellar that went on for miles and miles and miles,' says Parker, 'and some of the wines that we found had been left tucked away from Queen Victoria's time.' But when Philip turned his attention to other legacies from the nineteenth century, he ran into problems. Philip found himself without allies in his quest for modernisation because, as his cousin, Lady Mountbatten, explains, 'a lot of the so-called "old guard" did view Prince Philip with a certain amount of suspicion – was he going to try and alter everything and what did he know about all this sort of thing? So I think there was quite a lot of difficulty in the early days from that point of view.'

Pamela Hicks agrees, adding that 'there were several people who were more than slightly nervous or strongly disapproved. I think that something that is an old, established concern that seems to be running quite well is always very wary of a newcomer who appears very brash and would seem to be a new broom and full of new ideas – which were very good ideas but of course disturbing to the established way of things being done.'

Philip's attempts to make life easier and more efficient in the royal kitchens were a classic example. Percy Benham, who had been employed by Elizabeth's father as her nursery footman, was now Under-Butler for the Pantry and deeply attached to the old method of washing up the hundreds of dirty plates produced by each state banquet:

They were all wooden sinks with a duck board in the base and lovely plugs so that you could put the plates in tens at a time, let them soak, or if the sink was big enough I might put in four lots of ten. So you'd let them soak and they were washed off with good soft soap by sponges and then wiped and put on top of a hot-plate – not too hot – so they dried off immaculate. When they were completely dry, a leather was put between each plate to stop them scratching because of the beautiful paintings of bouquets of flowers or whatever is inscribed upon them.

For about a week, Philip had been going through the kitchens, bedrooms, housemaids, housekeepers and silver room with a man from the Department of the Environment. He eventually fetched up in Benham's domain and told him, 'The time-and-motion people are coming in to see you and I want you to describe to them how you wash up.' After hearing him describe the laborious, five-stage process for cleaning plates, Percy remembers, 'They said "We'd like to do this, we'd like to make it easier for you, we can install three huge washing machines with racks and shelves but nothing will rumble around, it will just pour water and flush down and then hot air and so on." So I thought to myself, well that's absolutely ridiculous, so I asked to see the Master of the Household and told him it's not feasible.' It was Percy Benham who won out against Philip and his time-and-motion allies: the washing up after state banquets is still done by hand today.

At the beginning of her reign, Elizabeth had neither the tempera-ment nor the experience to back her husband up. As soon as she came to the throne, she had announced her intention of continuing things as her father had done. And although her loyalty to Philip was absolute, it did not initially translate into taking his side in battles against the Palace *nomenklatura.* For Elizabeth, journalist John Grigg thinks, 'it was a natural soft option to keep things as they were because she'd been brought up in a very enclosed way. She'd not gone to school and people of a certain type were the only people she'd met, the only people she got even remotely close to. And it's understandable that she should want to go on having those people close to her.'

Even in the 1960s, when Barbara Castle had dealings with the Palace, she was struck by 'how isolated the monarch is. You see, they're surrounded by such Court etiquette, they're really prisoners,' adding that 'the Court retinue prevented her from giving Prince Philip the sort of role she would have liked to give him. So he is a rather frustrated man, always coming out with awkward remarks and difficult behaviour of various kinds, because he was not given the sort of job to do that his abilities merited.'

The frustration of Philip became front-page news in 1957, as he neared the end of a four-month tour of some of the furthest-flung parts of the Commonwealth. He left – with Mike Parker but without his family – in October 1956, and was away for four months, including Christmas. The point of the tour, according to Parker, 'was to open the 1956 Olympic Games in my home town of Melbourne and we never looked upon that as being a long time away'. Bolted on to the Melbourne visit were places like Tristan da Cunha and St Helena which, Parker thought, 'were now cut off because ships didn't want coal any more and there were not the necessary communication stations and so on. So we joined all these islands together and made a trip out of it. And it had a huge effect on the fact that they were being recognised and that they were going to be visited, and no less a person than the husband of the Queen was coming to see them.'

Whatever the original worthy aims of Philip's odyssey, they were soon overshadowed by rumours that all was not well in his relationship with Elizabeth. Mike Parker's own marriage was in trouble and the newspapers used the misfortunes of the Parker family as a means of hinting that all was not well with his employers. It was an American paper, the *Baltimore Sun*, which first reported that unidentified members of London society were 'talking openly of a rift' between Elizabeth and Philip, and the resignation of Michael Parker a week later only fuelled the speculation.

By early 1957, officials at the Palace were sufficiently alarmed that they took the unusual step of issuing an official denial, which only fanned the flames. 'Fly Home Philip!' called the front page of the *Daily Mirror* on 11 February 1957, while others pointed out that Philip had not seen his family for 119 days. 'Why didn't the Duke of Edinburgh fly home to be with the Queen during the "nine days" wonder of the Parker episode?' wondered the *Sunday Graphic* darkly. 'What prevented them meeting in Gibraltar, if not in London?' Mike Parker stresses that 'we didn't go away on purpose. We didn't want to get away from the Queen or anything crazy like that. We were making a sacrifice in going away.' At first he and Philip mistook the real purpose of the crowds of journalists who surrounded them at every stop: 'Naturally we had no idea that that was the sort of comment. We literally thought that they were going to comment on the fact that we were going to visit all these beleaguered people who were really out of touch with everything. We were astonished.'

Philip himself was 'very hurt, terribly hurt, very angry' at the press reports but hardly eased the situation when he failed to hurry home to see his wife and children. Parker, meanwhile, returned to London early, in time for a taste of the twentieth-century press in full cry. He found it unnerving and decided that his only honourable course was to resign:

It's a very extraordinary feeling for a person who doesn't like to be exposed to have that white-hot heat thrown at you from the moment you go out of your door or even sometimes in your door. I caught a chap going through my dustbin one night and I upended him into it. I found my apartment had been burgled by them on several occasions. There was always a car outside my house, waiting to follow me wherever I went and so it went on. How was I to carry on at the Palace with all that going on? No sir, I couldn't do it. But I'm very pleased to say that the Queen didn't want me to go and wanted me to stay and Prince Philip wanted me to stay too. I shall never forget their kindness and their helpfulness at that time.

This kindness and helpfulness was, however, limited to Parker's immediate employers, as he discovered when he first arrived back in London: 'As I descended the steps from the aircraft that had brought us from Gibraltar to London Airport, I saw a chap from the Palace who told me a press conference had been arranged. I was so pleased to see a friendly face, but then I was absolutely stunned when he looked at me and said, "Well, from now on you're on your own." '

With the departure of Michael Parker, Philip had also been deprived of a key friend and ally and Elizabeth did what she could to indicate her support for her husband. After four months apart, he and his wife were reunited in Portugal in February 1957. They travelled to Lisbon separately; Philip went to the airport to meet her and discovered when he boarded her aeroplane that she and all her ladies-in-waiting were wearing false beards in honour of the naval whiskers he had grown while he was off on his solo trip. That at least guaranteed that when the royal couple did appear in public, they were in good humour, and when they returned to Britain, Elizabeth underlined the serious regard in which she held her husband by promoting him from Duke of Edinburgh to the rank of Prince of the United Kingdom – he now became officially what he had always been known as: Prince Philip.

In addition, Elizabeth finally stood up for Philip in 1960 over the vexed issue of the family name. In 1953, when the question first arose, the idea of grafting Philip's surname of Mountbatten onto the Windsor dynasty had been firmly quashed by Winston Churchill. Seven years later, Elizabeth raised it again with Prime Minister Harold Macmillan, whom she found a less spectacular and awe-inspiring figure, informing him that she had 'absolutely set her heart'[60] on a change. It was nonetheless still an emotional and difficult issue for her. She knew how strongly her husband felt, yet she was still very loyal to the tradition she felt it her duty to uphold. She was also unused, after eight years on the throne, to forcing her own will on the elected government.

Harold Macmillan noted in his diaries that Elizabeth's uncle, the Duke of Gloucester, had warned him: 'I think she's in a bit of a state. Her sister wants to marry a man called Jones [the future Earl of Snowdon] and Philip wants to change her name to Mountbatten.' Rab Butler, who was Deputy Prime Minister and the man sent along to the Palace to discuss things with the Queen, recorded privately that she was very distressed when he spoke to her and almost in tears over the whole issue.[61]

The result of her intervention was something of a fudge: the Government ruled and the Palace duly proclaimed that immediate members of the Royal Family (those who could call themselves Prince or Princess and so had no real need of a surname anyway) should continue to call themselves Windsor. Their grandchildren, however, or any other distant relatives who were not princes or princesses and needed to call themselves something, should use the name Mountbatten-Windsor. It was not quite the dramatic shift that Philip

Elizabeth's engagement, July 1947. 'She was quite clearly very in love' (*Camera Press Ltd*)

'I can't believe it's really happening' (*Topham/Press Association*)

On the balcony of Buckingham Palace, 20 November 1947 (*Topham/Press Association*)

A family picnic: Elizabeth and Philip with their cousins Anthony Brabourne and Patricia Mountbatten (*private collection*)

Louis Mountbatten takes the prize, Malta 1949 (*private collection*)

The Coronation
photocall (*Camera
Press Ltd*)

'The Queen was very
happy.' A newly
crowned Elizabeth
returns to
Buckingham Palace
(*Hulton Deutsch*)

The young family – a difficult balancing act for a working woman (*Hulton Archive*)

The Queen's abiding passion: on horseback, June 1961 (*Hulton Archive*)

Watching a video of Charles and Diana's wedding with Lady Anson and Philip, 29 July 1981 (*private collection*)

At Claridges for the Charles and Diana wedding party (*private collection*)

Stirring the Christmas pudding aboard *Britannia*, October 1982 (*private collection*)

With Prime Minister John Major in Scotland, 1991 (*private collection*)

Elizabeth with one of the new royal breed (*News International*)

and his uncle might have hoped for in 1952, but it was a clear gesture of loyalty and recognition on Elizabeth's part – and one made all the more striking and significant by Elizabeth's usually passive, quiescent approach.

In 1957, Elizabeth also faced unprecedented criticism over her public style. Since the Coronation, the mood surrounding the monarchy – and Elizabeth personally – had been one of enthusiastic support. The gloss of Churchill's 'New Elizabethan' rhetoric was wearing off only slowly, and the Queen's popularity was at an all-time high – all of which made the publication in August 1957 of a single article in an obscure magazine called *The National and English Review* even more shocking. The article attacked her upbringing, her friends, her Court officials, even the way she spoke and what she said:

> She will not . . . achieve good results with her present style of speaking, which is frankly 'a pain in the neck'. Like her mother, she appears unable to string even a few sentences together without a written text – a defect which is particularly regrettable when she can be seen by her audience . . . But even if the Queen feels compelled to read all her speeches, great and small, she must at least improve her manner of reading them. With practice, even a prepared speech can be given an air of spontaneity. The subject-matter must also be endowed with a more authentic quality . . . The personality conveyed by the utterances which are put into her mouth is that of a priggish schoolgirl, captain of the hockey-team, a prefect and a recent candidate for confirmation. It is not thus that she will be able to come into her own as an independent and distinctive character.

The author of the piece was John Grigg. Grigg's father, Lord Altrincham, had once been a courtier – he served as one of Edward VIII's aides when he was Prince of Wales – and Grigg himself was no republican. 'I think the appeal of the monarchy is inherent in the institution,' he says today. 'It is an inherently romantic institution and the more people can relate to the particular individuals who embody it at any particular time, the better.' Defending himself on television in 1957, Grigg professed himself a loyal subject of the Queen, declaring only that 'I care very much for her future and I want her reign to be as successful as it possibly can be'. The problem, as Grigg saw it, was that Elizabeth's way of running things would made it very hard for people to relate to the monarchy, once the initial excitement of having a young new Queen had worn off. He thought the real character of the Queen was hidden by layers of protocol, tradition and elderly courtiers: 'I feel that her own natural self is not allowed to come through,' he told Pathé News. 'It's a sort of synthetic creature that speaks, not the Queen as she really is, and if she herself were allowed to speak, the effect would be really wonderful.'

On top of that, Grigg argues to this day that Elizabeth had surrounded herself with completely the wrong sort of people:

> In the 1950s, in the very early years of her reign, her Household was exactly what it had been in her parents' day and indeed in her grandparents' day. It consisted of the landed classes in the country. It was strictly a class thing. As far as the Household was concerned, I said then what I've never ceased to say, which is that I feel it should be more widely representative socially and ethnically of the vast world-wide community over which the Queen presides. There are no black or brown or yellow faces in the higher reaches of the Royal Household and I'm sure that

this is not due to any racism on her part, because everything I hear about her leads me to suppose that she's not in the slightest degree racist. It just means that there is a certain lack of imagination.

William Heseltine, who joined Elizabeth's Household as her press secretary in 1960, found Grigg's description on the whole an accurate one: 'It was still, I suppose, a rather old-fashioned establishment, fairly hierarchical and pretty much staffed at the upper levels by people who had served in the armed forces,' while Martin Charteris protests that 'the dear old Court is a long-established institution and we are the semblance of our predecessors and you can't change it overnight'.

Fifty years on, it hardly seems revolutionary to suggest that the Queen should not be surrounded only by ancient aristocrats, and it is almost commonplace for newspapers and commentators to call for a more down-to-earth sovereign who could be a bit less majestic and a bit more obviously human. In 1957, though, Grigg's criticisms were both new and outrageous. 'There was the sort of feeling of the Elizabethan Age,' Edward Ford explains, 'and so the Queen was on a pedestal from which criticism was thought to be bad form, really. I think everybody thought the criticisms of the Queen were slightly offensive and in bad taste.'

According to Martin Charteris, Elizabeth herself was also displeased – 'I don't think she liked it. I don't see why she should. And, of course, the courtiers disliked it very much' – but the biggest response came from the public and the media. 'Big Sneer, Little Peer' ran the loyal headline on the *Daily Sketch*, while the *Daily Mail* asked scathingly, 'Who is he to pit his mind against the experience of centuries?' In Australia the Bishop of Sydney gave a public sermon in which he castigated John Grigg as 'grossly impertinent and bad-mannered', and the town councillors of Altrincham passed a resolution 'dissociating the borough from Lord Altrincham's comments'.[62]

Robin Day continued the case for the defence on national television, asking Grigg on the *Impact* show, 'Aren't you falling yourself into the error of expecting the Queen to be endowed with superhuman qualities? To judge from your article, you expect the Queen to have the qualities of a wit, you would like her to be a better orator, you would like her to be a TV personality in addition to being a diligent, dutiful and devoted monarch and a mother. Isn't that a lot?' Grigg replied that he was asking only for 'spontaneity to be the key note', and repeated his loyal belief that 'I know that if her character is allowed to come through, the effect will be terrific. The effect at the moment, frankly, is not terrific.'

Most dramatic of all, when Grigg left Broadcasting House after a different interview with the BBC, he was slapped around the face by a man called Burbidge, who accompanied the blow with the words, 'Take that from the League of Empire Loyalists!' The League of Empire Loyalists are now, like the Empire, defunct, but at the time Burbidge became an instant celebrity. 'I realised that Prince Philip could not do it himself, or any other member of the Royal Family,' he explained in his own television interview. 'I thought that actions were needed, not words.' He was fined £1 by a Bow Street magistrate, who agreed with him that 'about 95 per cent of the people of this country are disgusted and offended by what was written'[63] and the fine was paid by an anonymous member of the public – 'The best investment I ever made,' said Burbidge.

Grigg himself claimed that, of the hundreds of letters he had received from members of the public, at least three-quarters were in his favour. His criticisms of Elizabeth's Court struck a particular chord. Martin Charteris admits that 'I did see that there was something of great importance in what John Grigg said. I wasn't as hostile to him as many of my colleagues and I think we were a bit stuffy. "Tweedy" was the word that John used. Quite a clever word.' Slightly more defensively, Edward Ford also agrees:

> It was true and we all recognised it was perfectly true. But it wasn't unnatural, for various reasons, really. One is the way, on the whole, that intimate members of the Household were selected: usually by the ones who were there. I think it really meant that one came from a certain cut in the population, so to speak. Of course, you were going to spend quite a lot of time as a house-guest of the King or Queen, whichever it was, so it was important that those should be the sort of people whom the Queen might have invited to stay with her whether they were in fact working for her or not. I think this goes back to treating their Household, those who work for them, as their friends and their guests, so it was rather natural that they should be in a small coterie.

The charge that Elizabeth had left things entirely unaltered since her father's day was slightly unfair. There were changes, but they were small and incremental. 'I think,' says Martin Charteris, 'that John was only ushering us in the way that we were going. He may have made it happen a little quicker. He may even have made it happen a little slower. That's the way of the world, isn't it?'

One of Elizabeth's reforms, which would have meant very little to the general public but which made a great difference to those concerned, was the ending of the practice of footmen having to powder their hair. While staff at the Royal Mews were provided with eighteenth-century-style wigs, the footmen at Buckingham Palace had to improvise their own by covering their heads with flour. John Taylor, one of Elizabeth's pages, explains how 'you had to get your flour allowance and bake it in the oven to kill any weevils. Then you kept it in big tins. You soaped your hair and sprinkled flour on it and it would dry like a crust.' Taylor and the rest of the pages all received extra money to pay for the soap and flour, but it was a hopelessly impractical tradition. It took ages to achieve the desired effect and then at least another hour to wash your soap-and-flour-caked hair at the end of the day. In George VI's time, when the footmen had to powder their hair before waiting at dinner, the Royal Family might turn in at 11pm, but, after clearing up and washing their hair, it would be 1am before the servants got to bed. It rained during the state procession for Elizabeth's Coronation and the footmen marching alongside her coach had to contend not only with damp clothes but with their wig-effect hair running in white trickles down the backs of their necks and over their uniforms. Elizabeth finally banned the practice in 1955.

There were other changes too. The social ritual of presenting upper-class young women at Court was ended in 1958. Instead, the idea of inviting a wider and more representative number of people to garden parties was introduced. In addition, from 1960, one or two of Elizabeth's staff were appointed from Commonwealth countries. None of it was very revolutionary, though. And according to Martin Charteris, 'Basically, the Court that she inherited was her father's – that's perfectly true. And I think that Philip led the way in saying, look, we've got to get into the second half of the twentieth century. And his influence was certainly strong in favour of modernisation and it wasn't long before they'd abandoned the debutantes' parties and that sort of thing. But the change was subtle, it wasn't violent. There was no breaking of old ties or chucking people out.'

Assessing the impact of his 1957 article today, John Grigg thinks that 'the worst thing, really, was that nothing happened. That in spite of all this interest, the people who could have changed things, who could have made things happen, on the whole didn't.' Of all the people who could have made things happen, Elizabeth was the most important – but her personality, combined with the nature of the institution she represented – made dramatic change all but impossible. Grigg had argued that the real Elizabeth had only to speak and all would be well, but in fact the real Elizabeth was quite at home with things as they were.

In some small areas, Grigg was probably right. One of Elizabeth's staff agrees that 'the people around her protect the Queen too much. For example, we had a gelding which made a squeaking noise from his sheath and they told her in the stable that it was the saddle noise. Once I was riding him and the noise started and she said, "Oh, you've got the squeaky saddle." "No it's not," I said. "It's the air in his sheath." Well, when I got back one of the Queen's equerries called me in and he said, "You have to remember who you are talking to. You can't tell her everything." '[64]

Even in the 1980s, the atmosphere of Elizabeth's Household struck some outside observers as distinctly old-fashioned. Bernard Ingham, press secretary to Margaret Thatcher, takes a dim view of the entire breed, arguing that 'it seems to me that if you are a courtier – and there are a lot of them about – then quite frankly you don't have opinions, do you? All you do is smooth and smarm and generally curry favour.' Meanwhile, Chris Patten, another former member of Lady Thatcher's own court, thinks that 'most of the Queen's closest advisers are professional, charming with a rather old-fashioned cut to their jib and I don't think that the Queen would care for too much flash and dash around. I think she'd get a bit suspicious of people with slightly too much cuff showing, so you'd get a decent sort of brogue, elderly and well-polished. You'd get a well-cut but rather elderly suit and you'd very often get a pretty smart professional mind on top of it.'

The problem lay not in the courtiers, though, but in the woman who employed them. By the late 1950s Elizabeth was not so much shielded or smothered by the Royal Household as a fully integrated part of their world. They, in turn, took their cue from an earlier age and 'I can't help feeling,' says Grigg, 'that she has very much looked to her grandfather as an example. The devotion to duty, the addiction to routine, which was very strong in George V and certainly very strong in her – and the fundamental decency and the upholding of decent standards – in all of that I think she's been following his example.' Her upbringing had prepared her for nothing else, and Barbara Castle, observing the Queen into the 1970s, maintains that 'the whole of the Court routine and the rest of it remained unaltered for so long in her reign because she'd never been encouraged to break free. You never get the feeling that she'd been asked, "Now what do you think? Do you think it should be altered? How?" No, she was correctly waiting to do her correct job but she nearly got fatally left behind.'

If Elizabeth only slightly altered the composition of her immediate Household, she altered her own routine even less – and has stuck to it throughout her reign. As Grigg points out:

> The very long summer holiday at Balmoral, the pretty long Christmas holiday at Sandringham and then the spring in Windsor – these routines are apparently set in stone. They are maintained and there's no question of establishing residences in other parts of the world or spending at least part of these very long holidays in other countries of which she is sovereign let alone other countries of the Commonwealth of which she is head. There has been a remarkable fixity. Perhaps excessive and unfortunate fixity.

It was a fixity, becoming apparent in the late 1950s, that would leave Elizabeth looking sorely out of touch as the rest of the country moved on. John Grigg's article may have caused public outrage in 1957 but he was only a few years ahead of his time. By the 1960s, the Queen would have to face the first major re-evaluation of her role. Bill Deedes recalls:

> Respect began to take a backward step and any form of being obsequious to anyone became out of order. Broadcasting became a great deal more lively. Television became more iconoclastic. There was a feeling that there were no holds barred. The media became more outspoken, the cartoons became rather more personal and ugly. In other words, it was an era in which everybody in authority began to feel the draught. I don't attribute that to the Royal Family – I think the Royal Family were simply part-victim of a much less respectful attitude towards authority. They were, in a sense, caught in the same gale.

CHAPTER SIX

Elizabeth's own approach to the business of the monarchy was fatalistic. The criticisms she faced at the end of the 1950s, like the wild adulation that had surrounded her when she was crowned, were to an extent like background noise that had little effect on the reality of her life. She was not impervious to criticism – or to praise – but, as Edward Ford puts it, 'I don't think the Queen was saying to herself, "I must modernise this institution." I think she was thinking, "Well, what is my duty as Queen and how do I best do it?" ' In reality, much of Elizabeth's life, according to many outside observers as well as her friends, was disagreeable. Bob Hawke, the former Prime Minister of Australia, thinks that:

Being the Queen is like being condemned to purgatory. I mean, you have to be nice to people who you think are absolute shits. You have to endow them with a wisdom that you know they're entirely lacking in and treat them as though they are next door to Einstein when you think that they really would get a mark-up of about 50. There comes a time in life when the last thing you'd want to do would be to go and open a Girl Guide function or Boy Scout function, but if it's on the list it's on the list. And as Queen you'd have to, as she had to, be nice to Idi Amin. Well, God, being nice to Idi Amin's got to be just about the worst job in the world, hasn't it?'

In fact, smalltalk with Idi Amin was something Elizabeth was spared (although he did once send a proposal of marriage to Princess Anne) but, among other heads of state, she did have to entertain the thoroughly unpleasant presidents Ceaucescu of Romania and Mobutu of Zaire, as well as burying the sword among the tea-cakes when Emperor Hirohito came to visit. The more monstrous highlights of the routine may even have come as a relief to her: chatting to corrupt dictators and other tricky guests may at least have given her some good anecdotes to tell. Far more depressing, as Hawke points out, would have been the prospect of making non-committal polite conversation with a succession of ambassadors, run-of-the-mill politicians, local councillors and military officers for as long as your life lasted. This was something about which Princess Margaret made her own feelings plain. On top of that, there was also a seemingly endless succession of new hospitals, bridges and factories waiting to be visited or opened (even today, the demand for members of the Royal Family to attend any number of minor civic functions far outstrips supply). From the very beginning, Elizabeth's instinctive response – and probably the only way of coping with the job – was not to expend too much mental energy on worrying about it all. As one of her friends, Lady Anson, puts it, 'I don't think she would ever stop to think what she would have liked to have been. I think her dedication to the job is such that that would be a negative thought.'

The result was that Elizabeth-the-Queen was indistinguishable from

Elizabeth-the-person. John Grigg's criticisms had touched a raw nerve, not just because of the deferential climate of the time, but perhaps also because many people sensed, then as now, that to criticise the monarchy was actually to criticise the person of the monarch. In previous reigns, there may have been a sense in which the character of the King or Queen stood apart from their advisers or the values that they represented. But under Elizabeth II the overlap was almost complete. If she stood for anything in public, it was for trying your hardest, upholding family life and setting a good, quietly decent example.

In private, it was exactly the same. 'I think the Queen has a very steady and loyal and steadfast nature,' says Lady Mountbatten. 'In her upbringing those characteristics were very much brought to the fore, and I'm sure she realised very early on how important it was to behave sensibly and loyally.' Nothing that Elizabeth did was an act. And, while many of her friends and those close to her agree that she does tend to separate her life into compartments, there seems to be no compartment in which she is not Queen. If there is one part of her in which she is an entirely private individual, it appears to be so tightly sealed and seldom visited that it may as well not exist. With no real life of her own to retreat to, Elizabeth's response has been to make the formal, duty-bound aspects of her role as domestic and normal as possible.

As Kenneth Scott, one of the Queen's former private secretaries, explains, Elizabeth's courtiers 'organise the Queen's life – other than her really private life (her life with her horses and her dogs and her family she organises herself) – but everything she does publicly is organised under supervision by the three private secretaries. And so everywhere she goes, whether it's for a weekend to Windsor or for a holiday in Balmoral or for a trip abroad, at least one private secretary is always there, feeding her with paper from Whitehall, which comes in every day.' Elizabeth's attitude to her staff, as to her job, is down-to-earth. 'She doesn't like pomposity,' says Scott. 'I've heard her describe somebody as being "much too grand for us", and she doesn't like side. She likes people who make her laugh and she likes people who are warm in their personality and people who are interesting.'

This is the same approach she has always taken to the formal, state side of her life. For a woman who is hardly ever seen in public without at least a pair of gloves and a hat on, and who has often appeared in formal gowns decked with fabulous jewellery and tiaras or crowns, Elizabeth has little personal liking for her official incarnations. 'I wouldn't think she's particularly interested in clothes,' says Lady Mountbatten. 'She is one of those people who does not wish to always be in the forefront of fashion and indeed it wouldn't really suit her. I mean, she wears clothes because it goes with the job and you have to wear the type of garments that people expect to see you in. But I think, for her own sake, what she would like is probably a jersey and a tweed skirt and something really comfortable to relax in.'

Margaret Rhodes believes that, given a choice, 'she would be a country lady with dogs and horses and a bit of shooting and leading a proper countrywoman's life. She's not innately an urban person.' Kenneth Scott agrees: 'I think if the Queen wasn't Queen she would like to live in a comfortable house in the country, surrounded by horses and dogs and friends who like the same thing. That's why she enjoys Sandringham so much – and Balmoral and Windsor – where she can ride every morning and visit her horses and follow the life of a country lady. I think she would prefer never to cross the threshold of Buckingham Palace if she could help it.'

As it is, the atmosphere that Elizabeth has tried to create in private reflects what might have been. She treats her Household almost as an extended family, though she never unbends to the point of real informality, let alone indiscretion. Nonetheless, as Kenneth Scott reveals:

The Queen does like sometimes to relax with her staff, very often in fact. The first time I met the Queen, when I was being looked at as a possible candidate for this job, I was invited up for a gin-and-tonic after work and that was a very relaxed atmosphere. Particularly when in Windsor or Sandringham or Balmoral, the immediate household – the private secretary, the lady-in-waiting, the equerry – are very much part of the social life as well. She likes to be surrounded by her intimate staff whom she knows well.

Edmund Grove was also struck by the close, almost familial atmosphere when the Court was away from London:

I found the Queen – in fact I still find her – extremely easy to get on with. She has a great feeling for people. She has a great memory for faces and people and when she comes to Sandringham she likes to relax and she knows nearly everybody here – the staff and the people living around. She likes to know everything about her staff, and whenever someone is ill or dies, we have to send a note to the Queen. And I remember well, on one occasion I wrote a note saying that one old lady at Balmoral had died and that there was no next-of-kin. I sent the note to the Queen and it came back very shortly and written on the bottom of it was a note by the Queen which said, 'Oh yes, she has. She has a niece, her name is Bunty and I met her when I was last in New Zealand.'

It is when she is in the country that Elizabeth has a chance to be most nearly herself. 'I've been at Sandringham when she's been there,' says Lady Penn, 'and she lives the life of any other country person. She takes her dogs for a walk, she'll go for a ride. She'll go and see people on the estate, she'll go and look at how the garden's getting on. She'll do her work in the mornings and probably have a picnic lunch somewhere and be with her friends. She loves doing jigsaw puzzles and plays Patience in the evening sitting at a table by herself.'

'I look upon the royal years as rather like a school year,' says Shane Blewitt, a member of her staff. 'You have your three terms interspersed with breaks – which are still working breaks. So you have the Balmoral break, which marks really the end of the school year, so everybody's sort of exhausted by then and we have a nice long break. And then you come back for the autumn term which ends at Christmas and then the Sandringham break. And then the spring term and then the (very hectic, usually) summer term after the Windsor break.' This routine has never varied for practically the whole of Elizabeth's life. 'She probably goes out for a ride in the morning,' says Shane Blewitt, 'comes back, does some work, goes out to a shooting lunch, comes back from that. Then there's tea, then after tea there's more work with her private secretary or whoever else happens to be up there – maybe the Master of the House coming to discuss staff or something. And then you're into the evening, which might be more often than not a barbecue.'

In 1957, John Grigg had criticised Elizabeth for staying so firmly rooted in the British Isles and had even suggested that she set up new residences in some of the Commonwealth countries. According to Kenneth Scott, though, 'she isn't really interested in exploring new places. She gets enough of that in her official life. The Foreign Office makes her go on state visits abroad, sometimes to very off places, and that's enough foreign travelling for her, really. The only two exceptions have been when she's been to visit stud farms in Kentucky and in France where she's had mares being serviced by local stallions.'

Horses have long been a passion of Elizabeth's and the childhood hours spent playing with her toy ponies or pretending to be a horse with her governess in no way diminished her enthusiasm as an adult. 'Her favourite weekends,' says Margaret Rhodes, 'would involve a trip down to see the horses in the stables and maybe get up early and see them riding on the gallops,' while one of her staff insists that Elizabeth has a particular empathy with and ability to communicate with animals. 'The Queen has something about her which the Duke doesn't have,' he says. 'I've seen her go into a field of ponies at Balmoral and they all just go to her.'

She breeds her own racehorses, which have won every classic race except the Derby. Michael Oswald points out that 'the big Arab breeders have 250 to 300 brood mares each and the Queen has only between 20 and 25, and they have far larger sums of money invested in the whole business than she does. She is now a minnow in a very big pool. But in 1999, for example, in terms of winners to foals born, she was the leading breeder in England and Ireland. Ahead of all the Arabs. So in terms of quality she's right up in the very top of the tree.' This was the only interest that Elizabeth could pursue without interference from anyone else. Undoubtedly a rich man's pastime, breeding horses was nonetheless something which brought its own rewards and which Elizabeth could take pleasure in as something that was entirely her own. It also brought the illusion of privacy and normality.

'She is happiest at Sandringham where she can walk privately,' says one of her trainers.[65] 'We would all have breakfast together and she would help herself. I would point out the plovers and once a little hare. She loved that. Once one of the horses broke free and she stood in the road to stop the traffic so that we could round him up and get them all across together.'

Perhaps because, like horses, they are generally more reliable than people and require less in the way of conversation, Elizabeth has an almost equal enthusiasm for dogs. As well as the corgis, she has seventeen labradors and spaniels (called, appropriately enough for dogs in a household that sets its clock by the 1950s, Flash, Spick & Span, Oxo and Bisto) that follow the Court up from Sandringham to Balmoral in their own special van.[66]

She is, according to Margaret Rhodes, 'terribly good at picking up when she's out shooting and using her dogs for dog trials and so on. She's very knowledgeable about all the techniques of making your dogs go in the right place using the right hand signals and whistles and it's almost like people who run sheepdogs. You can control your dog at a distance of half a mile by particular hand movements and whistles.' Bill Meldrum agrees that 'the Queen can control a dog by whistles at 800 yards, making him jump, go left and so on. One blast is stop, four is come back.' As well as training the dogs, Elizabeth also breeds them – a subject to which she brings the same knowledge and memory for detail that she applies to her horses. 'We've sometimes had dogs that are from her own dogs,' says Patricia Mountbatten, 'and it's quite possible that one might have forgotten oneself which dog was the parent of your dog, but she won't have. She'll say, "Oh yes, that was so and so's dog or bitch." '

Like anyone with very great private wealth, Elizabeth was never going to be able to share all the common experiences of most of her countrymen. One of her staff, who used to ride with her every morning,[67] recalls that 'she would ask about issues, like decimalisation. I said it would put all the prices up. She said that I shouldn't judge just on the price of a pound of butter. So I gave her chapter and verse on what we spent our money on – clothes, heating, something put by for holidays, etc. She said she had never considered that, as no one had ever let her handle money.' Perhaps, on this occasion, she was just being polite – she did, after all, pay her own bills, even if she did not count out the change herself – but she did try, when living on her own country estates, to live a less constrained and isolated life. At Windsor, a courtier remembers, 'we would go round the track at Ascot and she would stop to talk to people who had no idea who she was. If she saw someone with greyhounds, she would say, "Where do you race them?" There was a pigeon man and they would talk about his racing pigeons. She told him, "I have a racing loft in Norfolk." Afterwards he said to me, "Who's that woman? Bloody liar, she is." "She has got a loft," I told him. "That's the Queen." He didn't believe me.'[68]

At Sandringham, where the locals were apparently more observant, Elizabeth and her mother both joined the local Women's Institute. According to Lady Grove:

> Queen Elizabeth the Queen Mother is the President of the Sandringham Women's Institute, and the Queen is a member and they both always attend our January meeting, which is the highlight of our year as far as the W.I.'s concerned. The Queen pours out the tea and you talk about your families or other people in the village – people that the Queen herself has known since she was a child, people who have probably grown up with her. And the Queen Mother likes to talk about the older people and about other normal everyday things. I remember on one occasion talking to the Queen Mother about how often the dustbins were emptied and whether they were done properly.

With her family and guests, Elizabeth was notably more relaxed in the countryside than in London. Lady Anson explains, 'I think it's because you can get away from everything into the most amazingly beautiful scenery where you can hear a pin drop. And the hustle and bustle of life suddenly seems miles away and you can hear a bumble-bee and wonderful sounds of water, and I can totally understand why it's so special to her.' At Balmoral, in particular, says Lady Penn, 'indoor life doesn't come into it – one's out-of-doors practically all the time and they have picnic dinners during the day and even at nights, up on the hill with lovely fires and candles'.

It was there, if anywhere, that the Queen was in her natural habitat, enjoying what Queen Victoria described as 'a quiet, a retirement, a wildness, a liberty and a solitude'.[69] Like Victoria, Elizabeth and all her family were enchanted by the landscape. 'I miss the mountains deeply and that noisy silence of Deeside,' Prince Charles later wrote. 'Nothing has the same meaning and the soul-refreshing quality that Balmoral can provide.'[70]

Beautiful, remote and isolated as it is, the Windsor way of life at Balmoral is not for the faint-hearted. 'I think it's as difficult an environment as any country one for people who are actually what I call pavement people,' says Lady Anson, pointing to the robust approach that Elizabeth and her family have always taken to the pleasures of the countryside. 'I've seen them all after tea get booted and spurred up to go for a walk and it's not what you and I would call a gentle amble about. They love that Scottish way of life where you go for long, long walks, the muddier and rainier the better. The hall at Balmoral has every kind of raincoat and walking boot.'

The Balmoral picnics, though, were on a very grand scale. They involved the minimum of servants and formality but were organised with unbelievable efficiency and care. Their chief claim to picnic status was that the food was prepared outside but there their resemblance to the common experience of picnicking ended. In truth, a picnic at Balmoral was about as normal as Marie Antoinette's fantasy of living like a milkmaid at *Le Petit Trianon* but even so, for Elizabeth they provided a gratifying contrast with the starched routines of official banquets and dinners. 'They like to be completely on their own with their friends and do exactly what they want to,' says John Taylor, one of the Queen's footmen. 'When they're away from the staff they've got no prying eyes, nobody goes with them at all. And they just enjoy being normal people.'

'The Queen lays the table and does everything herself,' agrees Lady Anson. 'I think she really enjoys doing that and it's meticulously done. She is a housewife manqué. If you offer to help, she refuses.' Philip's role lies with the preparation and the cooking. According to Shane Blewitt, 'He goes out ahead with his Land Rover and the trailer. The trailer is a magnificent design with drawers and everything. Everything fits in, designed by him and he goes out ahead and gets stuck into the cooking.'

'There are compartments for the glasses,' says Lady Anson, 'compartments for the cutlery, compartments to take, you know, a beautifully decorated mousse. And even if it goes at an angle, the food doesn't slide off. Don't ask me how, but it really works. It's probably the most hi-tech picnic vehicle that I've ever come across.' In the first fortnight of August, Elizabeth and her family would vary the relaxation with a slow cruise up the Western Isles aboard the Royal Yacht, *Britannia*. Even then, though, the picnics continued: whenever possible, the Royal Family would be put ashore, clutching hampers of food and fuel for the barbecue. And the vicissitudes of the weather, as always, took second place to the pleasures of al fresco living. 'I think once a decision had been made that there was to be a picnic or barbecue, it almost went on regardless,' says Sir Paul Greening, one of the royal yacht's officers. 'Everybody put on their mackintoshes and boots and got on with it.'

Elizabeth has five official residences – Buckingham Palace, Holyrood House, Windsor Castle, Sandringham and Balmoral. Although the privately owned estates of Sandringham and Balmoral certainly have a place in her heart, it is Windsor of which she is most fond. 'I think,' says Lady Anson, 'that she probably regards Windsor as her home and she probably spends more time there, on a regular basis, than anywhere else and it's the nearest place in the country that she can get to.'

The Great Park that surrounds the Castle is redolent of the past. The 1930s houses carry the cipher of Edward VIII, the Post Office that of George VI. The park fences carry no barbed wire and the houses themselves are painted in the Queen Mother's favourite shade of pink. The whole atmosphere is like that of Britain before the war, and if ever old maids were to be found cycling through the mist to morning communion it would be there. The little kingdom of the last reign, Windsor draws the Queen comfortingly back into her childhood. 'The Queen can come there,' as Michael Mann points out, 'put on a tweed skirt and a headscarf, take the dogs and go out for a walk and she knows she doesn't have to worry. She can get complete privacy and that means an awful lot to her. She often used to refer to Buckingham Palace as the flat over the office and Windsor is always referred to as home.'

According to Kenneth Scott:

They feel in a way almost like curators of a lovely museum when they're there, as well as it being a family home. She's very proud of the rich history of Windsor and the rich collection in the royal library. When she lives down at Windsor, there are parties called Dine and Sleep where a number of the great and the good – the Prime Minister always comes to one of them – are invited to a dinner party and to spend the night at the Castle. And after dinner the Queen and Prince Philip conduct their guests to the Royal Library where a special exhibition has been laid out with a number of items for each of the guests – so if the President of the Royal Society comes, there will be George III's schoolboy essay on chemistry. I remember once when Mrs Thatcher was at one of these parties fairly soon after she had made her famous announcement in Downing Street, 'We are a grandmother', and they managed to find a note in Queen Victoria's diary saying, 'I have become a grandmother', which was rather nice. Mrs Thatcher took it very well.

However much she may enjoy country walks, picnics and quiet games of Patience in the evenings, though, it was not Elizabeth's fate to be left to enjoy her quiet, settled routine in peace. 'Her life does follow a pattern,' admits Shane Blewitt, the former Keeper of the Privy Purse, 'and certainly whether it be Windsor or Sandringham or Balmoral, each year is much the same and of course her life in Buckingham Palace is totally habitual. You've got investitures, you've got state visits, you've got her visits out from the Palace. It does follow a ritual.' By the 1960s the ritual was beginning to look not only bizarrely rigid but meaningless and out-of-date. Michael Mann thinks that 'the Queen herself is such a wonderful person and she is so disciplined and so contained that she is aware the whole time . . . Sometimes people may say that they think she's a bit stuffy or a bit reserved. But then that is the inevitable consequence of the intrusion of the media.'

It was not, in fact, entirely the fault of the press. As Elizabeth herself recognised, she was not a natural performer in the way that her mother was: neither (as the Princess of Wales was later able to do) could she present herself as a natural comforter of the poor and the sick. 'I'm always slightly amused,' says Lady Pamela Hicks, 'because her greatest horror is being with somebody who has a terrible cold or flu or illness – not that she's unsympathetic – but in case she catches it and then has to cancel all her engagements.' In private, many of her friends say, she could be relaxed and funny, but the lighter side of her character did not shine through in public and the notion of projecting a separate public image of herself was entirely alien to her. 'She's got a wonderful smile,' says Michael Oswald, 'and she looks serious when she's thinking about a problem. Now somebody once suggested to me that she ought to smile more on her birthday parade. But she's on a military parade and people don't smile on military parades. She's not a pop star, you know, currying favour with her audience.'

In fact, currying favour was exactly the task that awaited Elizabeth in the second decade of her reign. Throughout the 1950s, the mass adulation that surrounded the new Queen and the still deferential attitude of most of society had allowed the Palace to look on the demands of the media with a cold and distant eye. When Harold Nicolson had lunch at the Garrick Club in August 1959, he wrote later that 'it is announced the Queen is to have a baby in January or February. What a sentimental hold the monarchy has over the middle classes! All the solicitors, actors and publishers at the Garrick were beaming as if they had acquired some personal benefit.'[71]

The sentimental hold of the monarchy was such that, for some years, Palace officials were able to use selected, wholesome details of Elizabeth's private life as a means of increasing popular support, while simultaneously denying that the public had any right to such information. Newsreel cameras might occasionally be allowed into the Palace precincts to record happy scenes of Elizabeth and Philip playing with their children in the garden and throughout the 1950s the annual progress of the Court up to Balmoral was treated as an event worthy of national news coverage. The Palace press office, however, steadfastly refused to allow the media to set the agenda.

Richard Colville, Elizabeth's first press secretary, took a particularly uncompromising line with any reporters who wanted to write about his employer's private life. According to William Heseltine (the man who succeeded him in the job in 1968), 'Richard Colville's usual answer to that kind of question was "no comment", because he saw his role as providing facilities for members of the media to report on the official activities of the Queen and Duke of Edinburgh and the members of the Royal Family and outside that he really thought they had no business to stray. And he won his name of 'the Abominable No-Man' for the number of occasions on which he would turn down requests for information or facilities that he thought impinged on the private lives of the Queen and the Duke of Edinburgh.'

For the first years of Elizabeth's reign, Colville had a powerful ally in the Queen's private secretary, Alan Lascelles (known as Tommy). Even more than the impertinent questions they asked, Lascelles deplored the very existence of television and radio. As Harold Nicolson noted in his diary at the end of 1960, 'I lunch at the Beefsteak with Tommy [Lascelles]. He agrees with me that to broadcast the Queen's Christmas message on television is a great error. It destroys the mystique of monarchy. He says that when he was private secretary he even tried to stop the sound broadcast.'[72]

That Lascelles should have set his face against even the sovereign's Christmas broadcasts – which had begun on the radio in 1932 under George V and which were televised for the first time under Elizabeth in 1957 – reveals the depth of distrust with which many around Elizabeth looked on the media. In a sense, of course, they were right. Without the help of newspapers and television, Elizabeth would have been spared many of her more excruciatingly public agonies, particularly in the 1980s and 1990s, and some of the crises might not even have arisen in the first place. At the beginning of her reign, most newspaper editors and proprietors were naturally inclined to support the monarchy and some fifty years later some of them were openly committed to destroying it.

William Heseltine remembers the Duke of Edinburgh 'saying he found life a lot simpler and pleasanter if he didn't read the papers in the morning'. Elizabeth herself had no particular liking for television and, after her first Christmas broadcast, a BBC official noted that 'the final draft was actually Prince Philip's. I think the very fact that the Queen had nothing to do with the script made our job a tough one, since it is the most difficult thing in the world to give a personal message that is in fact not personal.'[73] Shane Blewitt admits that 'I think it took quite a long time to adapt to modernisation. There was not an easy relationship with the press. Instead of being seen as possible allies, they were seen as an enemy, almost, and I don't think we had the ability in those days to handle them perhaps as skilfully as we should.'

What men like Lascelles and Colville failed to recognise was that the media were not dispensable and not, in themselves, the root of the problem. 'The trouble about the press is you can't blame them for doing their job,' one of the Queen's advisers observes, 'and their job, as it is now conceived, is to find out everything and publish it if possible before it's happened.' Michael Shea, Elizabeth's press secretary in the 1980s, has 'a very mixed view about the media' but also accepts the key role that they play: 'The people's attitude towards the Queen is rather like the Queen's attitude towards the people. It's interpreted by the media. The media are there interpreting both ways round.'

By the 1960s, the question of how to handle the press presented Elizabeth with a dilemma. On the one hand, there were the more old-fashioned courtiers like Colville and Lascelles, arguing that the press threatened to destroy the mystique of the monarchy. If she chose to sup with the devil, their line of thinking went, she could scarcely complain if dinner turned out to be a hellish experience. On the other hand, there were the younger advisers who saw that, while the press did have threatening aspects, it was not going to go away. In fact, it was needed as a means of reflecting the monarchy to the public in an age when most people did not turn to *The Times* for the news, but to more populist newspapers or the television. 'I've always had the deepest personal sympathy for those who occupied the post with the Royal Family, advising them how to deal with the media, advising them how to deal with the press,' says former newspaper editor Bill Deedes. 'Colville was one of them. There were others. None of them really I think have quite caught up with the mood which they have to cope with.'

Perhaps, in retrospect, Elizabeth should have taken a longer-term view. Had she thought in terms of centuries and decades, rather than years and months, maybe she would have done better to stick to her jigsaws and games of Patience, her horses and her dogs, and left the press to snuffle around outside the castle walls while she got on with Trooping the Colour, opening Parliament and giving people medals. As it was, she saw that the world was changing and decided that the image of the monarchy had better change too. After ten years on the throne, she still enjoyed great personal popularity but the institution as a whole was looking slightly dull.

In 1968 she appointed a new press secretary who took a very different line from the haughty disdain of Richard Colville. Looking back, William Heseltine says:

> I didn't think it was going to be practical to hold that line for very long. The atmosphere in which the organisation moved and worked and had its being was beginning to change. The extreme interest and deference which was the common attitude to members of the Royal Family soon after the Queen's accession had begun to shift a bit. Prince Philip himself remarked at that time that as he and the Queen became middle-aged the amount of interest in their activities was bound to go down, and indeed I think that was beginning to happen. In the middle to late sixties, I think it would be true to say that

most of the news about the Royal Family was to be found in the newspapers only in the rather stilted phrases of the Court Circular or else in some of the less reputable gossip columns.

Heseltine thought that, rather than holding the press at bay, he should use the media to put some flesh back on the monarchy's bones: 'My own feeling at this time was, because of the way in which news coverage of their activities had been presented, the Royal Family had become what you might call cardboard cut-out figures, and I thought it could only do good if the public were able to see them as the three-dimensional and very human and in some cases very humorous and delightful figures that they were.'

In deciding to co-operate with the press, Heseltine was running before the wind. In 1968 a photograph taken by Princess Anne of her mother sitting up in bed with Prince Edward found its way into the hands of *Paris Match* and from there into the *Daily Express*. By the standards of later press photographs – usually involving Elizabeth's daughters-in-law rather than the Queen herself – it was innocuous enough. It was, though, Heseltine admits, 'obviously a matter of some concern and even, I think, distaste at Buckingham Palace. There was nothing very much that we could do about it. It was worrying to the Queen that the people who had for so many years developed her own private photographs should have allowed one out of their care in this way and I think it was quite shocking to a lot of people – perhaps less so to the Queen than to some others – that a photograph of the Queen actually sitting up in bed should have been published.'

However small the event was, and however much Elizabeth herself took it in her stride, all the ingredients of later press scandals were there: the apparent inability of the Palace to control events; public disapproval of the newspaper's intrusiveness which climbed in fairly direct proportion to the newspaper's sales; and the editor of the *Express*'s own rationale for running the story. 'It was,' according to Heseltine, 'in the best traditions of Fleet Street that he should have published it with expressions of great distaste that this photograph should have been (a) stolen and (b) that a foreign magazine should have been so reprehensible as to publish it. But these were both, in his view, perfect excuses for publishing it himself.'

Public interest in the Royal Family increased, particularly as the Queen's two eldest children, Anne and Charles, grew up. The depart-ure of Richard Colville, says William Heseltine, 'coincided almost exactly with the emergence of the Prince of Wales and Princess Anne on the public scene and this, in the way in which the Royal Family renews itself, meant that there was a new wave of interest in their activities'. When George VI was in his teens the mass press was still in its infancy and even radio had not yet made an appearance. When Elizabeth was the same age, Britain was at war and what demands the media did make could be usefully contained within the Government's own official propaganda. But how would the Palace contain the wave of interest in Charles and Anne? This was an entirely new problem, made all the more pressing by the announcement in 1968 that Charles would be formally invested as Prince of Wales at Caernarvon Castle the following year.

According to Heseltine, the Palace press office was 'bombarded with requests for all sorts of facilities leading up to the investiture and we had to decide how to go about meeting them, many of which seemed, on the face of it, to be absurd. There were suggestions that the then seventeen-year-old Prince of Wales should be the subject of innumerable biographies and films. I considered, and I think my view was generally regarded as being correct, that there was no material for such a work as that.' As Heseltine and his colleagues tried to negotiate their way through the tangle of press enquiries, 'the idea emerged that we might present a new view of how the Queen went about her business and went about fulfilling her role as Head of State and project forward the role for which the Prince of Wales himself was being prepared'.

This was the genesis of what same see as one of Elizabeth's greatest triumphs and others see as one of her greatest mistakes: the ninety-minute, fly-on-the-wall style documentary film *Royal Family*. It was not the monarchy's first step into the world of public relations – the wartime newsreels that made so much of George VI's happy and united family were really just another form of propaganda – but it was the first time the Palace had tried to counter bad publicity with such a lavish and revealing account of the Royal Family's private life.

The idea came from Louis Mountbatten, Philip's uncle. No enemy to publicity in the past, Mountbatten had recently co-operated on a lavish twelve-part series made by Thames Television that celebrated his own life and achievements. 'I think through the jobs my father had had,' says his elder daughter, 'where public relations really played an important part, and he had a pretty good understanding of the necessity of looking at things from the public relations point of view and it was no good just having an aura of secrecy around everything. I mean, you had to have good public relations.'

Seeing the success of the Mountbatten series, Louis' son-in-law, Lord Brabourne, suggested to Prince Philip over lunch that the Queen might like to try something similar and asked if he had ever thought of it. No, said Prince Philip, he hadn't. But he listened very carefully and became interested in the idea. That's how it first started. Brabourne's reasoning was similar to Heseltine's:

I was making films at the time. I wasn't working in television, which I did later, but I had – like a lot of people – realised that the public did not really have any picture of what the royal family were like. Here was this young couple and two young children and people didn't really know them. They had no idea what a wonderful sense of humour the Queen had and what sort of person Prince Philip was, let alone the children. I had heard this said a lot, and I thought it was a great pity.

Elizabeth's reaction to the idea was not overly enthusiastic. Films about the Royal Family had been made before but they were carefully controlled affairs that gave the impression of providing an intimate glimpse of the monarchy at rest without really doing anything of the kind. The plans for *Royal Family* were altogether more elaborate and potentially more intrusive: the film would last for ninety minutes and the whole point was to give the impression that the camera crew had been free to film whatever they wanted. In addition to wondering whether her family would benefit from having its backstage moments recorded and broadcast to the nation, Elizabeth was instinctively opposed to anything which might appear to be contrived or crowd-pleasing. Martin Charteris commented that 'the Queen has sometimes been criticised for not playing up to the press. I think that's misunderstanding the situation. The thing about the Queen is that she is a woman of golden honesty and she's jolly well not going to play up to the press or indeed to the public.'

This was an aspect of Elizabeth's character of which Heseltine was well aware. The central purpose of *Royal Family* was to raise the monarchy's popularity by emphasising the personal appeal of its individual members, but Elizabeth's advisers were quick to stress that it would not do so by holding up a distorting mirror. 'It would have been quite wrong and indeed I think it would have been counter-productive for me to try and start image-making for the Royal Family,' says Heseltine. 'They were very resistant to this idea and if I had tried in some way to project an image of them which did not reflect the reality, it would have been very soon evident that this was what was going on and would have been exposed and ridiculed.'

The success of the Mountbatten series did a lot to help soften resistance. Heseltine thinks that it 'created a slightly more receptive atmosphere to the idea that something of this sort might be done affecting the Queen and members of her family.' Her advisers were careful never to present the idea to Elizabeth in the language of public relations – 'I don't think,' says Heseltine, 'I ever put it quite so bluntly to the Queen as "You've got to project yourself".' But she nonetheless recognised that something had to be done to satisfy the enormous number of requests for media access inspired by her son's forthcoming investiture. William Heseltine believes, 'She realised that there was very little that we could do with an adolescent prince which would meet these [expectations] and that was the basis on which she finally accepted that we should make the film, *Royal Family*. If it got a little extended beyond that original concept as we went along, I think she was sufficiently pragmatic to realise that this was going to add hugely to the interest of the film.'

The film was to be made by a BBC documentary maker, Richard Cawston, and would be overseen by a committee of five, which was chaired by Prince Philip and included Lord Brabourne as well as representatives from the Lord Chamberlain's office, the BBC and ITV (who were allowed to broadcast the programme a few days after the BBC). Elizabeth retained the right to pull the plug on the whole thing if the end result was unsatisfactory but, for a year, Cawston and his team would be allowed to film what they wanted.

For all her own misgivings – and for all the criticism she would attract in the 1990s for appearing stuffy and out of touch – her decision to go ahead with *Royal Family* put Elizabeth firmly on the side of the

Court modernisers. 'There was a degree of caution among some of the more senior members of the Household,' Heseltine agrees. 'I won't say there was opposition, because having succeeded in persuading both the Queen and Prince Philip that this was a sensible way of tackling the situation, it would have been rather pointless for any members of the Household to object. But they did indeed have a slightly more cautious approach.'

Unless it is made secretly and with hidden cameras, any documentary that claims to reveal the reality of people's lives does so with an element of contrivance. *Royal Family* was a very long way from modern fly-on-the-wall documentaries and it was, in any case, understood by everyone involved that its primary purpose was to present its subjects in an attractive and popular light. Filming Elizabeth and her family as though they were the interesting and oblivious subjects of a wildlife programme was always only the means to that end, not the primary purpose itself. The result was an occasionally odd mixture of newsreel-style commentary (that did the heavy propaganda work) and off-duty glimpses of the Royal Family that sometimes seem strikingly truthful.

The programme was conceived as a 'year-in-the-life' portrayal, and opens with shots of Prince Charles water-skiing, cycling through Cambridge as an undergraduate, and fishing at Balmoral. As images of the athlete/scholar/pastoral prince flash by, the commentary warns that it may be many years before he becomes King – perhaps not even until he is seventy – then offers to take us behind the scenes to see what the job he will one day inherit is like.

The first we see of Elizabeth is on horseback, at a military review for her official birthday. Walking her horse slowly back into the courtyard of Buckingham Palace, Elizabeth finds a footman waiting with a bowl of carrots which she gives to her horse, before rather shyly thanking everyone for all their hard work. The scenes that follow all have a similar, staged feel to them. The Queen and Prince Philip are shown working at their desks; Philip lands an aeroplane; the Queen presents Robert Graves with a poetry medal ('I think you should do it more,' he tells her in an uneasy attempt at light banter. 'I hope I shall,' the Queen replies.) A Buckingham Palace garden party follows, at which the Queen's democratic credentials are stressed: she meets, we are told, 'town clerks, Nigerian research fellows, hospital almoners' (as social workers were apparently known in the late 1960s), 'industrial chemists – anyone, in fact, from a shop steward to a retired Commonwealth prime minister'. As luck would have it, the camera alights on Elizabeth chatting animatedly to the former Prime Minister of Australia and we are left to take the shop stewards and industrial chemists on trust.

At times, though, Elizabeth is seen to better and more human effect, and some of the scenes reveal a naïve trust in the kindliness of television that would be unthinkable in the more battered monarchy of today. Discussing her wardrobe for a forthcoming state visit to Austria with her dresser, Elizabeth says artlessly, 'I was wondering if we couldn't find something for the sapphires,' as she lifts an impressively bejewelled tiara out of a box on the table. Later in the same scene she produces another magnificent piece of jewellery, which appears to consist largely of enormous rubies, and wonders again whether she ought not to have another new dress designed to go with it. Supremely oblivious of the staggeringly opulent contents of her jewellery box, the Queen is then struck by a moment of doubt, looking up to ask, 'I have actually worn this, haven't I?' If she had, she was surely the only woman in the world who could have forgotten – even Imelda Marcos, the viewer cannot help but think, would have a better grip on the contents of her wardrobe – but the impression Elizabeth gives is not of a spoiled woman with too many baubles but of a practical businesswoman wondering how best to deploy her resources.

Later on, when she appears formally dressed and wearing yet more incredible jewels at the Royal Opera House, she again behaves as though she has been put on stage in a fabulous costume but is actually rather worried about whether her performance will be up to scratch. 'Are there a lot of people?' she asks, sounding slightly nervous as she makes her way up to the royal box where she stands rigidly acknowledging the waves of applause that greet her entry into the auditorium.

Neither did the film downplay the other luxurious trappings of Elizabeth's life. Thirty years on, the mood of the nation – at least as perceived by the Court – is such that Elizabeth's officials present as a minor triumph the fact that it costs no more to fly the Queen from one end of the country to the other than it does a junior minister, while the Royal Yacht has been a museum piece for several years. Not so in 1968, when the boats, trains, helicopters and aeroplanes all still had a whiff of royal mystique about them, which *Royal Family* happily dispelled in the interests of explaining what practical purpose they served.

The Royal Train, the audience is told, consists of ten coaches, which 'contain three working rooms, three dining rooms, five bath-rooms, three kitchens as well as Prince Philip's room and the Queen's room beyond.' If it were broadcast now, the viewer might be impressed by the fact that kitchens and dining rooms outnumber the offices by two to one; they might admire the ingenuity and care with which railway carriages had been converted into pleasant-looking offices and drawing rooms; they might more chippily wonder if it was really necessary to give over 60 per cent of the Royal Train to eating and why three separate dining rooms were necessary in the first place. The tone of the film, however, is that it is all rather a clever and convenient arrangement.

When it gets to the Royal Yacht *Britannia*, the programme again reflects the less critical, more curious tenor of the times. Elizabeth still has not been seen doing very much work, as most of her subjects would define the word (although a helicopter is shown delivering its daily consignment of state papers for the Queen to study), yet we are told that the Royal Yacht's crew wear special shoes with soft soles and communicate by hand-signals rather than shouted orders so as not to disturb the royal passengers below decks. Instead of work, the film shows Elizabeth's two eldest children being winched from the deck of *Britannia* to that of an escort vessel cruising alongside – Charles rather glumly, Anne more defiant – in preparation, presumably, for whatever naval emergency might require such a slow means of evacuating passengers. It is a scene which seems particularly unreal – is that really how they spend their time on *Britannia*, the viewer cannot help but wonder – and one which appears to project an action-man image of the royal children that has only ever rung true with Anne. That, at least, was something Elizabeth had been spared at a similar age when voyaging to South Africa aboard HMS *Vanguard*.

Elizabeth's family are seen to much better effect later in the year at Balmoral. In contrast to the water-skiing and other show-piece activities in the earlier parts of the film, the scenes in Scotland show a relaxed, natural-seeming family who appeared to get on with one another. Philip takes an imperious young Edward out on the lake, responding meekly and obediently when his youngest son tells him to get a move on. Elizabeth takes Edward to buy some ice-creams at the local shop and they both laugh as she jokingly complains about the mess he will make in the car. The whole family gathers for a barbecue at which Charles rather tersely makes the salad dressing before beaming happily at his mother when the job is finally done. Anne meanwhile gets the fire going and darkly warns her mother, 'You realise this is guaranteed failure? Absolute totally guaranteed failure.'

'You mean the fire's not going to work?' asks the Queen.

'Of course it's not going to work,' replies Anne with characteristic bluntness.

Philip meanwhile prods hopefully at some large steaks and dryly informs his wife, who has brightly come to tell him that the salad is ready, that 'this, as you see, isn't'.

The effect is rather like a modern survival show — as though a group of disparate people had suddenly been put in front of the television cameras and told that they have to build a suspension bridge using only a few pieces of string and some driftwood — but with a much more authentic feel. There is, in particular, a sense of Elizabeth and Philip and their two eldest children as distinct characters — at least when they appear briefly to forget that the cameras are there.

Once, Lord Brabourne recalls, 'the Queen had a reception for all the prime ministers, and she found herself talking and going about and she suddenly saw a microphone just below her. And, after all, one of the great things is the complete privacy between the Queen and all her prime ministers and suddenly she realised that the whole world might be hearing what she said. That was a real shock to her.'

It was even more difficult to act naturally when in an informal setting — especially so, according to William Heseltine, for Prince Philip, who 'found it rather more difficult than did the Queen to accommodate himself to the constant presence of the camera team. And in fact he was, as is sometimes his wont, a little impatient with them when they appeared, as he thought, rather too close for comfort.'

Royal Family's triumph was that when it was able to capture Elizabeth and her family acting naturally it gave the monarchy an agreeably human face. Charles seems serious, a bit awkward and rather kind; Anne is confident, impatient and slightly pushy ('Jump, you fool, jump!' she tells Prince Edward when he takes his time about getting out of the car); Philip is a contradictory figure, sometimes shown in action mode flying an aeroplane, sometimes pottering about with his watercolours in the countryside. At the Balmoral barbecue he is quite self-effacing; at an embassy reception he plays up to the breezy, off-hand image that has now become his trademark.

Meanwhile, Elizabeth is shown as a far more animated and good-humoured figure than anyone would have guessed from just her public appearances. Whenever she is pictured with her family, more often than not she is laughing, and at the end of the film she confesses that one of the biggest burdens she has to bear is that of keeping a straight face in public. After Philip has told the family how George VI used to wear a bearskin cap when he was out doing the gardening, Elizabeth tells of a formal audience when 'the Home Secretary came in beforehand – like they do – and he said to me, "There's a gorilla coming in". So I said, "What an extraordinary remark to make – very unkind about anybody". And I stood in the middle of the room, pressed the bell, the doors opened and there was a gorilla! I had the most terrible trouble – you know, he had a short body, long arms – and I had the most appalling trouble.'

Even when she is shown at public or state occasions, the Elizabeth of *Royal Family* has a refreshing naturalness about her – despite the fact that the flummery and protocol surrounding her are at times so elaborate that a block of wood would look animated by comparison. When the new United States ambassador arrives at Buckingham Palace – wearing full evening dress – to present his letters of accreditation, whatever poise and dignity the man may normally have had appear to be stripped from him by the phalanx of uniformed courtiers that lie in wait. As one man takes his hat, another surreptitiously starts brushing at his coat, while a chorus of well-bred voices talk him through the coming ceremony: 'First of all the permanent under-secretary goes in . . . we all take a pace forward with our left foot . . . you walk up to the Queen who is six or seven paces away, she holds out her hand, you shake her hand, bow again. You turn and walk to the door. You turn around, bow once more . . .'

The elaborate formula, the commentary explains, is designed to ensure that all foreign emissaries are treated the same: it is hard, nonetheless, not to suspect that it was originally designed to reduce them all to the same state of quaking nerves. When the doors are eventually thrown open, the American ambassador can barely string a sentence together. Asked by Elizabeth where he is living at the moment, he replies, 'We're in the Embassy residence, subject of course to some of the discomfiture as a result of the need for elements of refurbishing, rehabilitation.' Elizabeth, by contrast, and however hard she was trying not to laugh, is relaxed and almost strangely normal. 'Thank you very much indeed,' she says rather abstractedly as the ambassador hands over his formal documents. Without a second glance, she hands them to somebody waiting behind, rather as if the ambassador had brought some flowers she was not expecting and did not particularly like.

There is a similar gulf between the high-flown tone of the commentary and the manner in which Elizabeth deals with her other official tasks. 'Even today,' we are misleadingly told during a royal tour of a British city, 'it's the Crown which unites the UK.' A trip to see a factory is dignified with the comment that 'the emphasis has shifted from armies to defend the Empire to exports to defend the Pound', while a state visit to Chile prompts a deluge of royal facts that are meant to underline the serious and tiring nature of Elizabeth's job – 'Fourteen guards of honour, eighteen *God Save the Queen*s, nine speeches delivered, four wreath-layings, twelve journeys by air, seventy-nine journeys by road.' We learn that the Queen and Prince Philip shook hands two-and-a-half thousand times, attended 'twenty-three different receptions, lunches, dinners and banquets – eight finishes after midnight – a total of a hundred and four separate engagements in fourteen days'.

The fatigue and excitement is more implied than apparent, though. Returning from another, similar visit, Elizabeth leafs through the foreign news reports aboard her aeroplane, her only reaction being that it is a shame she cannot understand what is being written about her. Later on, when she is hosting a state visit to Britain by President Nixon, she sounds more like a thoughtful hostess planning a country weekend than one head of state preparing to receive another. The President will have had a very busy day, she tells the Court official responsible for planning lunch, so they had better make sure that things do not go on for too long.

Royal Family ends with a serious-minded summary of the Queen's constitutional responsibilities and casts Elizabeth as the 'Friend of Liberty', defending her people from the threat of politicians and generals alike. 'Justice is administered in the Queen's name,' we are told in a statement of classic monarchist propaganda. 'If politicians run the courts, liberty is in danger. While the Queen is head, judges are secure and changing governments cannot dismiss them . . . The strength of the monarchy does not lie in the power it gives to the sovereign, but in the power it denies to anyone else.' In fact, as the film made clear, the strength of the monarchy now lay in the character of its principal players and, on those grounds, both film and institution enjoyed considerable success.

Royal Family was shown twice in June 1969 – first on the BBC, then on ITV – and, according to the BBC's audience research figures, it was seen by over two-thirds of the population.[74] After the public apathy that many of Elizabeth's advisers had feared, it was an astonishingly large audience and one that would not be matched until Prince Charles's marriage to Lady Diana Spencer in 1981. Denis Healey – Secretary of State for Defence at the time – thought that it was 'the first time they were allowed to appear as an ordinary family and it did the monarchy a great deal of good, there's not the slightest question about that.'

Elizabeth's own advisers were delighted with the result. Says William Heseltine:

> Overall I think the impact was tremendously useful, but one of the individual scenes which stays with me is the scene of the Queen going into a shop on the Balmoral estate and ordering an ice-cream for her youngest son. This seemed to dispel several illusions about her, one of the popular ones being that she never carried any money with her under any circumstances, because she produced the money from her purse and proceeded to pay for the ice-cream. There was another scene in which the youngest prince, Edward, watching the Prince of Wales playing the cello, was badly stung on the cheek when one of the cello strings snapped. It caused first of all a sharp exclamation of pain and this was followed, not surprisingly, by tears. Some people thought that that scene was rather unkind and it should have been removed from the film. But it seemed to both Richard Cawston and myself that it gave a kind of authenticity to the scenes – which a few people were suggesting had been specially staged – which nothing else could possibly do.

The drawback of *Royal Family* lay in the precedent it set and the fact that it represented the trading of privacy for popularity. Now that Elizabeth had allowed the cameras in to show what she and her family were 'really like', it would no longer be possible to maintain the line that the private lives of the Royal Family were nobody's business but their own without appearing hypocritical. *Royal Family* was not the first time that the monarchy had tried to make use of the media but it was nonetheless a significant milestone on a route that would eventually take in an increasingly disrespectful press as well as television shows like *It's a Royal*

Knockout, the Prince of Wales discussing the breakdown of his marriage with Jonathan Dimbleby, and his wife's breathtaking retaliation on *Panorama*.

'All those blank windows that people have stared at year after year,' the *Royal Family* commentary runs at one point, over shots of Buckingham Palace, 'knowing perfectly well they could never see what goes on behind them. Now we can.' And now we would. The film may temporarily have boosted Elizabeth's public standing but it also whetted people's appetite for more, confirming the worst fears of Elizabeth's more conservative advisers. As the film-maker David Attenborough warned *Royal Family*'s director, 'You're killing the monarchy, you know, with this film you're making. The whole institution depends on mystique and the tribal chief in his hut. If any member of the tribe ever sees inside the hut then the whole system of the tribal chiefdom is damaged and the tribe eventually disintegrates.'[75]

It is an accusation which the film's advocates strongly reject. At the time, according to Martin Charteris:

> I don't think any of us had any feelings that it might lead to too open an approach to the life of the Royal Family. I certainly didn't. I loved it. I thought it was very good for this reason – that I thought it showed the public something of what goes on behind the scenes and it made it perfectly clear that the Queen and Prince Philip were a happy married couple with a happy family. And also I think it allowed people to see that the Queen was a woman of considerable character and humour, more than they would realise if they saw her just on public occasions. So I had no feelings that it was anything but a good thing.

As Bill Deedes points out, it is very easy to be wise after the event:

> I think it's quite easy to say, 'Well, given our time again I think
> I would not have gone into all that. The appetite grows with
> feeding and the more you throw your house open, etc, the more
> people expect of you and feel you're stuffy if you don't concede.'
> I think it was a good attempt to bring the monarchy into line
> with what people expected now. Unless you're on television, in
> a sense you don't count and I think the feeling was that they
> ought to become much more part of the modern media circus.

Even with the benefit of hindsight, William Heseltine, who had been
one of *Royal Family*'s prime movers, argues that the documentary did
nothing to alter the course of events: the idea that 'this had somehow
opened doors, both to intrusive coverage of their private lives and to the
lack of respect which gossip columnists and others came to show I
regard as a purely nonsensical theory. The gossip columns were quite
well on the way to becoming the kind of newspaper reportage they have
subsequently become.'

This dilemma has run throughout Elizabeth's reign: too much
majesty and mystique made her look stuffy and out of touch; too little
left her dependent on the whims of public affection and press cam-
paigns, without the support of old-fashioned deference. The public,
too, was inconsistent in its demands: on the one hand, the Royal Family
was meant to set an example to everyone (by not, for instance, marrying
people who were divorced); on the other hand, it was comforting to
think that the Windsors were, at heart, just like everybody else.

It is hard to think what else Elizabeth might have done at the time.
As Heseltine points out, 'It would be absurd for anybody to think that
in the late sixties and the decades that succeeded, the Royal Family

alone could have gone about their business without making some sort of accommodation with this new-ish medium of television which had become so important in the lives of everybody in this country and throughout the Commonwealth.' Yet television just accentuated the tension between the Royal Family's need to be seen as ordinary and the criticism it then drew if its individual members appeared too ordinary – particularly if they had too many ordinary human faults. What Elizabeth thought of her early experiment in public relations can, perhaps, be gauged by the fact that, after its first transmission in 1969, *Royal Family* was taken down to the film archives and has never been seen in public since.

CHAPTER SEVEN

Whatever its long-term effects, in the short term *Royal Family* did a lot to help Elizabeth relax her public image. It changed the style of her Christmas broadcasts, which had previously consisted solely of the Queen sitting in a chair and talking to the camera for five rather stilted minutes. Elizabeth had never liked solo appearances on television: it had taken her until 1957 to agree to a televised Christmas message in the first place and, while she could be charming and personable in any normal one-to-one, the intimate nature of television seemed to pass her by. People at home might feel that television had brought the Queen into their living rooms, but Elizabeth usually spoke to the cameras as though she was addressing a large and quite distant crowd. At heart, she had a great dislike of anything which might smack of putting on a performance, and until 1960 (after which her messages were pre-recorded) she had the added disadvantage of having to interrupt her own Christmas celebrations in order to read out her Christmas message live.

'I don't think she did relish the prospect of a Christmas broadcast,' says Edward Ford. 'It was a very difficult thing to do, out of the blue, to make a speech once a year which millions were going to listen to and which therefore had to have a certain amount of proper content.' The more often they were repeated, the more difficult it was for the broadcasts to avoid sermonising and pious platitudes. Almost as important as the content, though, was the delivery: if Elizabeth appeared wooden and cold on the one day of the year when most of the population were watching her, then that was how most people would think she really was. She would never have the skill of using television as a stage from which to put on a beguiling performance, but *Royal Family* at least suggested a way to camouflage the shortcoming. After 1969, when she discussed the issue with her husband and the *Royal Family* film-makers, Elizabeth agreed to the now-familiar device of including in the Christmas broadcasts extra film sequences from the royal year gone by. It reduced the strain on her – at least now some of her words could be done as voice-overs, rather than live to camera – as well as giving the broadcasts greater interest and immediacy.

According to John Grigg, whose criticisms of Elizabeth's public style had first sparked off a furious row over ten years earlier, the *Royal Family* film had another very valuable effect, encouraging 'the Queen to feel that she didn't need to be completely remote in order to maintain the dignity of the office and I think it's no coincidence that soon afterwards she started doing walkabouts, which she does very well and which have been an important feature of her reign'.

The invention of the royal walkabout came in 1970, during a state visit to New Zealand and Australia. For the first time, Elizabeth brought her two eldest children with her – something which William Heseltine believes had 'a very distinct aspect of novelty' – and in the aftermath of *Royal Family* the level of public interest in the royal tour was particularly high. According to Heseltine, who accompanied Elizabeth throughout:

> The New Zealand authorities had tried to suggest from a very early stage that we might try and find some new format which meant that the 'ordinary people' might have a rather more prominent role in the visit. To do this, they designed a great many outdoor events – civic receptions that were removed from the shut-up precincts of the town hall to streets and squares outside. And at a very early stage in the visit, the Wellington civic authorities had arranged that the Queen and the Duke of Edinburgh should alight from their cars some hundreds of yards away from the front door of Wellington Town Hall and complete their journey on foot. They walked, in fact, around Wellington Town Hall in order to get to the front door. This, needless to say, was an enormous success with the crowds who had been waiting to see them. They had been accustomed in the past to see a rather distant view of the Queen and Duke of Edinburgh driving past them in the street and then disappearing into the door of the Town Hall, to be seen again only when they emerged and departed. So the idea of walking around the Town Hall and making contact with lots of people in the street was a new and enormously successful one.

It might, in retrospect, also seem a rather obvious idea but, after the success of the first impromptu walkabout, Elizabeth was keen to repeat the experiment. Experiments were not usually her forte – 'She doesn't always want to change things,' says Martin Charteris; 'she rather likes to keep things the way they are, I think.' But Elizabeth had no great love for protocol or formality and was happy to have some of the starch taken out of her encounters with the public. The fact that, in the past, she had usually met the crowds from the back of a car was only a convention. The royal motorcade was seldom actually going anywhere; it was simply a device to expose the Queen to the people and the idea of doing so on foot promised to be less boring for all concerned.

It also promised to be less safe, but that was not something – then or ever – about which Elizabeth was particularly concerned. Margaret Rhodes observes:

> The Queen has always been adamant that nothing should interfere with her technique of walkabouts and meeting the people. I don't think she would ever allow American-style security guards rushing along on each side of her car. I think that she's looked at the danger that palpably exists for any public figure and has decided to disregard it. As a small instance of this, I was once staying at Sandringham and we were going riding together – on a very misty day – and she said something like, 'I've just heard that the IRA have got a very powerful new telescopic sight which can see through all sorts of fog and mist. But there you are.' And that's symptomatic of the sort of line that you probably have to take.

Every detail of royal tours was usually worked out months in advance, but as she prepared to leave New Zealand for Australia in 1970, one of Elizabeth's officials was told to call ahead to Melbourne with a change of plan. 'I went to the radio shack on *Britannia*,' he recalls, 'and called the Mayor of Melbourne. "You're the bloody fool who wants my Queen to walkabout with all those Aussies? Well, be it on your own bloody head," the Mayor told me.'[76]

The science of walkabouts was still in its infancy, and when the royal party arrived in Melbourne, all they could see was a mass of people completely blocking the length of street down which Elizabeth was supposed to walk. It was a welcoming crowd – 'they just wanted to get much closer to these people that they had seen on television,' says Lord Brabourne – but also an unruly one. It was all the more of a shock to Elizabeth, who was used to more sanitised encounters with the public. 'The Queen was with Philip and Charles and Anne,' remembers one of her staff, 'and said to me, "What shall I do?" "Walk, Your Majesty," I said. She faced the crowd and walked and they let her through. It was after that we learned that we had to use crash barriers.'

Elizabeth's own style was still not entirely in keeping with the age. She was naturally conservative and preferred to rely on the lessons of the past, rather than take bold leaps into the unknown. She did not think it was her business to keep the monarchy one step ahead of the times – better, on the contrary, to be one step behind – and her personal manner tended towards honest self-restraint rather than high-flown gesture. 'She's got a classical simplicity in the way she likes to speak,' says Martin Charteris. 'I mean, if you put a draft up to her and it says, "I'm very glad to be in Reading," she's quite capable of crossing it out and saying, "I'm glad to be in Reading." Which is true.'

As with *Royal Family*, though, Elizabeth allowed herself to be talked into events which her more innovative advisers thought would help update her image. One such was the knighthood she conferred on the sailor Francis Chichester, who in May 1967 arrived back in Plymouth after 266 days at sea, during which he had sailed around the world – the first man to do so single-handedly. At William Heseltine's suggestion, she performed the ceremony in public – the first time she had ever done so – on the riverside at Greenwich, using the same sword with which Elizabeth I had knighted Sir Francis Drake in 1581. It was a deliberate attempt to capitalise on the mood of national self-confidence, linking the Queen personally with one of the country's latest successes, making what had been a formal court ritual into a staged media event and positioning Elizabeth herself midway between the grandiose rhetoric that had greeted her accession to the throne and the realities of the New Elizabethan Age.

Similar contrivance lay behind the royal high point of the decade: Prince Charles's investiture as Prince of Wales at Caernarvon Castle on 1 July 1969. The ceremony itself was of doubtful antiquity. Since the title had been created in 1301 by Edward I, there had been thirty-one occupants of the throne, of whom only thirteen had ever borne the title 'Prince of Wales'. Of those, the majority had been invested in London, and since the time of Charles I most of the ceremonies had been carried out in private. The last Prince of Wales – who later became Edward VIII – had been invested publicly at Caernarvon in 1911 but the ceremony had been almost completely made up and offered few useful precedents on what to do over half a century later. ('What would my Navy friends say if they saw me in this preposterous rig?'[77] complained Edward at the time.) However, for Elizabeth and the Court modernisers, the 1969 occasion offered another chance to vary the royal menu, providing some pageantry to leaven the normal diet of official birthdays and state openings and also establish Prince Charles as a major new player in the royal drama. It would, in addition, provide an opportunity to strengthen the links between Wales and a monarchy that some saw as a predominantly English institution.

The investiture had been a long time coming. Elizabeth had created her eldest son Prince of Wales in 1958 when the nine-year-old prince was still at prep school. But when Elizabeth's advisers were planning the Caernarvon event eleven years later they did not foresee a rise in Welsh nationalism that would turn her son's investiture into a controversial and even risky affair. To the dismay of William Heseltine, 'the political situation in Wales had changed markedly. What was quite new in 1968 and 1969 was the emergence of the Welsh independence movement and the rather extreme manifestations of that movement.'

Throughout 1968 and 1969, there were explosions and bomb scares at railway and police stations and at the Temple of Peace in Cardiff. On the night before and on the day of the investiture itself there were more explosions – one near Caernarvon Castle itself – and the investiture was described by *The Times* as 'the biggest, most expensive peacetime operation in Britain'.[78] But Elizabeth's own reaction to the threat of violence was characteristically understated, mixing fatalist acceptance with gentle mockery of the situation. Standing by the lift in Buckingham Palace as she prepared to leave for Wales, she turned to her senior staff who had, as usual, gathered to say goodbye, and told them, 'I might see you again – if I come back alive.'[79]

Charles himself escaped any physical harm in the run-up to the investiture, but was also left in no doubt as to the strength of Welsh Nationalist feeling. In the months before the ceremony, he had been obliged to take time off his studies at Cambridge in order to spend a term at the University College of Wales at Aberystwyth where he was to learn Welsh. Greeted by nationalist demonstrators, hecklers and an anonymous threat against his life, he also learned, as he later wrote with characteristic earnestness, that 'these people feel . . . so strongly about Wales as a nation, and it means something to them, and they are depressed by what might happen to it if they don't try and preserve the language and the culture, which is unique and special to Wales, and if something is unique and special, I see it as well worth preserving.'[80]

However, Charles's understanding, his emollient response and his brave attempts to acquire at least a smattering of Welsh language and culture did little to soothe the ire of the nationalists, who maintained – with an elephantine memory for historical injustice – that a foreign English prince was being foisted upon them. To add insult to injury, as they saw it, the ceremony was being held not in the Welsh capital, Cardiff, but at Caernarvon Castle, symbol of their 650-year-old defeat at the hands of Edward I.

When the ceremony was eventually staged on 1 July it turned out to be a curious mixture of the medieval and the modern. In some ways, it showed how far Elizabeth had come in her willingness to adapt to the modern world but it also highlighted some of the pitfalls that lay in wait for a monarchy that tried unsuccessfully to be up-to-date. In 1953, before Elizabeth's Coronation, there had been prolonged arguments about whether to allow television cameras in to film the ceremony at all. In 1969, for the Prince of Wales's investiture, the ceremony was specially designed to be shown on television, and the open area in the centre of Caernarvon Castle was conceived more as a film set than as the solemn setting for rituals that were meant to be as old as the monarchy itself.

Most of the arrangements had been put in the hands of Lord Snowdon, to whom Elizabeth had given the title Constable of Caernarvon Castle. (Snowdon was a professional photographer who had once described himself as 'a sort of gypsy' but had nonetheless married Princess Margaret in 1960.) He was thought to be more in tune with the spirit of the times than men like the Duke of Norfolk, whose traditional job it was to organise royal events. And Snowdon had the added advantage of knowing about photography and the requirements that modern television crews might have. 'You know about art,' a cheerful Duke of Norfolk told him. 'You get on with it.'[81]

Snowdon accordingly devised a minimalist, camera-friendly set, consisting of three slate thrones on a raised platform, covered by a perspex canopy that had the heraldic emblem of the Prince of Wales – a coronet and three feathers – engraved upon it. There was space in front of the thrones for a few hundred people to sit within Caernarvon Castle, but the real audience would be watching at home. The see-through canopy meant that television cameras would be able to film from every angle, while the simple, uncluttered platform and thrones were meant to suggest a forward-looking, modern institution that could move with the times.

Unfortunately, although the stage was set for a modern cere-mony, the play itself was ill thought-out. Usually, Elizabeth's heralds and Court officers more or less looked the part when they were surrounded by the pomp and ceremony of old-fashioned state occasions. In Caernarvon, however, attending a contrived ceremony that was set against a simple and unpretentious background, the playing-card costumes of the heralds and the massed ranks of trumpeters looked over-the-top. 'It wasn't,' says Lord Brabourne, 'a thing that made a great impact on me,' and the clashing sense of old and new was heightened by the fact that at the centre of it all stood the small, neat figure of Elizabeth dressed in modern clothes and carrying a handbag, while her eldest son wore a velvet cloak that was too short to reach the ground and a spindly medieval-style crown that looked as though it had come out of a props cupboard for school plays.

'For me,' Charles later recorded in his diary, 'by far the most moving and meaningful moment came when I put my hands between Mummy's and swore to be her liege man of life and limb and to live and die against all manner of folks – such magnificent mediaeval, appropriate words, even if they were never adhered to in those old days.'[82] Neither, though, did they seem particularly appropriate to 1969. *The Times* mused on how 'Edward I's eyes would have started out of their sockets at the scores of television cameras perched on every available turret of his impregnable castle . . . at investiture mugs and dishcloths on sale in his moat . . . at the armadas of mobile lavatories called "rollalongs" all over town and at the "trendy" hunting-green uniform worn by the constable of his castle and designed by himself'.[83] And Elizabeth herself was at times struck by the absurdity of the situation, telling Noel Coward some weeks later that during the ceremony she and Charles 'were both struggling not to giggle because at the dress rehearsal the crown was too big and extinguished him like a candle-snuffer'.[84]

The same year, Elizabeth faced a much more serious test over what would turn out to be one of the most vexed issues of her reign: money. Then, as now, people held contradictory views of the Queen's attitude to worldly possessions. On the one hand, she was held to be a thrifty, almost parsimonious figure, never happier than when prowling around Buckingham Palace at night in search of unnecessary lights to switch off. At the same time, she was thought to possess untaxed personal wealth on such an enormous scale that it was an affront to any modern democracy. It was a new formulation of the monarchy's old dilemma, caught between the need to be remote and grand enough to command respect, while still seeming sufficiently down-to-earth to retain mass support. There was some truth in both ideas.

'The Queen is personally extremely frugal,' says Shane Blewitt. 'She makes very small demands on money – indeed would resent extravagance – and I think this is probably part of the culture of her upbringing, in that she was brought up in the Depression, followed by the War.' But however careful Elizabeth was about the little things, she was also the owner of two private palaces (Windsor Castle and Buckingham Palace belonged to the state, but Sandringham and

Balmoral were hers) and had enough cash left over from sources other than the Civil List to fund her notoriously expensive passion for breeding racehorses. Although the crown jewels also belonged to the nation, she personally owned a stunning collection of tiaras, necklaces, brooches and rings, and while she may not have been quite as fabulously rich as many people thought, the fact that the extent of her private wealth was kept such a closely guarded secret only served to inflate estimates of what she was really worth.

Elizabeth derived an official income from the Government in the form of the Civil List, which had been introduced in the reign of George III. Before that, the monarchy had drawn its income from the Crown Estates, which in 2000 were valued at over £1000 million,[85] out of which the sovereign was expected to pay for the Royal Household as well as for most branches of government, including the diplomatic service, the judiciary and the salaries of government ministers. In 1760, Elizabeth's ancestor, George III, had handed over the income and the responsibilities that came with the Crown Estates to the Government, in return for a smaller, guaranteed payment to cover his own expenses. In modern times, the Civil List took the form of an annual payment that was agreed between Palace and Parliament at the beginning of each reign, and which then usually ran without any alteration until the accession of the next king or queen, at which point the whole arrangement would be renegotiated.

During the nine reigns that preceded Elizabeth's, inflation was, by late twentieth-century standards, so low that any settlement agreed at the start of a reign could generally be guaranteed to hold its value until the end. Between 1758 and 1918, the purchasing power of the pound declined by only one-third, so that you would still need only £3 at the end of the First World War to buy something that had cost £1 a few years before the War of American Independence. In the years that followed, however, inflation rose at such a rate that the Civil List – like any fixed payment – could seldom be relied on to hold its value.

Elizabeth's Civil List payment had been fixed at £475,000 a year at the start of her reign, out of which she was supposed to be entirely self-sufficient, paying all her travel and entertaining costs as well as maintaining her palaces and her staff's wages. By 1969, thanks to inflation, £475,000 was not enough and Elizabeth was having to dip into her own pocket to make up the difference. The problem came to light thanks to Prince Philip, who gave an interview to NBC's *Meet the Press* in which he semi-seriously warned that the Royal Family might have to move into smaller premises in order to make ends meet. 'We go into the red next year,' he announced, adding that he had already had to sell 'a small yacht' and as a further economy measure was considering giving up polo in order to make ends meet. He was, he pointed out more seriously, on a different allowance to the Queen but one that, like hers, had been fixed for the last eighteen years.

Philip's remarks caused a flurry of concern among Elizabeth's advisers. Bringing the monarchy's private financial troubles out into the open seemed a high-risk strategy at the best of times, and in a period when a Labour government had been pursuing policies openly designed to favour 'those who earn money as opposed to those who make it.'[86] Philip's jocular cry for help seemed particularly foolhardy. Annual inflation was running at 36.7 per cent and financially the Government was lurching from crisis to crisis. It may have been a logical time for a royal family living on a fixed income to ask for a raise, but the subject needed to be approached with considerable tact and – from the Palace's point of view – discretion.

Given that Parliament was responsible for the Queen's income, Philip's comments could also be taken as indirect criticism of the Government, and the fact that he made them while he was out of the country added to the impression of insouciant high-handedness. According to Martin Charteris, 'that remark of his slightly worried us at home, I may say. It worried the secretariat. In fact I think it led almost directly to the renegotiation of the Civil List, which was very important.'

The Palace mandarins were right to be worried. At no time in history could any English king or queen expect to go to Parliament asking for extra money and have an easy time of it. Even in the 1970s, when the political power of the monarchy was practically nil and the basis of all effective authority was vested in Parliament or in the Cabinet, the prospect of the Queen coming to the Treasury cap in hand brought out, at the very least, an inquisitive streak in Elizabeth's parliamentary paymasters. Even if they had no quarrel with Elizabeth personally, it was hard for the representatives of one ancient institution to resist the temptation to lord it over another. At the same time, some sections of the public and the more republican-minded members of the Labour Government were outraged at the thought of paying out more to the Royal Family at a time when national cost-cutting and wage-restraint were the order of the day for everybody else.

'I think it was a mark of how far the attitudes towards the monarchy were beginning to change that the reaction of most of the Cabinet was one of fury,' says Barbara Castle:

For years, you know, nobody had dared query the finances behind the Royal Household. We knew vaguely that the Queen was a very rich woman, some said the richest woman in the world. I don't know. She paid no taxes and the Civil List was voting from the pockets of all the people in Britain to maintain the symbolism of the monarchy. That meant that they'd all got to be properly housed, they'd got to have their palaces and their clothes and their way of life and it not only covered the immediate circle but a wider circle, quite a large circle. And there was real anger and I remember discussing it with Joel Barnett, who was then Chief Secretary to the Treasury and he was saying that it was absolutely outrageous. We should refuse to vote any increase in the Civil List until we at least know the size of the Queen's fortune.

The main factor that helped Elizabeth in her first battles over money was the combined support of the major party leaders. At the end of the 1960s Prime Minister Harold Wilson was not only personally well-disposed towards Elizabeth, he was also facing a general election. For all the public uproar, there was no evidence that the majority of the country had lined up behind the republicans, and Wilson was keen not to alienate his more traditionalist supporters. According to Barbara Castle, 'The ice had begun to crack and you dared to be a bit irreverent, without, you know, the working man and woman saying, "Ooh, she's a Bolshie".' But Wilson knew the climate of opinion had not changed that drastically.

A poll in January 1971 showed that the Queen was still the most admired woman in Britain (Barbara Castle came second and Elizabeth retained her lead position until 1975, when Margaret Thatcher overtook her).[87] The question of how much money she should receive from the Civil List was referred to a parliamentary select committee which began its deliberations in May 1971 under a new Government led by Edward Heath. Elizabeth's private secretary, Michael Adeane, was despatched to defend the royal expenditure while his colleagues back at the Palace waited anxiously for the results.

'When the select committee was deliberating on the Queen's finances,' says Martin Charteris, 'I think there was considerable nervousness throughout the Household, certainly in the private secretaries' office . . . You see, the point really is this: that it wasn't a question of pounds, shillings and pence (as we had in those days) but it was really a question of how is the monarchy run and is it good value for money?'

The answer was a qualified 'yes'. According to Barbara Castle, 'Somewhere behind the scenes was stitched up this agreement that there should be an increase in the Civil List but that the Queen should contribute about a third of it from her fortune. Well, that was hardly a revolutionary step. It didn't involve the Queen accepting that she should be taxed like anybody else. But it showed a little movement in the ice-pack.' In 1972, Elizabeth's annual payment was increased from £475,000 a year to £980,000 – an amount which was supposed to remain fixed for the next ten years.

What was significant about the row that had accompanied her original request was that it should have taken place at all. Twenty years earlier, she had come to the throne amid scenes of unparalleled public rejoicing and protestations of loyalty, but by the early 1970s, much of the glitter had worn off. Although there still seemed to be a distinction between the things people disliked about the monarchy – the cost, the number of minor royals who sometimes looked like hangers-on, the prestige and privilege that the institution itself embodied – and the things they liked about Elizabeth herself, there was much less glamour about her.

The film *Royal Family* and William Heseltine's more innovative approach to royal ceremonial had undoubtedly helped freshen things up, but the root of the problem was staleness and familiarity – something which Prince Philip recognised in a television interview in March 1968.[88] 'The monarchy is part of the fabric of the country,' he explained. 'And as the fabric alters, so the monarchy and people's relations to it alters. In 1953 the situation in this country was totally different. And not only that, we were a great deal younger. And I think to you people, a young Queen and a young family are infinitely more newsworthy and amusing.' He and Elizabeth, Philip pointed out, were getting on towards middle age and although 'I daresay, when we're really ancient, there might be a bit more reverence again . . . I would have thought we were entering probably the least interesting period of the kind of glamorous existence.'

If Philip had known how little reverence he and his wife would be shown almost forty years later he might have been more sanguine about the tribulations of the 1970s. As it was, Elizabeth's public relations problems were compounded by the fact that inflation had eaten away at the worth of her Civil List payments but it had also greatly increased the value of her private possessions. This meant that the value of Elizabeth's fixed assets in property, and the income she derived from them, were greatly increased from their 1953 levels. Her investments in the stock market had benefited similarly – and nobody knew how much the Queen was really worth: estimates in the press varied from £2 million to fifty times as much.

Whatever the true figure, while the post-war economic boom and the rise in inflation that went with it may have left the monarchy in the red when it came to the Civil List – and Elizabeth was the first sovereign since Queen Victoria not to make a profit out of government payments[89] – it was clearly considerably richer when the private balance was taken into account. Officially, the monarchy was not subject to means-testing: as Elizabeth's private secretary, Martin Charteris, later complained, 'people don't understand much about the Civil List. They still wilfully call it the Queen's pay. It is nothing whatever to do with the Queen's pay. It is the money which the Queen uses to pay her household and I was one of them so I jolly well know. And to provide her cars, provide the carriages, to provide all the infrastructure things which make the British monarchy what it is – the most admired in the world.' The fact that Elizabeth was personally richer than she was when she came to the throne should have made no difference to the amount of money she received to keep the royal show on the road. But the thought of giving the Royal Family more money at a time when many in the country were beginning to feel the pinch created a storm of criticism and bad publicity.

The issue bubbled to the surface again in 1975, only three years after the first increase in the Civil List, when – blaming inflation once more – the Palace felt it necessary to put in another request for more money, this time for £1,400,000 a year. In 1975 a Labour Government was in power. It controlled the House of Commons by a very slim majority of three MPs and there was, as Denis Healey recalls, 'a revolt in Parliament. We had altogether something like 150 MPs either voting against or abstaining on the motion and there was great opposition from some of my colleagues, not just on the left.'

One Labour MP who had long been an outspoken republican, Willie Hamilton, received 7000 letters from members of the public, over half of whom were highly critical of giving the Queen more cash. 'I object to even One Penny of my husband's hard-earned money contributing to making the world's richest woman richer,' wrote one woman who was facing her own financial dilemma. 'Last week we had to choose between new shoes for the children and keeping up the payments on the telly. I'd like to see Prince Andrew or Prince Edward with holes in their shoes.'[90]

'It certainly proves,' thought another correspondent with a shaky grasp of what had happened to Emperor Hirohito, 'that countries like Japan and Germany without the monarchy are in a much better state financially than we are.'[91] That so many of the letters were critical of the Royal Family perhaps indicated more about the type of person who liked to write to their MP than it did about the feelings of the whole country, but many politicians at the time were more than ready to listen to the complaints.

The final ingredient in the row – a bit of added spice that would continue to flavour public discussions of the Queen's finances into the 1990s – was whether or not Elizabeth ought to pay tax on her private wealth. The constitutional precedents were mixed: Queen Victoria and Edward VII had both paid income tax, but Elizabeth's father and grandfather had managed to secure an exemption that continued under the current reign. It seemed to some that, by asking for more money while refusing to pay income tax, Elizabeth was trying to have her cake and eat it.

'I don't begrudge them what they need,' wrote one member of the public, 'but they ought to pay taxes like the rest of us. It's not fair that the Queen should be the richest woman in the world and not pay a penny tax on it.' Even loyal monarchists were capable of occasional chippiness when brought face-to-face with some of the monarchy's more luxurious trappings – when Margaret Thatcher, in later years, first visited the Royal Yacht *Britannia*, she was asked by a welcoming officer whether she had ever been aboard before: no, replied the Conservative Prime Minister, she just paid for it.[92] And in the mid 1970s there were plenty of people in Parliament who were not loyal monarchists.

Elizabeth faced danger on another front in the shape of her sister, whose romantic affairs were once again beginning to dominate the headlines. Since her agonising decision not to marry Group Captain Townsend in 1955, Margaret had fallen in love with a successful and talented young society photographer called Anthony Armstrong-Jones (later to become Lord Snowdon). There was intense public speculation about who and when Margaret would marry and she was at great pains during her courtship with Armstrong-Jones to keep the affair a secret.

Years earlier, in 1953, her feelings for Townsend had been betrayed to the press by so small a thing as the affectionate gesture with which she had picked a piece of fluff from his uniform. So her need for secrecy and discretion was something with which Elizabeth fully sympathised, especially as the Queen had hated the public hue and cry which followed her own early courtship with Philip. Years later, as the country worked itself into an hysteria over the wedding of the Prince of Wales and Lady Diana Spencer, when Elizabeth's then press secretary, Michael Shea, observed to her, 'Ma'am, I've never seen and I don't suppose you've ever seen such a huge amount of press interest about this forthcoming marriage,' the Queen replied simply, 'You don't know what Margaret and I went through when people were wondering who we were going to get married to.'

Margaret's relationship with Snowdon went back to the 1950s, and in the early stages of their affair Margaret had given her sister no cause for concern. Knowing that the slightest glance or touch might alert the public, she and Snowdon met each other only when they knew they were safe from prying eyes. On one occasion, Snowdon accepted an invitation to a private dinner at Lady Penn's house, only to pull out with a made-up excuse when he found out that Margaret was also going to be there. She recalls: 'He rang back about half-an-hour later and said, "I'm terribly sorry, I've suddenly realised I can't come to dinner because I've got another engagement." And I swallowed that and found somebody else. But in actual fact, it was very clever because they were unofficially engaged but I didn't even know and I knew them both. So it just shows how clever they'd been.' Rather than meet Margaret at his own home, Armstrong-Jones even rented a room from a friend in a run-down old house overlooking the Thames at Rotherhithe, where Margaret would sometimes cook dinner and the two of them could be relaxed and informal in a way that would be impossible anywhere else.

However, Margaret's affection for the young man was well-known within the Royal Family, and Armstrong-Jones was staying at Balmoral when she heard that her first love, Peter Townsend, was about to remarry. She and Townsend had seen each other a few times since their dramatic break-up in 1955 and the news of his marriage came as a great shock to her. She felt, according to Christopher Warwick, her official biographer, that it was 'a betrayal of an understanding they had reached concerning remarriage after divorce,'[93] but the news at least seems to have helped draw a line under the past. She told Armstrong-Jones about it while they were together at Balmoral and shortly afterwards he asked her to marry him. When their engagement was officially announced in February 1960 it was genuine news to just about everyone. It was, remembers Lady Penn, 'a great surprise when she got engaged. I don't think anybody had any idea that she was going to marry Tony Armstrong-Jones. They'd kept it very much under wraps, which was clever of them because they managed to pull a fast one on the press.'

The wedding was held at Westminster Abbey on 6 May 1960. Some of those who knew both Margaret and Armstrong-Jones wondered whether a marriage between such a senior member of the Royal Family and a faintly bohemian photographer was going to work. Armstrong-Jones' father warned him that his free-wheeling approach would not mix well with the hidebound conventions of life at Court,[94] while Noel Coward's diary entry for 28 February 1960 noted of the bridegroom that 'he looks quite pretty, but whether or not the marriage is entirely suitable remains to be seen'.

The reaction of the press, on the other hand, was entirely favourable. Armstrong-Jones was the first person to marry a senior member of the Royal Family who was not himself of princely blood and even if he was, as John Grigg points out, 'a fairly phoney commoner, really' (his

The ideal family. Queen Mother and princesses, June 1936 (*Hulton Deutsch*)

Elizabeth as Prince Charming in *Cinderella*, Windsor 1941 (*Hulton Archive*)

'I shall always work as my father did' (*Hulton Archive*)

The Royal Family. Making so much of family life stored up trouble for the future (*Camera Press Ltd*)

With the Windsor Women's Football team (*private collection*)

A Royal picnic. 'Indoor life doesn't come into it' (*private collection*)

'A countrywoman at heart.' Elizabeth and cousin Margaret Rhodes at Balmoral (*private collection*)

'She can control a dog at 800 yards' (*private collection*)

Beach-combing during a tour of the Western Isles in *Britannia* (*private collection*)

Outdoor living at Balmoral (*private collection*)

'My guess is that the weekends at Balmoral were purgatory' – Bernard Ingham (*private collection*)

'The two sisters have always been close' (*private collection*)

Elizabeth, Margaret Rhodes and lady-in-waiting Susan Hussey at Balmoral (*private collection*)

Elizabeth and her mother at Windsor, 1991 (*private collection*)

mother was married to an earl and he had been educated at Eton) he at least worked for a living and did a passable imitation of somebody who knew how life was lived on the majority side of the Palace walls. Like everyone else who was destined to marry into Elizabeth's family (with the possible exception of Princess Anne's husbands), he was expected to bring a breath of fresh air into stale royal corridors and gave every indication that he would be able to do so. 'Tony was wonderful company,' says Angela Huth, one of Princess Margaret's friends. 'He had that funny way of making the ordinary extraordinary. You knew no day was a dull day. He worked terribly hard, has always worked terribly hard. He's very talented. Princess Margaret admires talent no end and she loves people who work hard.'

Like Elizabeth, Margaret had been brought up with no real knowledge of life in the outside world and Armstrong-Jones seemed to offer a path out of the ivory tower. 'I think,' says Lady Glenconner, 'that Princess Margaret relies a lot on her girlfriends or ladies-in-waiting, like I am, and we have a very nice relationship. When we were in Mustique and I was just sitting in her bedroom she said, "Oh, is this like being at boarding school?" And I said, "Well, it is rather, you know. We used to sit on each other's beds and chat and all that sort of thing." She's always quite interested to know what happened at boarding school.'

That Margaret should not know how even the most privileged of Britain's children were educated only underlines the extraordinary isolation in which she and her sister had been brought up. But her new husband was not only well qualified to satisfy her curiosity about the mysteries of private education, he also introduced her to a world she could never have known if she had married a run-of-the-mill foreign prince. 'They went to all the most fashionable places,' says one of their friends, jazz musician John Dankworth. 'They were really quite something in those days – a very beautiful couple that went around London.'

Margaret was what her sister had never been and never wanted to be – fashionable – and, in the early years of her marriage, she was prepared to make allowances for her husband, who, as some of his friends had predicted, found the limitations of royal life irksome: walking a respectful pace or two behind his wife was not what Snowdon was used to. When he forgot, though, or could not be bothered with the niceties of Court etiquette, Margaret was unusually ready to forgive. 'On Monday night,' Noel Coward wrote in his diary for 11 June 1961, 'I dined with Princess Margaret and Tony at Kensington Palace . . . and after dinner drove secretly to Tony's place or "studio" in Rotherhithe where we banged the piano and threw empty Cointreau bottles into the river. Not an intellectual occupation but enjoyable. They were both very sweet and obviously happy.'

Alongside all the usual challenges of marriage, however, Margaret and Snowdon also had to contend with a world of difference in their upbringing and expectations. George V had encouraged the notion of commoners marrying into the Royal Family, but Snowdon, like all his successors, found that he had married an institution along with his wife and, perhaps inevitably, the couple's differences in background eventually overcame their personal similarities.

Margaret was happy to temper the formality of life as a princess with forays into the relaxed, artistic world of her husband's friends but in the end it was relief that she was after, not a sea-change. For her, as for Elizabeth, being royal was not a part-time act put on for the benefit of the public but part and parcel of her whole outlook on life. For Snowdon, marriage to a princess did not sit well with his desire to continue his professional work or to live life as any other married couple. To escape the boredom of royal life, he took a job on a newspaper and started making documentaries which often involved long absences from home. By 1967 the papers were running stories of problems in the Snowdons' marriage with gossip both about Armstrong-Jones' relationship with Lady Jackie Rufus Isaacs and Princess Margaret's friendship with Robin Douglas Home and the actor Peter Sellers.

Elizabeth viewed her sister's situation with sympathy and concern. The two did not, as Michael Mann puts it, 'always see things through the same set of spectacles' but they had always been close and since childhood Elizabeth had felt a sense of responsibility for her younger sister. 'I think her great concern would have been for Princess Margaret's happiness, above anything else,' says Lady Clayton. At the same time, now that Elizabeth was in her forties and head of the family, she had a real responsibility – as well as affection – for her sister and there was, according to William Heseltine, 'a good deal of trepidation about the prospect of Princess Margaret's marriage ending'.

It was still a very rare thing for any member of the Royal Family to be divorced and Elizabeth's nervousness stemmed as much from fear of what the public reaction would be as from any desire for her family to provide a moral example. The Abdication crisis and Edward VIII's marriage to Mrs Simpson may have happened over thirty years earlier, but the Townsend affair had happened barely a decade ago and there was, says Heseltine, 'a good deal of nervous anxiety that such a move by such a close member of the Royal Family would cause a good deal of unhappiness and disaffection among members of the public at large'. The only recent precedent for a royal divorce had been Lord Harewood, Elizabeth's cousin, and he was a good deal more distant from the throne than Princess Margaret: he had also married his divorcée in a quiet civil ceremony in the United States. The disintegration of Margaret's marriage promised to be a great deal more spectacular and explosive.

As with Townsend – and with practically every family crisis she has faced – Elizabeth refrained from heavy-handed interference in her sister's life, although in private the stress Margaret was under was obvious even to guests staying with the Queen. On one occasion, when Harold Macmillan was staying at Sandringham and enjoying a private conversation with Elizabeth, 'Princess Margaret came roaring in in high dudgeon and said to her sister, "Nobody would pay any attention to you if you weren't Queen!" and stormed out again. And he was both amused and a little bit shocked about that. I think it amused him because it showed that the Royal Family could have problems in their family life just the same as everyone else. But a little bit shocked because he felt that you shouldn't address the monarch like that even if you were her sister.'[95]

Barbara Castle, another Government minister who observed the sisters together, came to the conclusion that Margaret didn't need to be protected 'but Elizabeth needed protecting against Margaret because Margaret had a free range of expressions. She was brash, she was not going to play the routine and that was all right for her. She was only a princess, but for the Queen on the throne, it could be embarrassing.'

It was embarrassing because, by the early 1970s, Margaret and Snowdon were effectively living separate lives and doing so in a manner which only focused attention on their private difficulties. It was known that both of them were having affairs and, as William Heseltine remembers, 'there's always been a certain double standard about people who are quite reconciled to the fact that marriages break up in their own spheres, but for many years I think it was felt that these old-fashioned standards should be maintained by members of the Royal Family'.

Margaret was also living a life of conspicuous consumption that, coinciding with Elizabeth's own financial negotiations over the Civil List, gave the impression of a carefree princess who was happy to play idly while the rest of the country was tightening its belt. Margaret's friend, Lord Glenconner, had given her a plot of land on the island of Mustique as a wedding present and he received a telephone call from her as relations with her husband plummeted. 'Already her marriage was obviously not satisfactory,' he recalls, 'and so she must have rung me up I suppose and said, "Your present, was it for real?" I naturally said, "Yes, of course it was for real." It hadn't been formal-ised. And then she said, "And did it include a house?" "Of course," I said.' But, while Margaret's holidays in Mustique may have helped to sweeten the pill of a broken marriage, they did little for her reputation, or for that of the monarchy. Shortly after her Civil List allowance had risen to £55,000 a year, one Labour politician stated that 'if she thumbs her nose at taxpayers by flying off to Mustique to see this pop-singer chap, she shouldn't expect the workers of this country to pay for it'.[96]

The 'pop-singer chap' was Roddy Llewellyn – an attractive, upper-class young man with not very much to do, whom Margaret had met on Mustique in 1973. At a time when Margaret's husband was leaving inventively abrasive notes hidden in drawers for Margaret to find later on ('You look like a Jewish manicurist,' one of them read, 'and I hate you'[97]), Roddy Llewellyn seemed to offer a number of advantages – although most of them could be listed under the 'no hatred for Margaret' heading. 'Roddy was an angel really,' recalls Lord Glenconner, who had introduced him to Margaret. 'He was of course very, very supportive and not abrasive in any way. He's a very soothing person and Princess Margaret had been perhaps very bruised and to that extent he was of course you know just what the doctor ordered. He had an angelic nature and had allowed the world to take advantage of him at that point. He was at a very low ebb as it turned out. This was because he was so pleasing.'

Roddy was less pleasing to Elizabeth and her advisers. According to Sarah Bradford's authoritative biography of the Queen, she disapproved of what she privately referred to as 'my sister's guttersnipe life',[98] and on one occasion, when Margaret telephoned a friend threatening to throw herself out of her bedroom window unless he abandoned his house-party and came over to see her, Elizabeth advised him to 'carry on with your house-party. Her bedroom is on the ground floor.'[99] Her reaction was perhaps less heartless than exasperated: over her sister's marriage and the figure of Roddy Llewellyn, Elizabeth was torn, as always, between her devotion to her family and the idealised image of The Family for which the royal dynasty was meant to stand. Having just celebrated her own twenty-fifth wedding anniversary, she cannot have felt anything but sympathy for her sister's repeated and unsuccessful attempts to find love; but, as the Princess of Wales would later find out, responding to histrionic cries for help was not Elizabeth's strong point. On top of that, the image portrayed in the press of Margaret hanging out with a freeloading playboy did nothing but damage to the conscientious and painstaking version of the monarchy that Elizabeth preferred. Nothing, it seemed in the 1970s, could be further from the cosy, decent world of George VI and 'us four' than Margaret and Roddy.

Llewellyn's relationship with Margaret – which her official bio-grapher, Christopher Warwick, describes as a 'loving friendship' – hit the headlines in 1976 when a long-distance photographer snapped a picture of them at the poolside. The photo implied that their relationship was certainly loving and probably more than friendly but in fact it was doctored. It failed to show that Margaret and Roddy were surrounded by friends at the time and that, far from snatching a moment of illicit intimacy, they were both obviously in a public place and conscious of the fact. The implication was clear enough, though – 'Margaret and the Handsome Young Courtier!' ran the *News of the World* headline on 22 February 1976 – and it provided the catalyst for an official separation. In March, Kensington Palace announced, using a form of words with which the royal typists would become very familiar, that 'Her Royal Highness the Princess Margaret, Countess of Snowdon and the Earl of Snowdon have mutually agreed to live apart. The princess will carry out her public duties and functions unaccompanied by Lord Snowdon.'

Any relief Elizabeth may have felt that the running sore of the Snowdon marriage had finally been lanced was tempered by the fact that Margaret's friendship with Roddy continued after her separation from her husband. The original plan was that the Snowdons should separate, but not divorce – but the continuing scandal over Margaret and Llewellyn made it inevitable. 'It was a very painful thing for her to have to do,' recalls Lady Penn, 'but it was something that really had to happen and I'm sure that is one of the reasons why she's never married again – because she just doesn't believe in divorce. She believes that you marry and that's that – that's what you do.'

In the late 1970s, though, Margaret's position on the moral high ground was in danger of being overwhelmed by a tide of bad publicity. Her visits to the commune that Llewellyn shared in Wiltshire ('Neighbour John tells of the "funny ways" of Margaret's rustic pals!'[100] one newspaper headline hinted darkly), her holidays in Mustique and the fact that, as one columnist put it, 'One minute she is coming the royal "we" over some member of the lower orders and the next slugging gin and singing *Chattanooga Choo Choo* with friends far removed from her husband's set'[101] dealt her constant front-page damage. Her divorce was announced in May 1978 and whatever private sympathy Elizabeth felt for her sister's predicament took second place to protecting the reputation of the monarchy. 'Subsequent to the divorce,' William Heseltine remembers, 'there were elements of Princess Margaret's behaviour which attracted a lot of criticism and which I'm sure the Queen wouldn't have been altogether happy about.'

The Queen's strategy – which in years to come would become almost a set routine – was to avoid direct confrontation in favour of withdrawal and coded signs of public disapproval. According to Michael Shea, one of her later press secretaries, 'the Queen doesn't like rows. Margaret Thatcher famously said that the press only gave her one emotion, which was fury. I have constantly read in the press of the Queen's fury about things. I have never known the Queen to be furious about anything.'

In Margaret's case, Elizabeth's disapproval took the form of limited social sanctions. 'I think she perhaps found it prudent not to meet some of the people that Princess Margaret had established friendly relations with,' says William Heseltine, and in 1980, when her sister celebrated her fiftieth birthday, Elizabeth made it clear that she would not attend the birthday dinner if Roddy Llewellyn was there. Later that year, Llewellyn married somebody else and the clouds that had hung over Margaret gradually cleared, but the scandal had set a pattern that would be repeated within barely a decade. The personal life of any member of the Royal Family was now clearly established as fair game for the amusement of press and public alike. Meanwhile, the clean-cut and decent image of the Royal Family which Elizabeth tried to maintain had inevitably become less a moral example to the nation and more a yardstick against which the failings of her own relatives could be measured.

CHAPTER EIGHT

In 1977, Elizabeth celebrated her Silver Jubilee. A quarter of a century earlier, she had come to the throne as a young woman of twenty-five, the youngest sovereign since Queen Victoria, hailed with extravagant fanfares and hopes for the future. Since then, the country had changed almost beyond recognition and not, perhaps, as those who had heralded the New Elizabethan Age in 1952 had quite anticipated. The British Empire, which in 1952 had still included colonies in much of Africa as well as Malaysia, Ceylon, and Singapore, not to mention the self-governing white Dominions of Canada, Australia and New Zealand, had by the mid-1970s evaporated almost completely, and the imperial ideal had been replaced by the far fuzzier and more collaborative notion of the Commonwealth.

The transition from Empire to Commonwealth had been peaceful on the whole, and the amicable relationship Britain enjoyed with most of its former colonies was a cause for some self-congratulation, but in the wider world the country's standing had slipped disastrously.

If Britain was, in international terms, still a Great Power it was only by virtue of the fact that, in a world dominated by the Soviet Union and the United States, great power did not really matter any more: super power was what counted. In 1956, Prime Minister Anthony Eden had attempted to invade Egypt with the help of the French and the Israelis, only to be forced into a humiliating retreat in the face of military threats from Russia and economic sanctions from America. 'That demonstrated,' journalist John Grigg recalls, 'in the most brutal way, the power we'd lost and the people who now had it.'

Even in its own league, Britain appeared to be losing the economic race against France and Germany and in 1976, with inflation running at over 16 per cent, the Government had run out of money and was forced to ask the International Monetary Fund for extra cash. In return for the bail-out Denis Healey – the Labour Chancellor of the Exchequer – had to accept strict international control over government spending that further underlined how, far from running other countries' affairs as they were used to, the British could now barely manage their own.

Like everyone else, Elizabeth was dismayed at her country's fall from grace. As the former Labour minister David Owen recalls, after a private conversation with the Queen, 'she did express herself very clearly and straightforwardly about that issue. She definitely wanted Britain in the late 1970s to develop its economy, to stand stronger, to play a more active role.' Within the country, though, her own position had changed. At a speech she made at London's Guildhall to mark her Silver Jubilee, Elizabeth remembered her own twenty-first birthday, reminding her audience that 'when I was twenty-one I pledged my life to the service of our people and I asked for God's help to make good that vow. Although that vow was made in my salad days when I was green in judgement, I do not regret or retract one word of it.'

Now that Elizabeth was in her fifties, however, the country's attitude had shifted – to her and to the ideals and duty and dedication for which she stood. She was still widely admired but she no longer embodied the mood of the nation in the way she had in the more respectful, hierarchical Britain of the 1950s. At a dinner Elizabeth had attended in Downing Street for Winston Churchill's retirement in 1955, her elderly Prime Minister had proposed a toast with the words, 'I drink your health, Your Majesty: a toast I first drank as a subaltern officer in the 4th Hussars at Bangalore in India in the reign of Your Majesty's great-great-grandmother, and I drink to the wise and kindly way of life of which Your Majesty is the young and gleaming champion.' Twenty years on, as Prince Philip had predicted, Britain had new 'young and gleaming' champions, while the image of the monarchy had been tarnished by the recent rows over money and the state of Princess Margaret's marriage.

With this is mind, the question of how to celebrate twenty-five years on the throne seemed a delicate one. After a quarter-century of unprecedented national decline the country was scarcely in celebratory mood and, according to surveys of public opinion, many people were unsure quite what a Silver Jubilee was. Some people thought it marked a milestone in Elizabeth's marriage to Philip, others that it was in some way connected with D-Day,[102] and confusion was heightened by the decision to hold the main celebrations not on the date of the Queen's accession in February but on 7 June.

Major Michael Parker, who was in charge of planning some of the events, recalls that 'we actually started working on the Silver Jubilee in 1975 and at that stage, quite honestly, most people said, "What's a jubilee?" because they didn't know what it was and then everybody said, "Well, I don't think there's going to be much interest, do you know?" ' Elizabeth herself, whose professional caution coincided with a personal dislike of pomp and display, wanted to keep things as low-key as possible, according to Shane Blewitt. Her doubts were shared by members of the Government and by many of her advisers at Buckingham Palace.

Martin Charteris remembers quite clearly that 'the Government of the day wondered really whether this country would get excited about the Queen's Silver Jubilee'. And, according to William Heseltine, 'when we first started to think about ways in which the Queen's Silver Jubilee should be presented and celebrated the economic and political situation in Britain was not a very comfortable one. A lot of people felt that anything in the way of extravagant celebrations would be inappro-priate and that view I think was certainly shared by members of the Household.'

'It's a shame for the Queen,' one member of the public told the opinion pollsters, 'but I think people hold it against her for giving away the colonies, for there was gold in some of them countries.'

'We're going to be sick and tired of all this Jubilee stuff by the time it's over,' worried another.[103]

In the event, the scale of the public's response confounded nearly everybody's expectations – to the satisfaction of Palace officials like Martin Charteris, who had been in no personal doubt that once she was brought face-to-face with the people, Elizabeth would prove that she had lost none of her allure. 'I was in the position of being able to discuss this with them,' he recalls, 'and I jolly well knew the country would respond well, because I had spent the last twenty-three years following the Queen round this country, which they hadn't. And so I said, you'll find it will be all right, and of course I was actually right. It was a huge success. But the Government was surprised.'

The long build-up to the June celebrations perhaps helped. As Philip Ziegler points out in his study of the monarchy, *Crown and*

People, 'favourite projects – the planting of trees, a seat for the village green, an annexe to the school hall – were revived and latched on behind the Jubilee bandwagon'[104] and the media also played its part in whetting the public's appetite. From February 1977, newspapers published special accounts of Elizabeth's reign, film of the Coronation was repeated on television and was again watched by millions across the country. After years of economic bad news and a particularly harsh winter, the feeling that the Jubilee at least provided an excuse for a party eventually began to outweigh people's initial boredom.

Added to that, there was a genuine and undoubted affection for Elizabeth herself. There may have been arguments over the Civil List, and Margaret's unhappy and eventful love-life may have introduced an unwonted element of soap opera into the royal mix, but the Queen had escaped much personal blame. Given her innate conservatism, it would be wrong to think that the unchanging face she presented to the world was the result of anything like calculated strategy. But, even if it was by nature rather than design, there were clear advantages to being the still point in a turning world.

Elizabeth's careful and dutiful approach had, in 1977 at least, reaped rich rewards, and the corridors of Buckingham Palace leading to her private office were littered with sacks of congratulatory letters from members of the public. One of her secretaries, Jean Dowling, remembers that they had to hire extra staff simply to deal with the correspondence and public regard was matched by renewed curiosity about the Queen's character. At least thirty-one books about her were published that year, including Robert Lacey's *Majesty*, which sold over 200,000 copies by the end of the Jubilee alone. Even John Grigg, who had criticised the Court for being too dowdy and old-fashioned over twenty years before, admits that in 1977, 'I thought that she'd hardly put a foot wrong as far as dignity was concerned and showed great steadiness. On every formal occasion, laying wreaths on the Cenotaph and all that sort of thing, she behaved with consummate grace and in her personal behaviour she did nothing to embarrass or disgrace us. So I felt she'd done wonderfully in all those ways.'

As the country worked itself up into a frenzy of Jubilee excitement, nobody was more surprised than the Queen. Her low expectations of the event mirrored almost exactly the sentiments of her grandfather who, in 1935, had been the last British monarch to celebrate twenty-five years on the throne. The Silver Jubilee of George V had got off to the same shaky start, with much initial doubt about whether anyone would care very much or turn up for the processions. It had ended with massed crowds cheering on the streets and an amazed and gratified King saying with some wonder, 'I didn't realise they felt like this.'[105]

In 1977, the size of the crowds and the enthusiasm with which they cheered her took Elizabeth just as unawares and her reaction was identical to that of her grandfather. 'I am simply amazed, I had no idea,' she kept saying.[106] The centrepiece of the celebrations was a procession in London on 7 June and the night before Elizabeth was due to light a bonfire at Windsor that would set off a chain of beacons across the country. The organisers had expected only four or five thousand people to turn up. But in the end, according to Michael Parker, there were ten times that number and Elizabeth, who was driving up from Windsor Castle in a Land Rover, was held up by the crowds.

Afterwards she was driven back to London in one of the royal limousines which were usually used only for official tours and processions – a fact on which Philip commented, wondering why they were not using one of the less ostentatious cars since it was late at night and there could hardly be anyone still awake to wave at. As they reached Datchet at 11pm, though, they saw that the whole village had turned out to greet them. And as the car drew into London, the crowds along the central reservation of the motorway grew thicker and thicker until, at the end of the Mall, it could barely make the turn into Buckingham Palace. The mood in the royal car was one of simple astonishment, and at least one of Elizabeth's attendants began to get goosebumps at the sight of so many people unexpectedly cheering and waving in the middle of the night under the yellow London streetlamps.[107]

The next day, Elizabeth was still convinced that a little of her would go a long way. She was due to travel to a thanksgiving service at St Paul's Cathedral by coach – with Prince Philip sitting beside her and Prince Charles riding behind on horseback – and at first thought that a one-way state procession would be more than enough for the public. At the end of the service, Shane Blewitt remembers her arguing, 'They'll have had enough of me by then and I'll come back by car.' In fact, there were a million people lining the route – as many as there had been for her Coronation – and some people had slept on the pavement the night before to make sure that they had a good view as the Queen went past. As Shane Blewitt recalls, 'Everybody said, "You can't possibly do that, you must come back in the carriage." So she finally agreed to come back by carriage and the streets were absolutely lined all the way back. She thought that, having done the service, they'd all have gone away but they were there to pay tribute to her, which was touching.' When Elizabeth visited Liverpool, she was greeted with even more enthusiasm. William Heseltine remembers the visit as:

> a carefully constructed event which was almost overwhelmed by the number of people who turned out. What had been planned was a progress between the two cathedrals, with a few events staged along Hope Street. In fact, I think the police estimated that there were a million and a half people crammed into that street. And really it just became an

opportunity for a million and a half people to see and cheer and a few favoured ones to touch the Queen and Prince Philip as they went by.

Elizabeth's pleasure was obvious. It was a long-standing complaint of the public that the Queen usually looked too serious and occasionally even appeared to be scowling when carrying out her duties. Yet, as one of her staff admits, 'the Queen laughs all the time. She is always laughing. But when she is doing her job she concentrates and looks very serious.'[108] For the Jubilee, though, Elizabeth's surprised gratitude got the better of her. She clearly appeared to be enjoying herself, and the crowds in turn grew more enthusiastic, the more they could see the Queen's delight. 'We have come here because we love you,' one woman told Elizabeth. 'I can feel it and it means so much to me,' the Queen replied.[109] 'She is such a modest and humble person,' observes one of her staff. 'I don't think she ever felt that she would get such a triumphant reception. I think it must have been very morale-boosting for her.'

In private, the Jubilee also provided plenty of stimulus for Elizabeth's sense of humour. Like her father – who had a schoolboy's love of practical jokes and used to amuse his family by running his home movies backwards so that people would entertainingly appear to leap back on to diving boards or shuffle rearwards out of the room – Elizabeth had a keen sense of the ridiculous. 'Impish, I think, is the word I'd use for the Queen's sense of humour,' says Kenneth Scott. 'She's quite a good mimic and she enjoys making gentle and un-nasty fun of people. She enjoys playing charades and she can see the funny side of situations in which she is actually playing an unfunny role and can be quite amusing about them afterwards.' Her own unique status and the public's fascination with it also provided her with some wry amusement: dining in private with a friend once in a public restaurant, the Queen looked out of the window at the crowds of people who were staring at her outside and commented dryly, 'I think they've seen someone.'[110]

In 1977, Elizabeth was at least expecting to be seen, and was indeed fervently grateful for the size and enthusiasm of the crowds. With so many Jubilee-related public engagements and ceremonials, however, there were plenty of opportunities for things to go wrong – and, even if no one else noticed them, minor mishaps could always be counted on to keep the Queen engaged. On 6 June, when the first of the Jubilee beacons was lit at Windsor, almost nothing went right. Half the lights failed to work because the BBC's main generator blew up, the Olympic torch with which Elizabeth was supposed to light the bonfire went out, and the young boy who was holding it for her burst into tears. Everything was running late and when, in semi-darkness, the Queen finally found a blazing torch with which to set the beacon going someone behind the scenes pressed the emergency ignition button too early so that the bonfire roared into life before Elizabeth's flame actually reached it.

'It was,' recalls Michael Parker, 'one of many things that were going wrong at that stage and I'd like to think I wasn't responsible for most of them, but I did say something like "Ma'am, I'm terribly sorry to say this, but absolutely everything is going wrong." And I believe she turned to me and smiled and said, "Oh, good. What fun." And it was fun, actually, because it was a lovely gentle occasion and it didn't really matter, you know.'

There was similar confusion later on in the celebrations – this time in private – when the Military Knights of Windsor, along with the Dean and Canons of St George's Chapel, were meant to present Elizabeth with an address of congratulation and welcome. Michael Mann, who was Dean of Windsor at the time, explains:

The drill was that the doors opened and the Military Knights marched in until they got opposite the Queen, halted, and turned to face the Queen, then the address of welcome was given. Then they turned to the right and marched out the other end, and the Dean and the Canons followed in the same way. Well, the Military Knights duly marched in, in their wonderful William IV uniforms of red and cocked hats and all the rest of it; and these old gentlemen stumped along but the General forgot to halt them, so they just stumped past the Queen and marched out at the other end, when two rather astonished footmen had to open the doors rather more quickly than they were accustomed to. And they marched right out without ever doing anything. The Queen absolutely doubled up – she thought it was terribly funny.

Elizabeth had good reason to be light-hearted. Since her Coronation, the Jubilee was the biggest and most unmistakable display of public affection she had ever received. As William Heseltine remembers, 'I think that the way in which the public responded to the event took even the Household by surprise. It was a remarkable year in which quite spontaneous celebrations, street parties of all kinds took place and there was a remarkable feeling of resurgence of excitement and affection for the monarchy.' Part of the Jubilee's success may have been due to the public's liking for a party – there were 6000 street parties in London alone – and the opportunity it provided for a demoralised country to let its hair down.

However, as the Queen's experience with the crowds showed, it also reflected – in much greater measure – on Elizabeth herself and the illusion that her walkabouts gave to people that they had, very briefly, made human contact with the small, dutiful, decent woman whose lifelong insistence on dedication and personal sacrifice may no longer have struck much of a popular chord, but who was liked and admired for it nonetheless. It was the Queen's personal qualities, reckoned *The Times*, that lay 'at the root of this outburst of popularity'.[111] And, as one woman who stood among the crowd of families outside Buckingham Palace later told a reporter, 'the look on those kids' faces, you could never believe it. They'll remember those few minutes when they're buried in their graves. And what I want to say is, does she know the effect she has? Does she know how she can win people round?'[112]

The effect that Elizabeth had on people owed some of its power to the fact that her children – particularly Prince Charles – were of marriageable and therefore newsworthy age. It was true that the real focus of the Jubilee celebrations was Elizabeth. But, whereas in earlier years the Queen had had the royal stage pretty much to herself, there was now a growing cast of supporting characters. Her press secretary, Michael Shea, recalls that 'the real interest in that period was in the younger members of the Royal Family – you know, who they're going to marry, who they're dating, who would be suitable marriage partners and so on and so forth and there was a huge range of stories going round'. It was not an unwelcome situation, but it was a novel one: George VI had come to the throne with the ready-made Royal Family unit of 'us four' and cosy domesticity had been a constant theme of his reign. Under Elizabeth the Royal Family was larger ('us seven' if you included Princess Margaret), more unwieldy, and less amenable to the neat packaging that had wrapped up Elizabeth's own childhood and early adulthood.

The press, for one thing, was much more powerful and anarchic. Says Michael Shea:

I can remember almost my first day at Buckingham Palace, when the *Daily Express* ran a headline story, front-page: 'Prince of Wales about to marry Princess Marie Astrid of Luxembourg.' I was a newcomer and therefore checked with those concerned and I later issued a statement that not only was the Prince of Wales not intending to get married to Princess Marie Astrid of Luxembourg but he'd never even met her. This didn't daunt the *Daily Express*, because next day it just ran the headline 'Despite Buckingham Palace denials, rumours continue to abound that . . .' And that sort of story was a daily occurrence. We had a new girlfriend every week, true or false. The Prince of Wales and, indeed, his siblings would have had to have been very energetic to have dated as many young people as they were reported to have done.

Equally important was the fact that Elizabeth kept her family on a much looser rein than had either her parents or grandparents. She had always been very close to her own father and when she was a young woman, even after her marriage, George VI had been the fixed point around which her world, and her sister's, revolved. George V had exerted a similarly strong gravitational pull on his family, although his personal dislike of any display of emotion left him more dependent on the levers of paternal and regal authority than of love ('What do they mean by saying that "Buckingham Palace" is not me?' he used to complain when critics of the monarchy tried euphemistically to avoid direct attacks on the King himself. "Who else is there, I should like to know? Do they mean the footmen?" '[113])

Elizabeth's approach was quite different. She was not authoritarian like her grandfather and, although she was not emotionally cold, she seemed to have none of her father's need to construct an idealised, carefully protected, private world of the family in which she could take refuge from the pressures of the job. She was altogether more self-reliant. In the opinion of one of her courtiers, Kenneth Scott, 'She's not very demonstrative. Certainly since I have known her she's not been demonstrative towards her children. She's kind to them and enjoys their company but she's not a hugging and kissing sort of person, really.' Above all, when it came to bringing up her own family, the Queen was never an interventionist. When the children were very young – although more so with Edward and Andrew than with the two older ones – Elizabeth involved herself as much as she could, but once they were grown-up, she generally expected them to get on with their own lives. In this she was, as journalist Graham Turner points out, 'being rather modern . . . I think it's the politically correct attitude now. You don't interfere, you let them get on with it. Well, the Queen was there a long time before the rest of us.'

Of all the royal children, it was Prince Charles whose ability to get on with things was watched with the keenest interest. In 1977 Elizabeth's eldest son was twenty-nine. He had left the Royal Navy the year before, at which point he had rashly announced that thirty would be a good age to get married. His words had only piled fuel on to the fire of press speculation about who the future Princess of Wales might be, and with only a year to go before the expiration of Charles's self-appointed deadline, a large part of the population was almost beside itself with excitement. When Charles was staying at Sandringham with one of the women he was thought to be courting – Lady Jane Wellesley, daughter of the Duke of Wellington – a crowd of 10,000 people turned up to watch them go to church. 'Such was the obvious conviction that what they had read was true,' Charles said afterwards,[114] 'I almost felt I had better espouse myself at once so as not to disappoint so many people.'

If many of the stories about Charles's love-life were untrue, there were still plenty that appeared to hold water or that simply went unreported. The existence of either category seemed to many of Elizabeth's courtiers reason enough for grave misgivings. Meanwhile, Charles's own attitude towards marriage was further complicated by the fact that he was in love with a married woman – Camilla Parker Bowles. He had met Camilla before her own marriage in 1972 and found that, with her love of the countryside and hunting, her down-to-earth sense of humour and dislike of affectation, they were kindred spirits.

Unfortunately, he failed to press home his advantage in time and she married Andrew Parker Bowles, an officer in the Household Cavalry, while Charles was at sea. It left him aghast that 'such a blissful, peaceful and mutually happy relationship should have come to nothing'. 'I suppose,' he wrote, 'the feeling of emptiness will pass eventually' but, to the concern of Elizabeth's advisers, it was later rumoured that Charles's romantic friendship with Camilla had not come to nothing and that he was actually still pursuing an affair with her. This possibility was particularly shocking not so much because Camilla was by this time married, but because her husband was an officer in a regiment of which Charles was Colonel-in-Chief.

Elizabeth knew of the rumours about Charles but preferred to keep her distance. According to the journalist Graham Turner, 'when the Queen was told by one of her courtiers that Charles was sleeping with the wife of a brother officer in the Brigade of Guards, there was no reaction at all. I asked the courtier, "Was there anything in her face to show a reaction?" "No change whatever." So I said to him, "What do you think she did about it?" "Absolutely nothing," he said. Now, that is a classic case where intervention via the Queen might have made a big difference.'

As it was, Elizabeth left her son to go his own way and, in matters of the heart, the Prince's closest confidant was not a friend of his own age – and certainly not his parents – but his great-uncle, Lord Mountbatten, a man in his seventies whose attitude to women and marriage carried more than a whiff of an older, more cavalier age. 'I believe, in a case like yours,' Mountbatten told Charles, 'that a man should sow his wild oats and have as many affairs as he can before settling down. But for a wife he should choose a suitable and sweet-charactered girl before she meets anyone else she might fall for.'[115]

Charles's romantic problems were compounded by the fact that he did not have much to do in the way of real work. He had (as was the tradition in the Royal Family) done a stint in the armed services after leaving university. But he was not going to become a career naval officer and, as long as his mother was alive and well, his ultimate destiny would remain out of reach. Like Edward VII, he faced the prospect of many years as king-in-waiting and Elizabeth had no experience of her own to fall back on for guidance on how to help him.

'She herself had never been forced by her father into an occupation,' points out William Heseltine. 'In the early stages of his kingship it must have seemed to them all that her apprenticeship was going to be a long one.' When her son found himself in the same position, his own aimlessness coincided with the Queen's distanced inaction to produce what was, in the eyes of many of Elizabeth's advisers, a dangerously undirected state of affairs.

Charles was no sybarite, but his love of fox-hunting and polo marked him as one of the country's more leisured elite, while his continuing string of romances provided no sign that he might at some stage settle down and marry. As the 1970s went on, Graham Turner recalls, officials at Buckingham Palace became very concerned:

I mean, they knew perfectly well what Lord Mountbatten had
told him and that he provided the facilities for the spreading of
wild oats. But as the seventies went on and Charles became
older, they were desperately hoping that some of these oats
might turn out to be not wild but – to mix the metaphor –
some woman he could actually spend his life with. But it was
an appalling preparation for marriage. So they were very, very
concerned about that, and at least one person left him really
because he couldn't go on any longer with someone who was
living that kind of lifestyle.

By 1978, even Charles's devoted uncle, Mountbatten, was ticking
him off for being selfish and lacking direction and wrote to warn him
against 'beginning on the downward slope which wrecked your Uncle
David's [the future Edward VIII's] life and led to his disgraceful
abdication and his futile life ever after'.[116] Charles, who knew perfectly
well what was expected of him, was devastated at the rebuke but a
year later the man he called his 'honorary grandfather' was dead,
assassinated by an IRA bomb while out fishing with his family in
Ireland.

The loss of Mountbatten was a terrible blow to the whole Royal
Family. 'He was, if you like, the father figure, senior even to the Duke
of Edinburgh,' explains Michael Shea. 'He was seen as having brought
the Queen and the Duke of Edinburgh together. He was the sort of
guru in the background and if that person is wiped away so viciously
and violently, of course it's going to have a huge effect and it did have an
effect all the way through the Palace for quite a considerable amount of
time.'

The Prince of Wales was particularly affected. He had always
relied on his great-uncle for guidance and, as Michael Shea puts it, 'the

disappearance of Lord Mountbatten perhaps removed one of the stays to Prince Charles in terms of making him settle down to one particular thing. And there was certainly a fairly widespread view that Prince Charles had better find himself something proper to do and not spend too much time on the polo field. That was certainly an issue.' Now Charles had no one to advise him on the most important decision of his life – and by 1980 he felt under intense pressure from his family and the press to find a wife. That was the year that he seriously began to consider Lady Diana Spencer as a possibility.

From the Queen's point of view, Diana seemed close to the ideal choice. As Michael Shea recalls, 'the perception from Her Majesty downwards throughout the Palace was one of great enthusiasm for this match. Now, we had gone through a period of looking at other possible partners and each one of them the press had turned up something about, because the press aren't interested, dare I say it, in good news and happiness. They're going to look for the problems of the past and if they can dig out divorces or past boyfriends or whatever, by Jove they do it very effectively indeed. But with Diana it appeared we had the perfect bride-to-be.' She came from good aristocratic stock and her family had close links with Elizabeth's. Her grandmother was a friend of the Queen Mother's; her father had been an equerry to King George VI; and her sister was married to one of the Queen's private secretaries.

Thanks to her blood-family and her in-laws, Diana was no stranger to Balmoral, and when Charles invited her to stay there in the autumn of 1980, she showed a pleasingly New Elizabethan enthusiasm for the hearty outdoor way of life that the Royal Family so enjoyed. 'We went stalking together,' one of Charles's friends told his official biographer: 'we got hot, we got tired, we fell into a bog, she got covered in mud, laughed her head off, got puce in the face, hair glued to the forehead because it was pouring with rain. She was a sort of wonderful English schoolgirl who was game for anything, naturally young but sweet and clearly determined and enthusiastic about him, very much wanted him.'[117]

The real catalyst for their marriage, though, was the media. As Michael Shea remembers:

There was no particular pressure that I was aware of within the Palace that the Prince of Wales ought to get married in the next year, two years or five years. It was very much up to him, as I think it is in life – it's up to the individual concerned. I was never aware of anyone saying to him, 'Look, you've got to settle down and get married.' It was only when Diana came on the scene, and the huge press interest began that was almost overwhelming at the time, that the pressures on him began to show and people began to say, 'Look, are you going to get married to her or are you not?' The media hunted Charles and then Diana in such a huge and overwhelming way that it speeded up the whole process. If you got asked – as I did daily – 'When are they going to get engaged? When are they going to get married? Are they going to have babies?' then the pressures on the individuals concerned are obviously very large indeed. So the media played a huge role, in my view, in the build-up to Prince Charles's decision on when to get engaged.

The press attention was such that Prince Philip in the end wrote to Charles warning him that, for the sake of Diana's reputation, he should make up his mind quickly: either ask her to marry him or stop seeing her.

The Royal Family was used to being the focus of media attention, but even the Queen's own experience can barely have prepared her for the intensity with which newspapers and television, British and foreign, pursued Charles and Diana. She did, it is true, remind her press secretary that she and Margaret had been through it all before when they were getting married, but on those earlier occasions Elizabeth had kept a cool head in public and only given vent to her irritation or dismay in private. The pursuit of Diana left the Queen more obviously rattled.

'None of us who are ordinary citizens,' says Michael Mann, 'realise the pressure of the intrusion – that there's no privacy, that there's no private life at all. Nothing is sacred, everything is open to prying into.' After the engagement was announced, Sandringham was besieged by reporters and on one occasion when the Queen was out riding, her press secretary Michael Shea says, 'she got really quite annoyed because the press were jumping out of hedges in front of her and startling the horse she was riding.' 'Why don't you go away?' Elizabeth shouted at the press in exasperation.

If the Queen had known what the future would bring, she might have decided to invite the newspapermen in for tea rather than shout at them. They were prying and intrusive but in 1981 royal reporting had not yet turned into a national blood-sport and when the engagement of Charles and Diana was announced on 24 February it triggered an unprecedented wave of royal hysteria. It certainly eclipsed any earlier press stories about Charles's love-life. 'It was fairly widely known, or gossiped about,' Michael Shea remembers, 'that the Prince of Wales had a number of girlfriends both married and unmarried. How close they were was of course known only to them and there was, you know, a degree of speculation about it which extended both within the Palace and outside the Palace. I think at the time of the engagement, all that was swept aside in the euphoria of the announcement itself.'

More than that, their romance eclipsed Elizabeth herself, who for the first time in her reign found herself relegated to the second division

when it came to press coverage and public interest. It was Diana –
photographed standing against the light so that her legs could be seen
through her dress, fighting her way through reporters to get to her car,
and above all peering demurely from beneath her page-boy hair – who
reigned on the front pages and who had become an instant icon for
millions of people around the world.

If the Queen was sanguine about the levels of publicity surrounding
her family, Diana was not. The characteristics which endeared the
future Princess of Wales to the public – her youth, naivety and shy
inexperience – left her particularly vulnerable to the press and at times
the pressures became too much. On one occasion just before the
wedding, she was travelling across Vauxhall Bridge with one of the
Queen's advisers in a chauffeur-driven car when they passed a huge
advertisement, three bus-lengths long, emblazoned with the words
'Diana, The True Story'. At the sight of it, according to Michael Shea,
who was with her, she 'collapsed in the back and said, "I can't take this
any more." And I totally sympathised with her. She pulled herself
together very quickly, but it was totally understandable and we did
everything we possibly could to try and help her.'

Along with a number of his colleagues at the Palace, Shea was
'very worried as to how we would be able to, as it were, guard this
young lady from the worst pressures of the press and do something to
help her come to terms with what she was going to have to put up with.
So we went through a training process and I took her to various
newspaper offices and to ITN so that she could begin to understand
the sorts of pressures from the media's point of view.'

It was, as Shea admits, a strange experience even for him: it may
have been his job to deal with the press, but nothing had prepared him
or his colleagues for the furore over the Royal Wedding and, although
he had set himself the task of training Diana, he was often learning as

much as he was teaching. What was clear, though, was the support which the Queen wished her future daughter-in-law to have. In later years there was certainly mistrust and dislike between Diana and Elizabeth's officials, but at the beginning their relations were much more cordial. 'I have never understood,' says Shea, 'what the Princess of Wales meant when she said that she wasn't given approval, particu-larly in the early days after her marriage, because to my certain know-ledge within the Palace there was a huge degree of approval of what she was doing and I believe that came from the Queen downwards.'

On the morning of the wedding there was an eerie calm at Buckingham Palace. As Michael Shea remembers, 'I wrote a chapter of my book that morning because everything had been done. I was writing a novel at the time and there was a period of quietness in the Palace just before everything started, because we all sat back, dare I say it, with a degree of satisfaction, knowing that more or less everything was in place. The telephones, believe it or not, stopped ringing, the press were in their positions, everyone knew what they were meant to be doing. It was the most wonderful piece of theatre.'

Outside the Palace, over a million people lined the way to St Paul's Cathedral while, across the world, three-quarters of a billion more watched on television as Charles, accompanied by Prince Andrew as best man, and then Diana and her father rode in carriages to the cathedral. For all the doubts and worries behind the scenes, they made a stunning couple and the Archbishop of Canterbury captured the not-too-elusive mood of the nation when he pronounced it 'the stuff of which fairy-tales are made'. Martin Charteris, who had over thirty years of royal service to look back on, thought that 'it looked absolutely wonderful and I thought that the Princess of Wales looked divine. I remember her when she was getting into the train saying goodbye to the Lord Chamberlain and she kissed him and I thought, now isn't that

lovely, you know, what a lovely girl we've got here.' The Queen of
Denmark, one of the Royal Family's guests, recalls it as 'a wonderful
occasion. I remember the atmosphere of London was quite
extraordinary. There had been some rather down years in Britain, I
think, but here it felt that people were really all together and very
enthusiastic. It was lovely weather and the atmosphere was electric in
the most positive sense.'

If Elizabeth had any worries about her new daughter-in-law or
about the public clamour which surrounded the wedding, she kept
them firmly to herself. Throughout the day she appeared delighted and
happy and after Charles and Diana had left for their honeymoon, she
went to an after-the-wedding party at Claridges. It was, Lady Penn
recalls, a relaxed and carefree celebration. 'We had big screens with
films of the wedding going on in the background all the time. It was
lovely.' Another of Elizabeth's friends, Lady Anson, remembers an
atmosphere of 'just, you know, great happiness. It's rather nice to see the
Queen pointing at a screen saying, "Oh, look, there's So-and-So and
there's So-and-So." Because obviously she hadn't had a chance to see it
herself before and these were just running during the party, and it was
rather a nice way of sitting down and relaxing, looking at a bit of film.'

The rest of the world had watched a great state event, but now, in
private, Elizabeth could enjoy things on a more personal, family level.
As the crowds outside made their way home, the soldiers who had lined
the route returned to their barracks and the camera crews packed up
their gear, the Queen and her friends were celebrating – the Queen
shrieking with laugher at the video playback, Prince Philip and Princess
Grace of Monaco colliding in a doorway, everyone bowing to the
saxophonist because they thought he was the King of Tonga. There
was good reason for their high spirits: the heir to the throne was married,
the dynasty was that much more secure, and the monarchy itself had

never seemed more popular. After the dog-days of the 1960s and the bad publicity of the 1970s, the Royal Family seemed to have renewed itself once again – it was as popular as it had been at the time of Elizabeth's own Coronation.

In fact the 1981 Royal Wedding had a lot more to do with mass hysteria and make-believe than reality. A century earlier the Victorian journalist Walter Bagehot had pinpointed the important role the British monarchy played in bringing romantic colour to the life of the nation, placing royal weddings high on the list of popular diversions. 'A princely marriage,' he wrote, 'is the brilliant edition of a universal fact and as such it rivets mankind.'

When Bagehot wrote these words, however, royal marriages tradi-tionally took place in private – it was Elizabeth's father who had begun the new custom of public processions and ceremonies. Even so, when George VI had married – and the same was true of Elizabeth and Philip's wedding – the numbers of the crowds who turned out and the newspapers' cut-out-and-keep memorial photographs did reflect the popularity of the monarchy as well as the country's more basic desire to relax and celebrate after years of austerity or war.

Neither was true of the wedding of Charles and Diana. Over a tenth of the planet's entire population were not riveted to their television sets because of a sudden global upswing in the popularity of the British monarchy; nor were the countless profiles and commemorative photos of Charles and Diana snapped up because of any innately admirable or loveable characteristics in the bride and groom. Elizabeth's Silver Jubilee had been a grand success, but the Royal Wedding did not so much surpass it as create a new league of royal extravaganza and popular excitement. The Royal Family's own courting of the media – which had begun back in the 1960s – had combined with a new public mood that was much more voyeuristic and demanding. The country – and the rest of the world – now looked to Elizabeth and her relatives for entertainment as much as anything else. Rather than providing the occasionally 'brilliant edition of a universal fact', the Queen faced a future in which weekly if not daily updates were required. It would have required great powers of foresight to recognise it, along with an utterly alien dash of melancholic self-absorption, but as the Queen danced and laughed at Claridges her reign had reached its peak of popularity. The path down the other side would be a lot more treacherous and less forgiving than that which had brought her there.

CHAPTER NINE

One morning in the summer of 1982, the Queen was woken up by a strange man in her bedroom at Buckingham Palace. Prince Philip, facing an early start that day, had gone to sleep in a separate room and during the night Michael Fagan had scrambled over the Palace wall, climbed up a drainpipe and through an open window. The ease with which he did so – and it later turned out that he had broken into the Palace once before, on that occasion stealing a bottle of wine – underlined the flimsiness of the security surrounding the Queen. Fagan had set off one of the Palace alarms as he climbed through the window, but when the policeman on duty saw the flashing light in the control room he simply assumed that the alarm had malfunctioned and reset it. Fagan was then spotted walking barefoot down a corridor by one of the Palace maids – who also assumed that there was no cause for alarm – before making his way to Elizabeth's private rooms. There he woke the Queen up just after 7am by drawing the curtains before sitting down on her bed, his hand dripping blood and clutching a broken ashtray, and talking to her about the problems he was having with his family.

Elizabeth dealt with the intrusion with exemplary calmness. As she later told Michael Shea, 'I got out of bed, put on my dressing-gown, drew myself up to my full regal height, pointed to the door and said, "Get out!" and he didn't.'[118] She then pressed the alarm button by her bed and telephoned twice for a policeman, chatting to Fagan all the while. When no one answered any of her three calls for help she persuaded Fagan to come out into the corridor where, she said, she would be able to get him the cigarette he had asked for. Standing with Fagan in the corridor outside her bedroom, Elizabeth at last met up with one of her 500-odd employees – a chambermaid whose exclamation must have echoed the question going around the Queen's own head: 'Bloody hell, Ma'am! What's he doing here?' Policemen from the Royal Protection Squad then arrived and Fagan was taken away.

As Michael Shea recalls, 'All around her was chaos and people yelling and screaming and calling for heads to roll and so on and the Queen sat in the middle of it, the coolest person there.' Trapped in her bedroom with a deranged member of the public talking about his private worries, with no apparent prospect of rescue, must for Elizabeth have been an intimation of what hell might be like. But, as her friend Margaret Rhodes remembers, 'She didn't appear to have been frightened. I remember her saying, "Well, I meet so many mad people that it didn't surprise me so much." ' To another of her friends, Elizabeth confided that 'he just talked the usual sort of bilge that people talk to me on walkabout. I can handle that.'[119]

It was indeed the sort of crisis for which Elizabeth was well equipped. 'She's a very together, level-headed person,' says Lady Penn. 'When somebody broke into her bedroom she treated it in the way she would treat anything else, in a perfectly matter-of-fact way.' She had shown similar courage a year earlier, when shots were fired at her during the Trooping of the Colour. On that occasion the bullets turned out to be blanks but the Queen had not known that. After calming her horse, she carried on with the ceremony despite the fact that, as far as she knew, someone had just tried to kill her.

The 1980s, however, would test Elizabeth in new ways as well as the old ones. Personal crises and situations which called for personal sacrifice or bravery posed few problems for her, but she was temperamentally better suited to reacting to sudden crises rather than meeting human dramas head-on. In Barbara Castle's opinion, 'When her duty was outlined for her the Queen would always try to give all her strength to it, because she's been brought up to the concept of duty. But a spontaneous reaction isn't there, not because she doesn't feel it inside, but because she's never been shown how to latch it on to the other side of her duty.'

Her whole approach to life was essentially passive – not in the sense that she was weak or indecisive, rather in that, as Martin Charteris, one of her private secretaries, noted, 'She's not an innovator. She has a wonderful negative judgement, but she is not a person who is passionately stamping the ground to change everything or to take the initiative.' It was a lack for which Elizabeth could hardly be faulted. (It had not for over a hundred years been the business of British monarchs to stamp their feet and call for change. And the last one who had shown much sign of independent action had barely sat on the throne before he was bundled off it.) But it would leave her and the monarchy at a dangerously low ebb by the end of the decade.

The 1980s began with a public call to arms in the old style – one which, like the Fagan episode, showed the monarchy to advantage. In 1982 Argentina invaded the Falkland Islands and Elizabeth's son, Prince Andrew, was among those sent to recapture one of Britain's few remaining overseas possessions. Before Argentina's military dictators decided to take matters into their own hands, the British Foreign Office had been quietly preparing to hand the Falklands over anyway. And after the war was won, critics of the Government argued that armed foreign aggression would have been better met with a more emollient approach. While it lasted, though, the Falklands conflict was a popular war and one which naturally strengthened public regard for the Queen both as Head of State and Head of the Armed Forces, especially as one of her sons was risking his life in the line of duty. The Union Jack flags that had been mass produced for the wedding of Charles and Diana barely had time to gather dust before they were brought out again to wave the Fleet off as Britain's Taskforce sailed in defence of British territory and national pride.

There was particular delight that neither Elizabeth nor Prince Andrew sought special treatment on the grounds of royal privilege. 'Really it turned out not to be a question at all,' Margaret Thatcher recalls. 'It was made very clear that Prince Andrew was determined to go, he had a duty to go and he'd uphold his duty, and it was marvellous, absolutely wonderful. Wonderful for the whole of the British people. The son of the monarch carried out his duty as every other person did. I had wondered whether I should discuss it with the Queen. The Queen indicated her view and it was confirmed by Prince Andrew – he was going. I was thrilled.' The public was left in no doubt either. 'Prince Andrew is a serving officer,' read a Palace press release in answer to press enquiries about the Queen's attitude, 'and there is no question in her mind that he should go.'

Andrew was trained as a helicopter co-pilot and his job was to draw Argentine missiles away from the vulnerable Navy ships by flying decoy missions. It was a role which placed him in genuine danger and the Queen was as anxious as any mother about her son's safety. Michael

Shea remembers that 'she was given a blow-by-blow account of everything that was happening. This was made even more important to her by the fact that Prince Andrew was serving in the Navy out there and when I was press secretary I probably heard from her more during that period than at any other time because I was getting the up-to-the-moment news stories – which undoubtedly were coming to her by official means as well but she was interested in how the news was being carried by the media at that time.'

The public image of Elizabeth as concerned mother was strength-ened by an interview Andrew gave in Port Stanley in which he told how, just like the other servicemen, he had managed to put in a call home: 'My mother was in – it was about the right time in the evening,' he told reporters. 'She was surprised to hear from me . . . She just said to pass on her very best and say how very proud she is of everybody and of the magnificent work that is being done down here by not only the troops but by the Navy.' When Andrew's ship sailed back into Portsmouth Elizabeth went out to meet him and stood proudly at her son's side as HMS *Invincible*, surrounded by a flotilla of tugs and small boats, came back into her home port.

The role of war-leader was played by the Prime Minister, Margaret Thatcher – the only politician in Elizabeth's long reign with whom the Queen was rumoured to have differences of opinion. On a superficial level they appeared to have a lot in common: they were both women, both the same age, both powerful figures within a political and social system that was generally still dominated by men and both were dismayed by the sharp reversal of fortune their country had suffered since the end of the Second World War. Beyond that, though, they were utterly different. Mrs Thatcher was an imperious, iconoclastic figure who, despite being leader of the Conservative Party, found little in the country's recent past that she wanted to preserve. Elizabeth, at least when she was not wearing her crown, was a much less regal and commanding figure, and in fact stood for much that her Prime Minister wished to destroy, representing as she did the apex of the amorphous 'establishment' – the City old-boy network, the Civil Service, the Church, the comfortable and settled old Britain that, along with the trade unions and the old Left, found itself outflanked by the new Conservative Party.

Elizabeth had always taken her political role extremely seriously. The monarchy had no real executive powers left – whatever rights and prerogatives had not been formally taken over by Act of Parliament were exercised by senior Government ministers in the Queen's name – but it was still at the centre of the political web. Nothing that Parliament wanted could become law without the Queen's assent. The Privy Council (a collection of senior politicians that historically had offered advice to the sovereign) had for generations been nothing more than a rubber stamp for whatever the prime minister of the day wanted done, yet it was still presided over by the Queen. It was an arrangement that left the monarch with no power, but a great deal of influence, should she choose to use it. There was no question that real authority lay with the Prime Minister, but the sovereign nonetheless had – in the well-worn maxim of Walter Bagehot – the right 'to be consulted, the right to encourage, the right to warn'.

Elizabeth's approach was characteristically conscientious. 'She works every day on her paperwork,' says Lady Penn. 'They come every single day, her red boxes, and she has to work on them. It doesn't matter whether she's on holiday – in fact she never has a holiday because they follow her even to Balmoral or Sandringham at Christmas or wherever and she has to get on with it.' The red boxes contained everything the Head of State had to know – appointments, orders, government reports, new laws that required the royal assent. While a less diligent, responsible person might have simply signed papers without bothering to read them – it was not, after all, as though the Queen could alter the tiniest detail of government legislation once it had been through Parliament – Elizabeth gave them her full attention.

Mary Francis, a member of her staff, says:

She's very, very effective. She always turned around the boxes of documents that we sent up every night. I'd previously worked at 10 Downing Street, I was used to sending up just the same sort of boxes of documents to the Prime Minister who actually in my day was also very good at turning his boxes around. But the Queen was as good as any minister I'd ever come across. She liked to deal with business during the same one-to-one and to talk things through and to sign things off very quickly there and then. She didn't sit on things and she didn't have long, agonising meetings about things.

Another of her advisers, Kenneth Scott, had worked for a number of employers before coming to the Palace, 'including ministers when I was in the Foreign Office and I've never worked for anyone who it was so easy to get decisions out of quickly when you needed to. She said to me once, "I'm a rather executive person," and she is. Sometimes, if it's a very new or difficult problem, she'll say, "I'd like to talk to Philip about this," and come back with the answer the next day. But she never faffs about and that is a great advantage for her private secretaries.'

Elizabeth's command of detail also kept government officials on their mettle. 'Never tackle the Queen on a point of detail,' says Michael Mann. 'She is nearly always right.' Her forte was more to advise and encourage than to warn, but as former Conservative minister Nicholas

Soames recalls, while 'everything else about the Queen is extremely friendly and very open and warm and receptive, the daunting thing is that you know she's incredibly well-informed and she does know about everything and I think this is something that her prime ministers have all admired very much.'

Harold Macmillan, according to his grandson, Lord Stockton, 'was tremendously impressed with her grasp of state affairs and he pointed out that she'd read every state paper since before the King died and he always said she was the best informed person about state papers of anyone he'd ever met – possibly even better informed than the Cabinet Secretary.' Even republican-minded politicians like Barbara Castle were impressed by Elizabeth's dedication: 'I thought she worked terribly hard at her job, because not only does she have to meet every new minister for the kissing of hands but she also has to say goodbye to anyone who is leaving the Cabinet and she doesn't just mouth routine things like "Thank you for what you've done for your party," or some baloney like that. She's really thought about it and will manage to give you the impression that she knew you as a person. I think that's a terrific job and so I didn't find it hard at all to give her the respect that was her due.'

Throughout her reign, the Queen has also held a weekly audience with the Prime Minister of the day: it has always been an entirely private meeting at which no notes are taken and nobody else is present and in which the Prime Minister can talk freely about anything he or she wishes. For the politicians, as many former leaders have attested, it has been a unique chance to unburden themselves in complete privacy and without fear of party political repercussions. For Elizabeth it was a chance to offer advice if it was wanted and to add to her store of political knowledge.

Says Kenneth Scott, of the weekly audiences:

All we know about them is that the Prime Minister is received by the private secretary at the door of the Palace, taken upstairs, ushered into the Queen's presence, sometimes looking rather preoccupied, and always comes out much more relaxed than when he went in. He sometimes stays for a glass of whisky with the private secretaries afterwards, but one never knows what goes on behind those doors. I think it is an important function because the Queen is the only person that the Prime Minister sees who doesn't want something out of him.

By the 1980s, Elizabeth was on her seventh Prime Minister, and according to Margaret Thatcher, 'I never remember any occasion on which the Queen and I did not get on,' adding that 'she had far more experience than I did. She had already had Prime Ministers, she'd already dealt with practically every other head of state or government that came to Britain. She is tremendously experienced and for me it was quite a challenge.'

The Queen's attitude to Britain's politicians was in general one of distanced correctness. As Head of State, the cardinal rule for Elizabeth was to stay out of the political fray and this was something that she scrupulously observed. Courtier Michael Oswald has known the Queen for thirty-two years, and has 'never once heard her say anything which could let anybody think she favoured one political party over another, or one political personality over another'. Douglas Hurd, whose responsibilities as Foreign Secretary included accompanying the Queen and her officials on state visits, notes that her reticence extended to overseas politicians as well as British ones – 'At the end of the day on a state visit after the evening function, they have a whisky and an informal chat about the next day, what's happened and then the conversation does get quite personal, but still she doesn't express political views.'

She approached the more solemn rituals of her political role with the same delight in minor mishap that she took in any royal ceremonial – at one meeting of the Privy Council, where new members had as usual been provided with stools on which to kneel as they took the oath of allegiance, Barbara Castle recalls that 'one chap was so overwhelmed, he picked up his stool and sort of clasped it to his knee and galloped up to the throne and the Queen could barely keep a straight face' – but she was never in any doubt about the uniquely exalted position she occupied. For much of the country, the formulaic way in which the Queen referred to 'my' Government or 'my' ministers may have been no more than a convention. But to Elizabeth, who spent hours each day reading government papers that may as well have been written in Chinese for all the difference her study would make to the course of legislation, it was an article of faith that ultimate authority rested with her. 'She treats everybody the same because everybody beneath her is the same,' thinks David Owen, a Cabinet minister in the 1970s, and from the very beginning Elizabeth had the distinction clear in her mind – even with so distinguished and experienced a premier as Winston Churchill.

'Just before she became Queen,' journalist Bill Deedes recalls, 'I'd attended a dinner party given by the Speaker and Winston was there. Winston couldn't take his eyes off her. He was obviously profoundly moved by the sight of this young woman who was going to become the Head of State. There was something that deeply moved his spirit. I think he felt that everything he'd fought for was worth preserving just for her, you know, and she, incidentally, I think, reciprocated the affection. I have a feeling that the Queen formed a deep affection for Winston without necessarily taking his advice very seriously.'

By the 1980s, though, Churchill's heir as leader of the Conservative Party threatened to upset the political neutrality which Elizabeth had spent her life carefully preserving. It was a bizarre turn of events, for – although she wished to tear down much of the old British Establishment – Thatcher had no personal animus against the Queen or the institution of the monarchy. The depths to which she would curtsey when meeting the Queen were always looked forward to by the more snobbish Palace courtiers, and the former Prime Minister herself describes her first visit to Buckingham Palace after the 1979 general election as 'more etched on one's mind than any successive election victory'. Charles Powell, one of the former Prime Minister's special advisers, states that although 'I would never regard Mrs Thatcher primarily as an intellectual – the great strength of Mrs Thatcher was the force of her personality and the vigour of her argument – I can't believe that was any great disincentive for the Queen. I am sure she is used to mixing it, shall we say politely, with world leaders.'

Mixing it with Mrs Thatcher, however, put the relationship between Elizabeth and her Prime Minister under new strain. Whether or not they had differences in political outlook, there was certainly a difference in style, and the press were quick to exploit any rivalry, real or perceived, between the two women. As Michael Shea recalls, 'almost from day one with Mrs Thatcher we had stories about "Oh, Mrs Thatcher had turned up at a state banquet wearing a long blue dress. Won't the Queen be furious?" "No, why should the Queen be furious?" "Because she's wearing the same colour, it's royal blue and she's wearing the same colour dress as the Queen." And there was a willingness, a determination particularly among the tabloid press to stir up this remarkable situation where you had a Head of State and the Head of Government who were both determined women.'

Their tastes were certainly quite different and the annual pilgrimage that every Prime Minister was obliged to make to Balmoral for a country weekend with the Royal Family was a source of wry amusement even among the political entourage at Downing Street. 'I think the slightly outdoor, outward-bound ethos at Balmoral was not one in which Mrs Thatcher felt naturally comfortable,' says Charles Powell, one of the former Prime Minister's advisers. 'She tended not to find her recreation in cold weather, freezing rain, outdoor picnics and so on and I think the country life in that sense was not one she particularly enjoyed.'

Bernard Ingham, the No. 10 press officer, found it equally hard to imagine that the Head of State had much in common with the Head of Government – 'Indeed, it is very difficult to imagine that anybody had much in common with Prime Minister Thatcher at weekends. My guess is that the weekends at Balmoral were purgatory to be gone through in the interests of convention but I don't think they were there to be enjoyed. My main concern while she was there was that there wasn't a crisis because that would greatly disrupt the Royal Family. I think that the second concern was that they didn't play charades.'

More importantly, the radical political agenda that the Government was pursuing polarised British society and heightened speculation about the Queen's own position. The Thatcher brand of Conservatism emphasised self-reliance and the unforgiving forces of free-market economics as the cure for the country's ills. It was a recipe which within a few years of her first election victory had made Margaret Thatcher the most unpopular Prime Minister of modern times. While she maintained that the best thing a government could do was to create a social and economic climate in which the poor could help themselves, her critics argued that her policies favoured the powerful over the weak and transformed greed from deadly sin to cardinal virtue. She had come to power quoting the words of St Francis of Assisi – 'where there is peace let us sow harmony' – but her mission to tame Britain's trade unions led to pitched battles between striking miners and armoured police in riot gear that were played out every night on television for twelve months.

Whatever the political merits of the Government's cause – and Britain's trade unions had for ten years enjoyed disproportionate power and influence over the nation's affairs – the manner in which it was pursued, and the relish with which some Government ministers defended their policies, left a bad taste in the mouths of some people. It also created an awareness in the minds of many more that the early years of Thatcherism were opening up new reservoirs of hatred and bitterness within British society.

Elizabeth's mother may have been unashamedly right-wing ('Now you be nice to that Mr Smith,' David Owen remembers her admonishing politicians who were sent out to try and encourage Rhodesia's white Prime Minister to accept black majority rule) but the Queen was concerned to maintain a united kingdom in fact as well as name and was thought to view the missionary zeal of her Prime Minister with some trepidation. Her press secretary, Michael Shea, regularly downplayed the idea that Elizabeth and Margaret Thatcher were personally at loggerheads, but the rumours became front-page news in 1986 when the *Sunday Times* reported that the Palace and Downing Street had had a major disagreement about the Commonwealth.

To many people in the country – particularly those born after the Second World War – the Commonwealth was something of an irrelevance. When sentiment was stripped away, its critics argued, it was at best no more than an international talking-shop; at worst, it was a way for self-important British people to convince themselves that they still had an empire, while ignoring the more important task of making friends and influencing events in Europe. To Elizabeth, though, the Commonwealth was of great importance. At the age of twenty-one, she had spoken of the 'great imperial family to which we all belong' and when she became Queen, newspaper headlines had accurately proclaimed 'Elizabeth II – Dedicated to the Empire'.[120]

Even though the Empire was now gone, according to Edward Ford Elizabeth still thought of the Commonwealth as 'in a way, her large family'. It was a family with which she had an affectionate but informal relationship. Some of the countries, like Britain, Australia and New Zealand, had Elizabeth as their Head of State; others, like Kenya, Nigeria and Ghana, had their own presidents but recognised Elizabeth's honorary position as Head of the Commonwealth. The only criterion for Commonwealth membership was to have been ruled at some point by Britain.[121] But there was no rule to say that the Head of the Commonwealth had to be the British Head of State, and the romantic, well-meaning idea that it could function as a brotherhood of nations which had nothing in common beyond their former imperial ties to Britain might well have withered on the vine had it not been for Elizabeth's personal interest and enthusiasm. As Margaret Thatcher recognises, 'she is the thing which keeps it all together', while Bob Hawke, then Labour Prime Minister of Australia, was struck by how 'she could speak about any countries of the Commonwealth not just as a tourist, but quite expertly in terms of their political structures, their economic resources and their relationships with their neighbours'. As the journalist Trevor MacDonald recalls, 'I once talked to about fifteen Commonwealth Prime Ministers, and they all sang from the same hymn sheet: that her presence is desperately, desperately important, as they put it, to the survival of the Commonwealth idea and of the Commonwealth ideal'.

The first tensions between Elizabeth and her new Conservative Government had become apparent as early as 1979. The Commonwealth Heads of Government were due to meet in Lusaka that year and the problem of how to deal with Rhodesia was high on the agenda. Rhodesia's white Prime Minister, Ian Smith, was engaged in a long civil war with black nationalists who refused to accept either Smith's rule or that of a black compromise candidate, Bishop Abel Muzorewa. Most of the Commonwealth leaders wanted to force Smith into negotiations with the nationalists – apart from Margaret Thatcher, who argued that they were terrorists and was lukewarm about maintaining economic sanctions against Ian Smith.

Fearing that the Lusaka conference would only expose how isolated she was, Thatcher initially wanted to stay away and at one point even threatened to stop the Queen from attending. Elizabeth, however, was determined to go. The argument over Rhodesia and Britain's diplomatic isolation threatened to tear the Commonwealth apart but, as David Owen recalls, 'for the first time to my knowledge [the Queen] was ready to risk and perhaps even allow it to be placed in the public domain that she disagreed with the Prime Minister and was not prepared to take her advice on this particular thing. And the argument used was that this was a Commonwealth responsibility.' Elizabeth was convinced that her absence from the meeting would only heighten the sense of crisis, while her presence might help to defuse some of the tension. As Charles Powell, one of Margaret Thatcher's advisers, admits, 'I do think that the presence of the Queen in Lusaka must have been a positive influence generally. It would have been an extraordinary situation for her not to be there and the fact that she was there enabled it to proceed in all normality.'

In 1986 there was a similar row, although the argument this time was over whether economic sanctions should be applied to the apartheid government of South Africa. Margaret Thatcher thought not:

I said I was absolutely against it for the reasons that they, I believe, had not thought out. They were mouthing the words, 'Sanctions, sanctions, sanctions.' It made them feel good, and I said, 'Look, just look, wait and see what it means. It means that South Africa would not be able to sell her goods overseas,' therefore her people would suffer because they couldn't get the income in. It would mean that many other countries would not be able to sell goods to South Africa, so *their* people would suffer. So when you say, 'Sanctions, sanctions, sanctions,' and mouth this phrase, what you're doing is to say by your diktat and agreement, you're going to make a lot of people suffer, and I said, 'It will not help South Africa.'

The rest of the Commonwealth, however, thought it would, putting Elizabeth in the same quandary as in 1979: should she keep quiet and support the British Government or make clear her unease for the sake of Commonwealth unity? As David Owen recalls, 'it was the style, it was the manner of Thatcher's objections that was the problem and it was doing harm to Britain's standing within the Commonwealth and thereby indirectly damaging the Queen's standing within the Common-wealth. And she had to distance herself from her British Prime Minister – which was not something she wished to do, but she chose to do it and she was right.'

The distance between Queen and Prime Minister was made public on the front pages of the *Sunday Times*, which claimed in July that 'sources close to the Queen' had made clear Elizabeth's displeasure not just over the question of South Africa and sanctions, but over the whole drift of the Conservative Government's policy – that the Prime Minister's approach was 'uncaring, confrontational and divisive' and damaging to the fabric of the nation and that the Queen was shocked and dismayed at the impact the Government's policies were having.

When the story broke, Elizabeth was at an official banquet in Holyrood House. While dinner went on, her press secretary and two of her assistant private secretaries frantically called Downing Street, Buckingham Palace and the *Sunday Times* in an attempt to minimise the damage. According to one of the officials, Sir Kenneth Scott, 'We were very worried about it. The Queen was very worried about it, because we were anxious it should not spoil the relationship between Buckingham Palace and 10 Downing Street – which had always been a very easy relationship at both the top level and the private secretary level.' There was equal consternation in the Prime Minister's office. 'She thought it damaging for the impression to be given that the Prime Minister and the Queen were at odds on something, that the Queen was unhappy about something,' recalls Charles Powell, 'and I think she had a vision of cleaning ladies all over Britain saying, "That Mrs Thatcher, she's been annoying the Queen – you know we can't vote for her next time." '

The journalist who had written the story, Simon Freeman, had been briefed beforehand by the Queen's press secretary, Michael Shea, who strongly rejected the construction that had been put on his comments. He admitted he might have said that the Queen disliked anything that was socially inflammatory, or that she preferred the countries of which she was head to rub along together, but, Shea argued, that did not add up to a condemnation of the British Government's policies. 'I was asked, for example, about the Queen's attitude to the miners' strike. I said, "As you know, the Queen doesn't get involved in politics, but she is concerned about anything that is divisive in British society." Therefore that is interpreted by the media as being another issue, along with the Commonwealth and blue dresses, that is antagonistic between these two people.'

Mrs Thatcher's advisers also did their best to play down the idea that there was a dangerous constitutional row in the making. 'I don't for a moment believe that the Queen expressed any view,' says Charles

Powell, 'but of course people round the Head of State sometimes can't resist the temptation to gossip away and let their own views emerge as potentially those of the Queen and I suspect that is what happened in this case.'

Mrs Thatcher, for her part, is scathing about the idea: 'It was absolute nonsense,' she says. 'Where they invent these ideas I don't know. Absolutely absurd. I served the Queen, it was my prime duty. Her advice was valuable because her experience was greatly in excess of mine. I was very fortunate to have such a wonderful Queen and such a wonderful adviser and if there was anything particularly deep we discussed it. I went at 6 o'clock to the Palace every Tuesday evening and had about an hour with the Queen. It was probably the most valuable hour of the week.' Sitting next to Michael Shea at lunch the day after the Commonwealth row, Thatcher kindly reassured him, 'Oh, I wouldn't worry about that, dear,' when he apologised for the whole mess.

Although the Palace quickly poured cold water on the idea that Elizabeth had directly authorised Michael Shea to provide the *Sunday Times* briefing, the Queen did not go so far as to sack him, which would have been the surest way of indicating that he had been speaking out of turn. Both the Prime Minister's office and the Queen's were keen to hush up the whole affair, but many insiders remain convinced that, authorised or not, the *Sunday Times* article was an accurate reflection of Elizabeth's political views. The Commonwealth leaders – along with other people who were opposed in some way to the Government – were certainly delighted with the story. 'I was very glad about the Thatcher row,' says Sir Sonny Ramphal, Secretary-General at the Commonwealth's London headquarters. 'What was in the *Sunday Times*, what Michael Shea was saying to the press, was what we knew to be the reality and it needed to be said.'[122] According to Nelson

Mandela, 'I have no doubt in my own mind that the Queen was too enlightened to support the attitude of the Conservative Government on the question of sanctions,' and Bob Hawke, the left-leaning Prime Minister of Australia, also reckons that:

> it's fair to say that the Queen didn't have a great affection for Mrs Thatcher. She had the odd expression about her which I found rather fascinating and I think this reflected not just something as simple as jealousy. I wouldn't accuse Her Majesty of that. But I think there was a sense in which she was not at ease with some of the attitudes and policies of Mrs Thatcher and she, I think, saw Mrs Thatcher as being somewhat danger-ous to the cohesiveness of the British structure. And that was reflected in her attitude and I saw it on a number of occasions.

For all the irritation and annoyance that the Conservative governments of the 1980s may have caused the Palace, Elizabeth could at least comfort herself with the thought that the then Prime Minister, like all her predecessors, would one day be replaced. The press, on the other hand, were always with her, and they kept the monarchy company increasingly on their own terms. The situation now was the exact opposite of the 1960s. Twenty years before, Palace officials had felt obliged to lure the public back into the royalist fold with carefully planned public relations exercises such as the *Royal Family* film and the Prince of Wales's Investiture. Under the more relaxed direction of officials like William Heseltine, the Queen's children had given interviews to newspapers and on television and had even appeared on chatshows like *Wogan* (where an apparently bashful Selina Scott had asked Prince Andrew whether there was any truth behind his nickname, Randy Andy).

In the 1980s, by contrast, press coverage of the Royal Family had passed out of the control of Palace officials and taken on a life of its own. The informality and accessibility of the Queen's children had inevitably removed some of the mystique and respect that surrounded the monarchy — not always to the monarchy's benefit. If, after one interview with a royal prince, people felt that they had been granted a privileged glimpse into an intriguingly different world, by the fourth or fifth they began to wonder why they had bothered to pay attention in the first place. There was a huge public appetite for the fairy-tale, golden-coaches side of the monarchy but it was not based on any real love of the monarchy or its principal characters — rather on the belief that Elizabeth and her family were there to provide constant diversion and gossipy amusement for the rest of the country. What had begun as an attempt to make the Royal Family appear more likeable and human had ended by turning them into Hollywood-style celebrities who were expected to pay for their fame.

It was a position from which retreat seemed impossible. To an extent, Elizabeth had perhaps brought the problem on her own head by allowing more open dealings with the press in the first place. But the media themselves were more inquisitive and less respectful and some were in the hands of editors or proprietors with an openly republican agenda. One tabloid's photographers referred to the Royal Family simply as 'the Germans' and described the business of snapping photos of them as 'whacking the Germans'.[123] Above all, every newspaper was after bigger and bigger audiences, and a front-page image of one particular member of the Royal Family could always be guaranteed to sell more copies — that of Diana. The Queen was particularly concerned about the effect the media were having on her daughter-in-law.

After the Waleses' honeymoon, Michael Shea recalls, 'we had

hoped there might be a slight respite. In practice there wasn't. In fact the degree of press harassment grew and grew and grew, to such an extent that I eventually summoned a meeting of editors at Buckingham Palace.' Elizabeth took the unprecedented step of coming to the meeting herself, in order to add weight to her officials' pleas for greater discretion and restraint in Fleet Street. But if she had hoped that a personal appeal would make any difference, she was disappointed. 'If Diana wants to buy some sweets, why doesn't she send a footman?' one of the editors asked the Queen, who had pointed out that being constantly photographed was making any sort of normal life for the Princess of Wales impossible. 'What a pompous remark,' Michael Shea remembers Elizabeth replying sharply.

For all her indignation, there was little that Elizabeth or the Palace could do. The days when sympathy or deference could be relied upon to keep the press in line had long gone. Indeed, the more junior members of the Royal Family often seemed intent on making a spectacle of themselves even without the help of the tabloids. In 1986 Prince Andrew had married Sarah Ferguson in another lavishly public ceremony at Westminster Abbey. But for all the enthusiasm and flag-waving which surrounded the wedding, the new Duchess of York, as Andrew's bride became, was as a red rag to the media bull. She did not have either the seniority or the manipulative skill of the Princess of Wales, and her honeymoon with the press soon turned sour. The Fergie formerly-known-as-fun-loving was transformed into an alliterative disaster-zone: in the tabloids she was fat, she was frumpy, she was feckless, she enjoyed too many free holidays and perks. Even worse, many Palace officials shared the media's dislike. One courtier revealed that he found it almost physically impossible to bow to her, while Martin Charteris gave an incautious interview to the *Spectator* in which he labelled her 'vulgar, vulgar, vulgar'.

Other members of the Royal Family fared almost as badly as the Duchess of York. In 1987 Elizabeth's youngest son, Prince Edward, resigned from the Royal Marines in order to pursue a career in the theatre. In the unforgiving climate of the time, what must have been an agonising and brave decision provided most of the media with an easy opportunity to characterise Edward as a wimp and his father – who was Captain-General of the Marines – as an outraged tyrant.

Later that year Edward came up with a disaster genuinely of his own making in the form of one of the most ill-advised Windsor ventures ever attempted – the television show, *It's a Royal Knockout*. Designed to raise money for charity, the programme featured Edward, Anne, Andrew and the Duchess of York as the captains of four celebrity teams who had to win deliberately ludicrous races – which usually involved falling over and getting wet – in order to gain points. Everyone wore medieval fancy-dress and the show was hosted by Les Dawson and Rowan Atkinson (in sub-*Blackadder* mode), accompanied by Barbara Windsor. It was meant to be funny, but even for fans of the *It's a Knockout* series, the Windsor variation had all the charm and spontaneity of pro-wrestling. Of all the royal participants, only Anne came out with her dignity anywhere near intact. Edward heaped further humiliation on his own shoulders by pettishly walking out of the concluding press conference after the assembled reporters had made clear just how little they had enjoyed the afternoon.

Elizabeth's courtiers had been vehemently opposed to the idea from the start, but the Queen herself had refused to listen to their advice. 'The one thing the Queen will not allow is any criticism of her children,' says one of her officials. 'No matter what has gone wrong, she thinks they are wonderful.'[124] What was an admirable characteristic in Elizabeth as mother, though, was less desirable in her as Head of State and, as so many times in the past, the overlap of public and private left her in a quandary.

To an extent, her dilemma was not unique. As Michael Shea points out, 'the Queen was like a large number of mothers in the land – not necessarily always prepared to say to her offspring "You must do this" or "You must not do this." You don't necessarily *tell* your children. You can advise, you can warn but you don't dictate and it's only when you come to an extreme position that the Queen perhaps says, "No, enough is enough." ' The problem was that the extreme position – the point at which the minor royals' ineptitude, frivolity or simple misfortune threatened to tarnish the dignity of the Crown itself – was only arrived at gradually so there was no obvious point at which Elizabeth could put her foot down.

Her natural tendency, in any case, was always to sit things out. According to Michael Shea, 'If a member of the Royal Family was not pulling his or her weight or was doing something wrong, the Duke of Edinburgh was very, very capable in my experience of making that view known,' but Elizabeth was not. 'The Queen does tend to be perhaps too kind, too trusting and too believing of people who perhaps shouldn't be given quite so much rope,' comments another member of her staff.[125] It was therefore her husband or her officials who attempted to impose some order on the royal children, not Elizabeth herself. She was naturally sympathetic to their position – 'I think,' she said in a television interview she gave in 1992, 'that this is what the younger members find difficult, the regimented side of things'[126] – and above all she disliked confrontation.

As Michael Shea recalls, 'on behalf of the Queen I would and did on a number of occasions say to members of the Royal Family, particularly junior members, "I do not think you should do this." And they would say to me, "Are those the Queen's wishes?" And I would say, "No, I haven't actually discussed it with her, but I know that would be her view".' It was an understandable and, from a purely private point of view, harmless way of running a family – if the remonstrations of Prince Philip or the Palace officials had had much effect. As it was, though, and with the press ready to magnify even the smallest slip into a major disaster, Elizabeth's *laissez-faire* approach contributed to the impression that the minor royals were running amuck. And what might have been written off as farce, if it had involved only the more junior members of the family, turned into tragedy once Diana and Charles took their turn under the spotlight.

There were problems in the Waleses' marriage from the very beginning. They spent the first part of their honeymoon aboard the Royal Yacht *Britannia*, where Charles happily painted or read while Diana listlessly wandered about the ship trying to disguise her boredom. The second part, at Balmoral, was not much more successful. They arrived in high romantic style – 'All the estate came to the main gates to receive them,' recalls Shane Blewitt, 'and there was a beautiful carriage garlanded in honeysuckle and heather. I think something similar might have been done for the Tsar's visit at the end of the last century. Anyway, the Prince and Princess of Wales were decanted from their grand limousine and put into the carriage and were then drawn up to the Castle by estate staff. It was an enchanting moment.'

The reality of her married life depressed Diana. For one thing, the newly-weds were hardly ever alone and one guest who was staying at Balmoral during the honeymoon was himself dismayed at the unimaginative way in which Charles was treating his new wife. 'Balmoral is so formal and they were on honeymoon and there were all these endless meals. I sat next to Diana and said, "You must be longing to go to Craigowan" – a house on the estate where they could curl up in front of the fire. "Can't wait," she said. Then coffee came and she said under her breath, "Why can we *never* have it out on the terrace?" There was that beautiful girl with a man fifteen years older and she was stuck in her mother-in-law's house.'[127]

Elizabeth had guessed at least some of the problems that Diana was facing. The Queen did not, at the beginning, know quite how bad personal relations were between the Prince and Princess of Wales but she did know how grim life at Court could be. At the age of twenty-five, Elizabeth had cried in the back of her royal limousine as she was driven up the Mall for the move back into Buckingham Palace when she became Queen.

Thirty years on, Diana was in much the same position and Elizabeth felt a natural sympathy for her. 'I trust,' the Queen wrote to a friend just before the Waleses' wedding, 'that Diana will find living here less of a burden than expected,'[128] and after the marriage, Elizabeth continued to do what she could to smooth Diana's way. 'I am very fond of all three of the Spencer girls,' she once told another of her friends,[129] and she was by nature eager for those around her to be happy.

'Her greatest talent,' says one of her relatives, King Constantine, 'is that she is a great listener and I have never hesitated at any time in my life, when I have had difficulties, to go and consult her and ask advice and she's never once said, "I'm too busy." ' Diana did come to Elizabeth to talk about her problems and even after the divorce she continued to stress how kind the Queen had been to her.[130] 'Certainly in the year that I had anything to do with Diana,' says Michael Shea, 'she was getting a huge amount of praise both within the Palace and without the Palace and everything she did was applauded.'

However hard Diana and the Queen tried, though, the differences between the two women were too great for any real friendship to flourish. According to John Taylor, who was Elizabeth's personal footman, 'the

Queen spoke to her many times, I know. But it just fell on deaf ears. She was a young girl, she couldn't adapt to Balmoral, she couldn't adapt to Sandringham, really. Although she lived at Sandringham as a young girl she couldn't really adapt to the way of life the royals had.' Many of Elizabeth's advisers shared his opinion. 'The fact that you are never off duty,' says Kenneth Scott, 'the fact that you are never outside the public gaze, the fact that you have to spend a good deal of time doing slightly boring things because of your position, the fact that you can never really let your hair down – it's a very demanding role for all of them. And I think it's difficult for people who haven't been brought up to it to adapt to that.'

Elizabeth's world was one of tradition, continuity and formality and even at Balmoral, where the Royal Family were at their most relaxed, people still dressed for dinner. Diana, by contrast, was warm, lively and spontaneous and she found it almost impossible to adjust to the sudden restrictions of royal life. 'I think the Duchess of York enjoyed it more than the Princess of Wales,' says John Taylor. 'The Princess of Wales didn't seem to adapt to that way of life at all. The Queen and the Duke of Edinburgh, as well as all the rest of the Royal Family, tried to get the Princess of Wales to adapt to it, but she just didn't like it at all. And she would really make any excuse to get out of it if she could.'

There was also a personal gulf between the Queen and the princess. The Windsors, as Michael Shea admits, 'are not a family that immedi-ately pour out their feelings to one another'. Elizabeth, however hard she tried to be friendly, always retained a certain distance. 'The Queen is a very amusing person to work with,' Shea continues. 'Nonetheless, no matter how informal you were, you always stepped back from too much familiarity and I believe that attitude extended to other members of the Royal Family as well. Obviously not to immediate children, but to those who had come in – and it's not only the Princess of Wales, but also Sarah Ferguson has talked about it – you can go so far, but the Queen remains the Queen and formality has to begin somewhere.'

The Queen was also ill equipped to deal with Diana's emotional problems – which included post-natal depression and a bulimic eating disorder. According to Lady Penn, Elizabeth 'found her ill-health or her mental instability very hard to understand, because she's a very matter-of-fact, down-to-earth person and I think it probably tried her patience a little bit'. Whether or not Diana was unstable – and in later years she would pour scorn on the idea – she was certainly unhappy and living in the midst of a family for whom unhappiness was generally seen as a cue for greater effort at self-control rather than tea and sympathy. 'The Royal Family are not good at recognising mental illness. None of *them* have post-natal depression,' observes one member of Elizabeth's staff,[131] while Michael Shea adds that 'until I left the Palace, I'd never heard the word *bulimia*. It was a new illness to me and therefore it doesn't come as any surprise to me that it would be a new illness to the Queen and other senior members of the Royal Family.'

Worse than any of this was the fact that Diana's relationship with her husband was plagued by jealousy and misunderstanding. The new princess found it hard to accept that Charles, like his mother, appeared to put his public duty before his private life – and when they *were* together, she was haunted by the ghost of Camilla Parker Bowles. Her anxiety was not dispelled by the occasionally cavalier and thoughtless way in which Charles treated her, and, although he swore to her that he had dropped his old girlfriend, Diana was convinced that he had not. 'Poor Diana had got it into her head that she was still important in his life,' says Lady Mountbatten, 'and absolutely nothing he could say or do would disabuse her of the idea that somewhere she was lurking in the background, which was an absolute tragedy, because it was totally untrue.'

True or not, to old friends of Prince Charles, it was evident that the marriage was not working. 'Those of us who knew him well were aware quite early that things were not really very happy,' continues Lady Mountbatten. 'For one thing, suddenly the easy relationship and friendly visits stopped. I realised of course it wasn't Prince Charles, but I understood that Diana had decided that she didn't want his older friends around and, because he was so keen to try and make it work, he agreed. So one didn't hold it against him because you knew the reason why this was happening. But it was very sad, because you felt that you couldn't give any support.'

The difficulties in her marriage made the Princess of Wales feel even more isolated within the Royal Family and, from the point of view of those close to the Queen, Diana actually seemed to welcome her exclusion. 'She wanted to be on her own, really,' says John Taylor. 'The Queen and the Duke bent over backwards to accommodate her, but she just didn't really want to know. Didn't want to know at all. They'd ask her to join them and try to get her to come out and that sort of thing, but she'd always got a headache or something of that nature. She never really wanted to come out at all.' Often Diana would telephone Elizabeth's office to say that she was too unwell to accompany the Queen on some official function – and then be found later on playing in the Palace swimming-pool with her children.[132] The Queen's response, after her initial efforts had been rebuffed, was to leave her daughter-in-law alone. According to Michael Shea, 'There was a growing awareness among officials at the Palace that there were problems in the marriage. Of course there were. But it was decided to leave these to the individuals concerned.'

For one thing, Elizabeth hated arguments of any kind. 'There are times when it really is easier to take a decision and get rid of the problem, because the problem's going to have to be tackled at some time at any rate,' believes Michael Mann, the former Dean of Windsor. 'But if it involves people, the Queen will put it off in the hope that that person can be helped or assisted in some way, when really the decision should have been taken a bit earlier. I think she really is a very kind person and hates doing anything that is of a disciplinary nature.' For another thing, confrontations of any kind were harder for Elizabeth than for most other people. 'The rest of us,' Michael Oswald points out, 'can have a fall-out with somebody and it's no big news. If the Queen has a confrontation with somebody then the press get hold of it, blow it up and make perhaps far more of it than need be. So I think the Queen does try — and probably wisely — to avoid a confrontation wherever she possibly can.'

In fact, Elizabeth at first sided with Diana rather than with her son. She and Prince Philip both 'felt that Prince Charles should try harder', says Lady Mountbatten, 'because it took a long time for people to realise that there were sides to Diana that were very different from what was seen on public occasions and in public photographs. Therefore they felt that Charles should try harder.' It was only gradually that Elizabeth came to believe that, however hard Charles tried, it was simply not going to be possible to make a success of the marriage — and even then, the realisation left her at a loss. Lady Mountbatten, who was one of those who discussed the problem with the Queen, recalls that 'we talked about it and we talked about what one could do to alleviate the situation and sadly there was no conclusion'.

As long as the problem remained private, the Royal Family's inability either to please Diana or to contain her did not affect the monarchy's public standing. Inevitably, though, stories about the unhappiness of Charles and Diana leaked out, and in 1992 the leaks became a flood when Andrew Morton's book, *Diana: Her True Story*, was published. Diana at first denied that she had co-operated with

Morton, but it later became clear that she had, recording on the journalist's tape recorder the grisly details of her unhappy marriage.

The Morton book was a body blow to the monarchy and under-mined an image of the Royal Family which the Queen had spent her life building up. Elizabeth was never criticised directly by Diana. But she suffered the humiliation of seeing her family portrayed as a cold, unfeeling clan who had never appreciated the princess or understood her difficulties. One of Diana's 'friends' was quoted saying that 'the whole royal business terrified her. They gave her no confidence or support,' while the monarchy itself was described as 'a white-gloved, stiff-upper-lip institution with a large "Do Not Touch" sign hanging from its crown'.[133] Much more seriously, the book made it clear that, as far as Diana was concerned, Camilla Parker Bowles was firmly back in the Prince of Wales's life. 'The whole prospect of Camilla drives her spare,' another of the book's sources said. 'You can't blame Diana for the anger she must feel given the fact that her husband appears to have this long-standing friendship with another woman. The marriage has deteriorated too much to want to have him back. It's just too late.'[134]

Confronted with this catastrophe, the Queen showed no outward reaction. She continued with her normal summer programme and expressed no hostility towards the woman who had broken one of the Royal Family's most important rules — never to talk about family problems in public. 'The Queen is always professional,' says Charles Anson, who had succeeded Michael Shea as Elizabeth's press secretary, 'and after fifty years in her role, she's very experienced. Her reaction to dealing with bad news or any particular set of events is a very practical and professional one. "How do we deal with this in the best way?" '

Privately, though, she was aghast. According to Lady Mountbatten, 'It was a feeling of disbelief that somebody within the family could do something like that and be so disloyal and unkind really. One knows from what you read recently about Diana herself, that she lived to deeply regret what she'd done, but it was a horrendous event really. Very unpleasant, very unkind, horrible.' Elizabeth's feelings were mirrored by the rest of her family. Princess Margaret – who until then had been friendly towards Diana and whose own experience had taught her just how unforgiving the demands of royal duty could be – was icily shocked, while the Duke of Edinburgh made no secret of his anger and distaste, openly snubbing Diana when the two of them found themselves alone in the royal box at Ascot.

The problem Elizabeth faced was that there did not seem to be any obvious way of dealing with the situation. Since the days of Queen Victoria and Prince Albert, the monarchy as an institution had relied heavily on maintaining an image of respectable family life. The fact that Elizabeth's uncle, Edward VIII, had abdicated in order to marry a divorced woman had dented that image, but the two sovereigns who succeeded him – George VI and Elizabeth herself – had done all they could to repair the damage and restore the idea of a monarchy that was as much about family as it was about crowns and sceptres.

The ups-and-downs of the 1980s and the arrival of the Duchess of York had done a lot to strip away the respectability of the Royal Family; and now Diana, by going public with her misfortunes, had in the minds of much of the population destroyed any idea that the Windsors were a happy family. It was clearly not a situation which called for half-measures – but equally, any measures directed against Diana at all threatened to make a bad situation even worse. The revelations she had given Andrew Morton may, from the Queen's point of view, have been biased and unfair, but Diana had the sympathy of both press and public, and she was still the Princess of Wales, mother of the future king. 'I think,' says Lady Mountbatten, of the dilemma Elizabeth faced, 'that she genuinely felt she would like to do what she could to help, even

though this was an intolerable situation made worse by Diana's behaviour. But she still wanted to keep it friendly from that point of view,
and as the mother of her grandchildren, which meant a great deal to
her. I think she's the sort of person who would not wish to be on bad
terms.'

The Queen's usual response to any problem was to sit tight and ride
out the storm, but the one thing that she refused to contemplate was an
end to Charles and Diana's marriage. In March 1992 the Palace had
announced the separation of Prince Andrew and the Duchess of York.
In April it had announced the divorce of Princess Anne and Captain
Mark Phillips — who had been separated since 1989. To see all her
children's marriages wrecked in one year was more than the Queen
could bear, and she insisted in a meeting with the Prince and Princess
of Wales that they put off any idea of separation or divorce in favour of
another attempt at reconciliation.

For Elizabeth, it was an unusually firm intervention and the sharp
encounter with her mother-in-law, according to Diana's later account,
had left her 'shaken rigid'.[135] But try as she might to keep a lid on things,
the dramas of 1992 were by no means over for the Queen. The marriage
of Charles and Diana remained under relentless public scrutiny, the
drama heightened by the publication of a private telephone conversation
between the Princess of Wales and a male friend in which Diana
referred to how her husband 'makes my life real torture' before com-
plaining bitterly how 'I just felt really sad and empty and thought,
"Bloody hell, after all I've done for this fucking family . . ." ' Meanwhile
the marriage of Andrew and the Duchess of York received another
enormous blow when photographs appeared of the Duchess and John
Bryan, the man she described as her 'financial adviser', enjoying what
appeared to be an inappropriately intimate moment while on holiday
together. And at the end of the year, as if to symbolise the chaos that

Princess Anne on her engagement to Mark Phillips, 1973 (*Hulton Getty*)

With her second husband, Commander Tim Laurence, 1993 (*Topham/Lionel Cironneau*)

'Whatever "in love" means...' Prince Charles' engagement to Diana Spencer, 1981 (*Topham/Press Association*)

A fairytale wedding (*Hulton Archive*)

'The Queen found Diana very hard to understand' (*Photographer's International*)

'She wanted to be on her own, really' (*Topham/Press Association*)

Prince Andrew with his fiancée, Sarah Ferguson (*Hulton Getty*)

More family trouble: the Duchess of York in tears, 1992 (*Camera Press Ltd*)

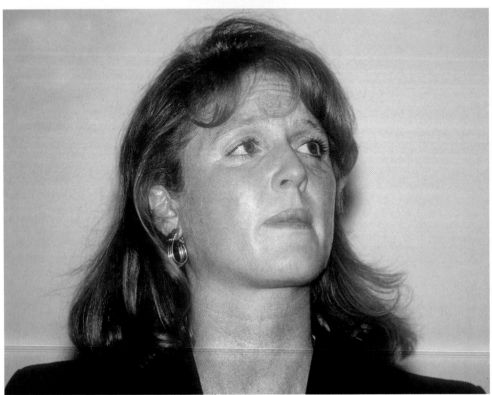

Annus Horribilis
(*Topham/Press Association*)

Inside St George's Hall,
Windsor Castle, November
1992 (*Topham/Press
Association*)

The moment the Monarchy faltered. The Queen at Princess Diana's funeral (*Rex Features*)

The Earl and Countess of Wessex: a modern media couple and a problem for the Monarchy (*Topham/Press Association*)

The hope for the future, Elizabeth II with the future William V (*Camera Press Ltd*)

'She's been doing this for years' (*PA Photos*)

Taking tea on a Glasgow council estate – a gesture towards modernisation (*PA Photos*)

had descended on Elizabeth's family, a fire broke out in Windsor Castle and threatened to destroy the entire building.

The fire started on 20 November – the same day as Elizabeth's wedding anniversary – when a spotlight in the castle's Private Chapel started a curtain smouldering. Smoke was spotted at 11.20am, but the fire was already well established, and by the time the fire brigade arrived twenty minutes later it was too late to save the Chapel. 'Beams were falling . . . the whole of that decorated ceiling was going,' one of the firemen said later. 'There was lots of smoke and I couldn't distinguish everything, but as you came from the Equerries' Staircase into the Chapel, the beams were falling, which meant it must have been burning for quite a while.'[136]

Parts of Windsor Castle had recently been modernised and had fire breaks installed, but there was none in the area around the Private Chapel. Once the fire took hold in the roof, it easily spread along the rafters and behind wood panelling to other parts of the castle where it grew and fed until a total of thirty-six fire engines and over 200 firemen were needed to prevent it destroying the entire building. By the time the blaze was finally extinguished, over a hundred rooms had been destroyed and £35 million worth of damage had been done, including the almost complete destruction of St George's Hall. As well as the vast damage caused by the flames, over 1.5 million gallons of water had been poured into the castle, saturating whatever had not been burned and leaving a sodden, charred ruin that would take five years to restore.

The Queen and most of her household were at Buckingham Palace at the time. David Airlie, the Lord Chamberlain, immediately left for Windsor, 'and halfway down I could see billows of smoke rising high into the sky, so I realised that this was really a serious matter indeed. When I got there and went into the forecourt to see this Castle ablaze it really was horrific, absolutely horrific and immensely distressing. An hour later the Queen arrived and there we stood in the forecourt and it was a perfectly miserable November afternoon, dark, dingy, drizzling with rain, and this ghastly fire spreading right across the Castle.'

Elizabeth was, her friend Margaret Rhodes recalls, 'totally knocked sideways by it'. Of all the royal residences, Windsor was the one the Queen had most looked on as home; although her private apartments had been spared by the fire, all of her possessions had been moved out for safety and the Castle was in turmoil. 'Even things like her medicine cupboard in the bathroom had been taken out,' says Margaret Rhodes, 'everything had been taken out. And she had to ring up to get hold of some medicament she wanted that we'd got.' After all the stress of her children's disintegrating marriages, the fire at Windsor must have seemed like the final straw to Elizabeth. At the end of the first day, Kenneth Scott remembers her looking shattered and sad, and adds, 'I don't think I've seen her really so emotionally affected by anything as by the Windsor fire.'

There was worse to come. Throughout her reign, Elizabeth herself had never been the focus of sustained national dislike but in the aftermath of the Windsor fire the public turned on her. The issue was, who should pay for the damage the fire had caused? Technically, it was the Government's responsibility: Windsor Castle may have felt like home to the Queen, but it did not belong to her. Sandringham and Balmoral were her personal possessions, to keep or sell as she wished, but Windsor – like Buckingham Palace – belonged to the state. Since, on the Government's advice, the building was uninsured, the repair bill should have been footed by the taxpayer. Even if it had been Elizabeth's responsibility, according to David Airlie, she was scarcely in a position to meet it. 'Of course, people did say, "Why can't the Queen pay?" the Lord Chamberlain recalls. 'Now, you know, the Queen couldn't possibly have afforded that sort of money. It turned out to cost, in fact, in the order of £37 million.'

Elizabeth had known that her personal wealth was a matter of great speculation and some envy. Even before the Windsor Fire her staff had been studying whether she should pay tax on her private fortune – the exact amount of which was kept a closely guarded secret and which was estimated by journalists to be anything from a few million to over a billion pounds. She had not paid any tax since 1952 but, by the end of the 1980s, it had become clear that the Queen's personal exemption from an imposition that everybody else in the country had to accept was straining public goodwill towards the monarchy. 'She recognised,' says David Airlie, who was in charge of reviewing the Queen's finances, 'that some time the change had to take place. She was perfectly content to go along with that proposal.'

The fire at Windsor, though, happened just before the Palace had completed its tax plans, and when the Government announced that it would pay for the damage itself there was a public outcry that took both Downing Street and the Palace entirely by surprise. To be sure, the country was in the middle of a recession, and the antics and marital catastrophes of the younger royal generation had exposed the monarchy to unprecedented ridicule, but nobody anticipated the rage with which people greeted the idea that the taxpayer should pay. It was the Queen's own fault, some of the news reports implied, for not insuring her castle in the first place. Nobody else in the country could go running to the Government for help when their house burned down, the argument went, so why should Elizabeth? And where she was not attacked for being negligent, she was accused of greed: reportedly the richest woman in the world, one who had never paid a penny of tax but who was still too mean to pick up the tab for a paltry £35 million or so. As John Major, then Prime Minister, admits, 'I misjudged what seemed then to be the media and public reaction. I was astonished, absolutely astonished, at the mean-minded vindictiveness of much of the hostility that arose at the time – to the thought that the taxpayer generally should contribute to the restoration of what is one of our national treasures.'

Elizabeth herself was horrified. On her twenty-first birthday she had dedicated herself to a life of duty and service – a dedication which she had renewed at her Coronation – and that, says her cousin, the Queen of Denmark, 'was what she was there to do. And I think that she's followed that through and that is the reason why it's hurt her more than I'd imagine she's shown anybody when things have been difficult or have gone wrong.' Even so, some of those close to her did get a sense of the extent of the Queen's dismay. According to Kenneth Scott, 'She was deeply hurt by the fury with which the press greeted the idea that public money should be spent on the restoration of Windsor Castle. She didn't think that people thought she was grasping in that way.'

The immediate response of the Palace was to try and limit the public-relations damage. The Queen had intended to announce the fact that she would pay income tax for the first time early in 1993, but – with such uproar over the costs of the Windsor Fire – the Palace decided to issue a press release much earlier. If it had hoped that this would mollify the public, though, it was to be sorely disappointed. The effect was to strip away any credit that Elizabeth might have expected to receive for the move. Before the announcement she was criticised for being selfish and miserly; after it she looked as though she was running scared from the public, which seemed to be gaining a taste for royal blood.

Her response to the disastrous events of 1992 was to appeal for public sympathy. In a speech at the Guildhall four days after the fire, speaking through a heavy cold, the Queen described 1992 as an *'annus horribilis'*. She acknowledged how unpopular the Royal Family had become, stating that 'no institution – city, monarchy, whatever – should expect to be free from the scrutiny of those who give it their loyalty and support, not to mention those who don't'. Even more remarkably, she revealed the hurt and anxiety that many of the press attacks had caused her, calling for 'a touch of gentleness, good humour and understanding'.

It was not the words themselves that struck people with such force but the fact that it was Elizabeth who was saying them and, to those who were well disposed towards the monarchy, there was great poignancy in the fact that a long-serving and dutiful woman who should have been celebrating forty years on the throne was reduced to trying to shame her enemies by appealing to their better natures. John Major, who was sitting next to Elizabeth as she made her speech, thinks that 'people saw a human side of the Queen, a public acknowledgement by the monarch – perhaps for the first time that people could ever remember – of some of the personal difficulties that she faced. And I think it drew from people an understanding that, monarch or not, here was someone who had a family, who had concerns, who faced difficulties, who wasn't isolated and insulated from the normal problems and vicissitudes of life.'

For all the good her speech did, though, Elizabeth might have been a pheasant appealing to the better nature of the guns at a Sandringham shoot. 'That Guildhall speech,' says Kenneth Scott, 'was an indication of the fact that something had gone wrong in the relationship between the Queen and her people, and insofar as this was because of the way the Queen was behaving, she would have to do something about it.' The problem was that 'insofar' did not cover much distance. If some of the disasters that had befallen the Queen were of her own making – her inability or refusal to keep her children on a tighter leash perhaps, or the slowness with which she had reformed the Palace finances – most of them were out of her control. Whether the press were leading public opinion or simply giving voice to it, the media took an increasingly cynical approach to the Royal Family, whose new purpose, it was becoming clear, was simply to provide entertainment for the rest of the country. At the same time, it was undoubtedly not something for which the press alone could be blamed, for the Royal Family's star turn – the tragicomic life of the Prince and Princess of Wales – showed no signs of running out of steam and at times even seemed to need the attention of the public in order to reach its conclusion.

Not surprisingly, it was Charles and Diana who provided the finale to the royal performance of 1992. Elizabeth had insisted that they try to bury their differences but by the time the Prince and Princess were pictured together on an official visit to Korea it was clear to everyone that they could not bear to be in each other's company. By December, even the Queen was persuaded that the Waleses' marriage was unwork-able and on 9 December the Palace announced that Charles and Diana would separate. Elizabeth's son and daughter-in-law appeared in public on the day the separation was announced, but the Queen stayed out of sight at Sandringham.

'It must have been very sad,' thinks Margaret Rhodes. 'Apart from being Head of the Church, as a mother anything that goes wrong in one's children's marriages is inevitably a huge sadness and there's no escaping the sadness.' It was certainly a fitting end to the worst year in the Queen's reign, but whatever Elizabeth's true feelings, she kept them characteristically hidden. Earlier that year, when Shane Blewitt saw the Queen after another catastrophic royal week, he found her looking 'absolutely grey and ashen'. But the next day, when he went to say goodbye, 'There was the Queen, unlike the night before when she had looked distressed, beautifully made-up, with a silk scarf on and a lovely incandescent smile again, and do you know what they were going to do? They were going ferreting. And I admired her enormously. She was saying, "I must get out and get some fresh air and then I will go home and be of more practical use in dealing with these problems. No point in sitting at home mooching." '

According to Lady Penn, 'She has a deep religious faith which has helped her and sustained her, I think, through all these difficult times,' and perhaps it was as well for Elizabeth that her faith was not of the questioning sort. Amid all the crises of her reign, 1992 had been by far the most disastrous, but the Queen would need all her powers of emotional discipline and self-reliance to deal with what was still to come.

CHAPTER TEN

In May 1995 Britain celebrated the fiftieth anniversary of VE Day – the day on which Germany had surrendered, granting victory in Europe to the Allies. It was a day for both commemoration and nostalgia – an opportunity to honour those who had fought for their country and to remember, through the softening haze of half a century, a time when Britain seemed a stronger, more heroic and decent nation. The insistent notion that the Second World War had been Britain's 'finest hour' (the phrase Winston Churchill had originally applied to the defeat and evacuation of the British Army at Dunkirk) was a source of puzzlement and some irritation to many other countries, perhaps because their own encounters with Nazi Germany had been either more horrific or less creditable. Nonetheless it was central to the way many British people viewed their own national identity and at the heart of all the wartime memories and myths, few images were more enduring than those of Elizabeth and her family.

The Second World War had been the making of the modern twentieth-century monarchy. The abdication of Edward VIII had done much to undermine the prestige of the Crown and the respect in which it was held, but the outbreak of war three years later provided an opportunity for George VI to do more than repair the damage. From the most cynical point of view, six years of fighting and hardship were an ideal means of erasing the memory of one selfish king and replacing it with the image of his hard-working successor, devoted to duty and sharing the suffering of his people. Looked at more generously, it was the real virtues of Elizabeth's parents – her father's shy determination and quiet patriotism, her mother's warmth and charm – that endeared them to the public and made them emblems of the nation, just as much as Churchill himself.

Whereas earlier twentieth-century sovereigns had been distant, formal figures, George VI had introduced a more intimate and familial tone: not so much 'the Father of the Nation', more simply a man with a wife and children of his own who also happened to be King. Elizabeth's mother's celebrated comment when Buckingham Palace was bombed – 'Now we can look the East End in the face' – may, in reality, have caused a few hollow laughs from Londoners who did not have four other palaces to retreat to when their homes were destroyed. Nevertheless during the war, and for a long time after it, the image most people carried of the House of Windsor was not of a grand dynasty at the apex of society, but an ordinary family at the heart of it.

By 1995 that family had disintegrated – as had most of the commonly shared values it was supposed to protect and embody. The *annus horribilis* of 1992 had not marked the end of Elizabeth's troubles, only a milestone on the way. And by the time it came to planning how to celebrate VE Day – an event in which Elizabeth would play a leading role – there were serious concerns that the cascade of royal divorces, scandals and embarrassments had so damaged the Queen's standing that the whole event would be a flop. There were concerts, parades and fly-pasts planned, but one of the most worrying questions was whether sufficient people would bother to turn up.

In 1945, crowds had massed outside Buckingham Palace to cele-brate the end of the war, so many that they stretched down the Mall and into Trafalgar Square, chanting 'We want the King' and cheering madly when the Royal Family appeared on the Palace balcony. Fifty years on, those in charge of the VE Day commemoration wanted to begin the day's events with another assembly outside the Palace, but they did so with some trepidation. Lord Cranborne, the Government minister in charge, remembers that 'there were people who were extremely nervous – including people at the Palace – who thought, well perhaps under the present circumstances we couldn't fill that huge space and what we ought to do is be less ambitious and try and fill Horseguards Parade, which we certainly could do.' On Cranborne's advice, the Queen decided to stick with Buckingham Palace, but just in case the crowd did turn out to be too thin, royal officials made contingency plans to send a couple of military bands to march around Hyde Park in the hope that this would encourage more people to turn up.

In the event, the emergency bands were not needed. As Lord Cranborne recalls, 'We got a message from the police about midday saying, "For God's sake, whatever you do don't bring anybody down from Hyde Park. We've got more people here than were here in 1945." ' Perhaps because VE Day and the memory of the monarchy's wartime role touched a particularly deep and nostalgic chord with the British, perhaps because it was the sort of celebration (as much national as royal) for which Elizabeth's version of the monarchy had been designed, the 1995 celebrations were a grand – and surprising – success. Over 700,000 people turned up – many of them war veterans but also many who had been born after the war and were just out for the day or had turned up out of curiosity – and the warmth with which they received the Royal Family was particularly gratifying to Elizabeth. 'She was pleased by the reaction and the way in which, as in 1945, the Royal Family was seen to be personifying the celebration of the country,' says Kenneth Scott. 'Coming as it did after a number of rather unpleasant experiences in previous years, it was very reassuring for her.'

Even more reassuring than the large and good-natured crowd was the fact that, for once, it was just the Queen, her sister and mother who were the centre of attention. At Elizabeth's own suggestion, they were the only members of the Royal Family to appear on the Palace balcony, just as, in 1945, the three of them had stood next to the King. With mass singalongs led by Vera Lynn and Cliff Richard, the whole day was an unabashed saunter down memory lane but one that all the senior members of the family genuinely appeared to enjoy. 'We've been rehearsing this for about three weeks,' the Queen Mother told one of the performers, and afterwards, Cliff Richard recalls, 'I'd never seen them so animated. They were absolutely arms in the air and so thrilled to have sung these songs. They loved it because it brought out all the best feelings about what had happened and how grateful they were, we are, for the sacrifice that was made on our behalf.'

A poignant reminder of the days when the Royal Family was looked up to as a model family, the 1995 VE Day celebrations also recalled the happy times when it was still just 'us four'. The modern monarchy, far from being a small, orderly constellation of a few bright stars, now had a number of minor satellites in more or less erratic orbit, as well as a scattering of separated or divorced wives and husbands that at times threatened to eclipse the central figure of Elizabeth herself. Of all of them, the figure of Diana loomed largest.

People like the Duchess of York or Prince Edward in his less fortunate moments at least promised nothing worse than severe embarrassment. Diana, by contrast, was a much more powerful threat. As mother to the future king, whatever her titles or status, she would always have an influence and seniority that could easily be denied to more peripheral figures. Beyond her official prestige, she also possessed such personal warmth and magnetism – a glamour and excitement that every other member of the Royal Family lacked – that her international fame alone provided her with a formidable base. 'She had this unbelievable star quality which resonated all over the world,' says Nicholas Soames, one of the Prince of Wales's friends. 'And of course this is very difficult to handle, because the Royal Family had never had to deal with anything like this. It isn't that they resented it, I think. It was just, "How do you deal with this? How do you deal with it properly and decently?" '

It was not a question that was ever really answered. Diana was separated from her husband but not divorced, and for all that she had become a semi-detached member of the Royal Family there was no lessening of her popularity at home. If anything, the image she projected – of a trusting, naïve woman who had been betrayed by her husband and let down by her heartless in-laws – made her all the more attractive. Though she no longer officially represented the Queen when she went abroad, there were very few foreign rulers who did not wish to meet her anyway. Within Buckingham Palace there was, as Mary Francis, a member of Elizabeth's staff, admits, 'undoubtedly a feeling of competition. That if she went on a very high profile foreign visit to undertake a charitable activity, for instance, and that rather overshadowed the reporting of an official visit that one of the members of the Royal Family was undertaking, there was disappointment that there'd been a clash and that there hadn't been sufficient co-ordination of time-tables to avoid that.' Even at home, there was a constant danger that the Princess of Wales would upstage the Queen – when, for instance, a speech by Diana about bulimia stole the headlines from the state banquet that Elizabeth was hosting for the President of Portugal – and at times some Palace officials found it difficult not to conclude that she had done so on purpose.

Diana was only part of Elizabeth's problems, though. If the Princess of Wales had been the only loose cannon careering about the royal decks then it is not hard to imagine that, eventually, some sort of workable compromise would have been reached. She had no love for the Queen's family but equally she was no republican and had little interest in destroying an institution she hoped her son would one day take over. What did turn Diana into a focus for public discontent with the Royal Family – as individuals and as an institution – was the series of own-goals that her in-laws achieved. And of all Elizabeth's family, nobody's reputation was plummeting faster than that of her eldest son.

The Prince of Wales had barely had a chance to recover from the collapse of his marriage in 1992 when, the following year, newspapers published details of a taped conversation between him and Camilla Parker Bowles. Readers of the newspaper which broke the story could hear for themselves what the prince and his mistress had to say to each other by dialling a special premium-rate telephone number. And by the time the rest of the media had got hold of the transcript, the whole country knew that Diana's claim that Charles had been unfaithful to her was true. What was perhaps worse than the simple confirmation that the Prince of Wales was an adulterer was the embarrassingly intimate nature of his conversation with Mrs Parker Bowles. As a result, Charles found himself not just drained of public sympathy but of public respect as well.

Unlike his mother, whose instinct in times of trouble was usually to lie low, Charles was unable to resist the urge to do something. Feeling the need to improve his image in general, as well as to put his side of the story with Diana in particular, he agreed to co-operate with the journalist Jonathan Dimbleby on a book and television programme about his life which came out in 1994. Both book and film were intended as serious and weighty accounts of the heir to the throne's career to date but both created the sort of publicity which the Queen and her advisers feared most.

The serialisation of the book began on the eve of Elizabeth's state visit to Russia. It was the first time any British sovereign had visited the country that had gone from wartime ally to Cold War enemy to new democracy in the space of just fifty years, but press coverage of the Queen's historic meeting with Boris Yeltsin was almost entirely overshadowed by the Dimbleby account of the prince's childhood. The Prince of Wales was never quoted directly criticising his parents but there were revealing details scattered throughout the book – images of a bewildered young Charles feeling left out of family discussions about horses, authoritative statements that 'though he was too proud to admit it, the Prince still craved the affection that his father – and his mother – seemed unable or unwilling to provide',[137] and the revelation that by the time Charles was in his twenties he communicated with his father mostly by memo. These provoked another flurry of disastrous royal headlines. 'The Prince's Agony – Father's a Bully and Mother Never Talked to Me', the front page of the *Sunday Times* proclaimed on 16 October. And although neither he nor the author had ever said any such thing, Dimbleby's book was another nail in the coffin of the old idea that Elizabeth's family provided any sort of moral example to the nation.

The television documentary that accompanied the book provided extra and even more explosive ammunition for critics of the monarchy. Although most of the programme, like the book, was a sympathetic and uncontroversial assessment of the public role Prince Charles had fashioned for himself, the publicity it generated was dominated by the prince's admission that he had had an affair with Camilla Parker Bowles. 'Did you try to be faithful and honourable to your wife when you took on the vow of marriage?' asked Dimbleby. 'Yes, absolutely,' Charles replied, 'until it became irretrievably broken down, us both having tried.'

Charles had hoped that a reasonable explanation of his conduct – that he had tried to make his marriage work, that he had only resumed his relationship with Camilla once he and Diana had reached the point of irretrievable break-down – would gain him public sympathy. But his decision to speak so openly about the failure of his marriage horrified the Queen and her staff. As well as waving a red rag to his wife, Charles's admission ensured that a row the Queen had wanted to keep private now became a public war, with both sides using the media as the battleground. There was also a world of difference between everyone knowing that the Prince of Wales had committed adultery and the man himself saying so on television: if nothing else, it certainly removed any chance that Camilla Parker Bowles would remain an aspect of royal life that could be tactfully glossed over. It also led people to wonder what sort of an impact the prince's admission would have on his children. 'I think personally it was a most unfortunate exercise,' says Shane Blewitt, Keeper of the Privy Purse, 'and I think it has subse-quently been agreed by those directly involved in it, that it was unfor-tunate and unwise. And of course it triggered off a reaction from the other side which again was counter-productive.'

The Princess of Wales's retaliation took the form of another television programme. Diana recorded her interview with *Panorama* in total secrecy, without even telling her own staff. It was broadcast on 20 November 1995 – tactfully enough, the anniversary of Elizabeth's own wedding – to the horror of everyone at the Palace. In a series of answers that appeared to be carefully rehearsed (Diana later claimed that they were spontaneous but one of the foreign broadcasters who had bought the rights to the interview and discussed it with the princess said they were not[138]) the Princess of Wales took the war with her husband and his family to new depths of bitterness. Her own private secretary and one of her ladies-in-waiting, with 'groans and exasperated laughter [rising] like nausea to our lips',[139] watched as Diana referred to the Queen's advisers as 'the enemy' and made it clear that she saw herself as the embattled victim of an unjust war. 'She won't go quietly,' warned the princess, referring to herself in the third person and going on to remind everyone of her two trump cards – 'I'll fight to the end because I believe I have a role to fulfil and I've got two children to bring up.'

As Charles had done, Diana spoke frankly about her marriage. But whereas the Prince of Wales had said that Camilla Parker Bowles had only entered the scene after the breakdown of his marriage, Diana said that she had been there all along. 'There were three of us in this marriage,' she said, 'so it was a bit crowded.' Having established that the collapse of their marriage was Charles's fault, his wife went on to administer the *coup de grâce* with the mock-sympathetic suggestion that he would not make a good king. 'Because I know the character,' Diana said, 'I would think that the top job, as I call it, would bring enormous limitations to him and I don't know whether he could adapt to that.'

The *Panorama* interview was the final straw for Elizabeth. Since 1992, when Charles and Diana had announced their separation, the Queen had kept up her official duties and avoided any open interference in the lives of her son and daughter-in-law. 'Life has to go on, work has to go on,' points out her press secretary, Charles Anson. 'My recollection is that there were difficult times, very difficult times, but it never interrupted the flow of public business, or royal business. It couldn't.' But for all her public composure, in private Elizabeth had been desperately hoping for a reasonably positive outcome.

Since Elizabeth was ten years old, Divorce had been a monster that haunted the Royal Family, lurking at the heart of every major crisis the Queen had had to face. It had lain at the heart of the scandal that had placed her father on the throne, and ever since things had turned sour between Charles and Diana, Elizabeth had hoped that she would not be remembered as the only member of her family for three generations who had succeeded to the throne without the spectre of divorce hanging over them. Even though she accepted that the future King and Queen might never live happily together, she had hoped that Charles and Diana, while separated, might at least keep their marriage going on paper – if only to avoid the prospect of a divorced Charles taking the Coronation Oath alone.

Panorama put paid to those hopes. Whatever the merits of the Queen's plan, it had depended on Charles and Diana at least being civil to one another so that, when public duty demanded, they could appear together as man and wife. Diana's interview made that impossible, and at the end of 1995 Elizabeth finally bowed to the inevitable. Not only had *Panorama* and the Dimbleby documentary injected insurmountable levels of rancour and bitterness into the Waleses' marriage, the fact that Diana had publicly raised doubts about Charles's fitness to be King had broken one of the most important rules of the Royal Family. No hereditary monarchy could survive if everyone went around openly wondering whether the next king or queen would be any good: the whole point – atavistically charming for monarchists and repellently ludicrous for republicans – was that the prestige and dignity of the Crown descended irrevocably on the most senior heir. If a general debate started about whether William would make a better successor to Elizabeth than Charles – or whether perhaps Anne might like to step in as Regent until William came of age – then there was scarcely any point in having a monarchy at all. That the Princess of Wales should lead such a debate was both farcical and threatening.

'The Queen must have realised at that moment that there were real dangers in this situation,' says Lady Mountbatten, 'and that if this really was going to go on – with these statements, quite unwarranted, about Prince Charles not being fit to be King and that sort of wild idea – then perhaps things should be brought to a close. Whatever the cost – and I don't mean financially, but whatever the cost in feelings and in amazement or surprise – that the time had come when something serious had to be done.' In December Elizabeth wrote separately to Charles and Diana to let them know of her 'desire for an early divorce'.[140] Eight months later, on 28 August 1996, the marriage of the Prince and Princess of Wales was finally over.

A year later, Elizabeth was at Balmoral, enjoying one of the regular royal holidays that had taken place nearly every year for the whole of her life. At the beginning of her reign, the Court's progress to Scotland was treated as a piece of major news, with cinema newsreels relaying pictures of the young Charles and Anne toddling off the royal train at Ballater station and newspaper reports of the Royal Family's attendance at the Highland Games at Braemar. Nearly fifty years on, the media barely paid any attention at all to what the Queen did during her summer break. The modern monarchy had become not much more than a personality contest, and in the summer of 1997 it was the newly divorced Princess of Wales who still dominated the headlines, summering in the South of France with Dodi Fayed, the playboy son of an Egyptian businessman. Diana's was not a low-profile holiday, but at Buckingham Palace there was still an element of relief that, whatever Diana got up to, it was no longer really the Court's problem. As Mary Francis recalls, 'There were a few raised eyebrows, but she was a divorced woman. It was her life.'

The relief was to prove short-lived. After a few days on Mohammed Fayed's yacht, Diana and Dodi flew to Paris. In the early hours of 31 August, the Queen was woken by the news that they had both been killed in a car crash after their chauffeur had collided with a pillar in the centre of a Paris underpass. The report of the disaster came, as the Lord Chamberlain, David Airlie, remembers, 'as an appalling shock. I was woken up in the middle of the night to be told about it and frankly, when I first heard it I didn't believe it. I just couldn't take it on board', and the Royal Family was thrown into utter disarray.

Elizabeth's reaction was one of bewildered disbelief and her first comment, according to one journalist, was that 'someone must have greased the brakes'.[141] Prince Charles, who was also staying at Balmoral, faced the immediate and terrible task of breaking the news to his sons, who were still asleep. Unsure whether to wake them immediately or let them sleep until morning, he turned to his mother for comfort and advice. Elizabeth told him that William and Harry should be left until the morning, but in the meantime the televisions and radios were taken out of the children's bedroom in case they woke up and heard the news when they were on their own.

However, the problems that Elizabeth and her family faced were more than personal, and much worse than any of them could have anticipated. Diana's death unleashed a storm of public fury and resentment against the monarchy that found its first target on the first day of the tragedy, Sunday, when the whole Royal Family – including William and Harry – went to church. 'The boys were asked if they would like to go to church,' recalls Lady Penn, 'or would they rather stay behind? Because the Queen would have understood whichever they wanted to do, and their father too. And they both said they would rather be with them, which is what they did.'

Neither of Diana's sons looked as though they had been dragged into church against their will, but the fact that Elizabeth had taken them there at all – along with the absence of any prayers for the late Princess of Wales during the service – was interpreted by the media as evidence of the Royal Family's cold and heartless reaction to the princess's death. 'What on earth was the Queen meant to do?' wonders her stud manager, Michael Oswald. 'She asked them if they wanted to go to church and they said, "Can we come too, Granny?" ' But the implication in many of the news reports was that Elizabeth and her relations were not mourning at all and that the two young princes were trapped in a cold and heartless family.

In fact, the Royal Family could barely bring themselves to do anything and, although many of the news reports on Sunday were spiteful or unfair, Elizabeth did bring many of the later attacks upon herself. Diana's death was received by millions, perhaps by most of the country, as a national calamity and yet, when facing the most testing challenge of her reign, Elizabeth could not or would not bring herself to act as Queen. Throughout her life, duty had routinely come before personal satisfaction and she had seldom hesitated in the past before sacrificing her maternal or sisterly affections to the interests of the Crown. In 1997, as never before, Britain needed the Queen to resume her role as Head of the Nation, to provide a comforting focus and expression of the country's grief – and yet, for once, Elizabeth refused.

For five days, she remained silent at Balmoral while the public's anger and sadness whirled about her, and it fell to the new Labour Prime Minister, Tony Blair, to carry out the duties that should have been Elizabeth's. It was the Prime Minister, not the Queen, who played the role of national mourner-in-chief. According to journalist Andrew Rawnsley, before Blair made his celebrated 'People's Princess' speech:

he kept saying both to his wife and to Alastair Campbell in those early hours, 'But is it my place? Is it really *my* role to do this?' And what finally made up his mind that he had to say something on behalf of the nation – that large numbers of people were grieving – was when he had a breakfast-time conversation with the Queen and it was made evident to him by the Queen that the Royal Family were planning to say nothing at all. And it was at that moment that Tony Blair finally made up his own mind – 'Well, if they're not going to do it, somebody's got to do it and the only person who can do it is me.'

For one thing, the Royal Family was, perhaps for the first time, running scared. Only a year after the Princess of Wales's divorce, they knew that the monarchy would be blamed for casting her out and that responsibility for her death would be placed unmistakably at the door of the Palace. 'She's going to be canonised,' one of Elizabeth's most trusted advisers warned her, and as Mary Francis, one of the private secretaries, recalls, 'there was considerable concern. Nobody had seen that kind of outpouring of public grief. Looking back on it now, it was a very, very strange period and I think people are now asking whether the kind of public emotion that was being shown at the time was entirely healthy. But it happened and it was very concerning.'

While Elizabeth and the rest of her family stayed at Balmoral, the crowds in London kept an astonishing vigil outside Kensington Palace and Buckingham Palace, where the flowers they had brought piled up five feet deep. And the longer the Royal Family remained out of sight, the angrier and more bitter the mood of the crowds became. Every morning, according to Andrew Rawnsley, two of the Prime Minister's closest advisers – Alastair Campbell and Anjie Hunter – would take a walk from No. 10 down to Buckingham Palace, along the Mall, past the crowds, and then return to Tony Blair and warn him just how ugly the mood was getting.

If Diana was becoming a saint, Prince Charles knew exactly who the sinner would be. Senior staff in the Prime Minister's office later told Andrew Rawnsley that 'to start with, Prince Charles was really no more enthusiastic than the Queen about breaking the internal exile in Balmoral – perhaps for different reasons. I know he expressed it directly to the Prime Minister in a conversation when Tony Blair was gently trying to persuade them to come down to London. Charles said to Tony Blair, "But won't we look like hypocrites?" '

Charles knew that he would be blamed for the Princess's death and his team felt that they had to pull out all the stops to defend their man. Months later, they stressed how he had to fight tooth and nail to persuade his mother to come out of seclusion and, in the opinion of one insider, it was also the Prince of Wales's own supporters who were responsible for some of the most damaging and untrue stories about Elizabeth's part in the preparations for the funeral. According to these reports, Elizabeth was firmly opposed to granting her former daughter-in-law any royal honours at all. Diana was no longer a member of the Royal Family, the Queen is meant to have argued, therefore she should not be flown home in one of the official royal aeroplanes: her coffin should not be covered by the Royal Standard, nor should she be granted a state funeral. It was, allegedly, only the intervention of the Prince of Wales and Elizabeth's own advisers that tipped the balance. 'Would you rather, Ma'am, that she came home in a Harrods van?' one of the Queen's private secretaries is supposed to have asked in exasperation. In fact, the private secretary in question said no such thing and the plan for the Prince of Wales to go in person to Paris to retrieve his ex-wife's body was given full support by everyone at Balmoral.

What was true was that there were no initial plans for a state funeral. The Royal Family had no blueprint for the burial of the divorced wife of a future king and the Spencer family wanted a quiet family service. At first the Queen was happy to go along with their wishes. Mary Francis was on holiday in Greece when the crisis broke, but 'when I phoned the

Palace and said, "Do you want me back?" the first reaction was "Probably not." ' It soon became evident, though – and it was something that struck Elizabeth's officials rather than the Queen herself – that a private ceremony was not something the rest of the country would accept.

The Lord Chamberlain, David Airlie, played a key role in planning the alternative, public event. By Monday morning the Palace had come up with a plan which combined the dignity of a traditional state funeral with modern touches which would reflect the spirit of the princess. 'We didn't look at any past files in relation to past funerals. We decided that this had to be something which was *de novo*,' says Airlie. 'I rang up the Queen's private secretary who was on duty at the time at Balmoral and put the outline proposals to him and asked him whether he would talk to the Queen about it, see what her reaction was. I also wanted to get this proposal to the Spencer family to see what their reaction was. This was early in the morning – half-past six, seven – and I had the answers back by nine. "Go ahead, that outline is fine, perfect." I then called a meeting of all the interested parties.'

Where Elizabeth did fail was in keeping herself hidden away at Balmoral. She was quite clear in her mind that she would only come back to London on Saturday, the day of the funeral and seven days after Diana's death. But by Wednesday, there was no let-up in the flowers piling up outside the royal palaces and by Thursday the mood of the crowd was turning ugly. 'It was something that we've never seen in this country before,' says Lady Penn, 'and I'm not sure it wasn't fanned by the media. It was something that I found rather distasteful and I think a lot of people did. Of course it was tragic and of course it was sad, but people went absolutely over the top and once it started it was like a tidal wave.'

To many of her friends and sympathisers, the attacks on Elizabeth seemed unfair and selfish. 'How could it help the children for her to go down and have them sitting in Buckingham Palace with nothing to do but think about losing their mother?' asks Margaret Rhodes. 'It seemed to me a totally natural reaction to keep them quiet and let them assimilate this tragedy before facing the public.'

'I feel very strongly about this,' adds Bill Deedes, 'because I think the Queen was fulfilling a tradition of many families, which is that death is a private matter to the family involved and in a sense not to be used as a demonstration of weeping and wailing, and you keep your distress to yourself.'

In fact, as the public insisted (or at least that section of the public for which most of the newspapers and the mass of London mourners spoke), death was no more a private matter for the Royal Family than birth or marriage. The demand, as one newspaper headline put it, to 'Show Us You Care' may have seemed callous, but it was really no more than the routine call to the colours that Elizabeth had, up to that point, spent her life obeying. This time, though, the Queen was wrong-footed when her advisers suggested that she might have to leave Scotland and return to London to console her people. It was only after the strongest, repeated advice from the Government and her own officials that she changed her mind – 'Some might argue belatedly,' says Lord Airlie – and agreed to return to Buckingham Palace a day early, on Friday.

There were still fears that she might meet with a hostile reception, so Andrew and Edward were sent on ahead to London to test the crowds' reaction. As it turned out, though, the response of the people massed outside Buckingham Palace was, on the whole, bizarrely appreciative. 'About bloody time too!' one man shouted.[142] And yet, as Mary Francis remembers, 'as their car came into Buckingham Palace, the whole crowd started clapping as they passed. It was a sort of wave of acknowledgement that the Queen had come back and done the right thing.'

She may have done the right thing, but she had left it dangerously late and had compounded the error by refusing to allow the Union Jack to fly at half-mast over Buckingham Palace. It was a decision for which Elizabeth alone was responsible, and it perplexed and dismayed many of her staff. 'There's a perfectly good Union Jack which is always flown at Windsor Castle, another one at Sandringham when the Queen's not there,' points out Michael Oswald, 'and I could never understand why somebody didn't show a bit of initiative and put a Union Jack halfway up the flagpole at Buckingham Palace. That could have been done by Monday morning if somebody had thought of it.'

As it turned out, nearly everybody else in the country *had* thought of it, and the fact that Buckingham Palace was not only empty for most of the week, but also the only public building with no flag flying at half-mast, became a symbol of the Queen's apparent lack of feeling for Diana. It also indicated a misplaced and excessive concern for royal protocol that was entirely at odds with the public mood. The Union Jack only ever flew over royal palaces when the monarch was not in residence, Elizabeth's reasoning went: when the monarch was in residence, the Royal Standard flew instead, but it could never be lowered to half-mast on the principle of 'the king is dead, long live the king'. The one time that the Union Jack had flown at half-mast (with the Royal Standard flying at full-mast above it) was for the death of George VI. But Elizabeth seems to have balked at paying the same respect to her daughter-in-law that had once been afforded her father. Once again, it was Elizabeth's advisers who talked her into changing her mind – but it was still not until the day of the funeral itself that the Union Jack finally crept halfway up the Buckingham Palace flagpole.

It may as well have been a white flag. It is hard to think of any other occasion on which the mood of the entire country has been more shaped by the emotions of its most impressionable citizens. Even though Elizabeth had dug her heels in over the flag and the retreat at Balmoral, she was eventually forced to do exactly what the public and the press wanted. Diana may have been, in the Prime Minister's phrase, the People's Princess but in the week of Diana's death the Queen was little more than the People's Pawn.

'At the end of the day,' reckons one Palace official, 'the royals are just puppets. If they're told to go in to tea, they'll go in to tea. They might protest a bit, but when the foot's down they do as they're told. Their strings are pulled for them.'[143] Nonetheless, by the end of that week, the Government and the Queen's advisers were seriously concerned that she was getting dangerously behind public opinion. They urged her more and more strongly that she must do something, and now that she was back in Buckingham Palace, the courtiers went into over-drive with a range of gestures to make up the ground she had lost.

The most important of these gestures was the live broadcast to the nation which Elizabeth had failed to make at the beginning of the week. It was a daunting prospect for her. She disliked appearing on television anyway – after forty years of making them, she still hated having to do her Christmas broadcasts – and found live performances a particular trial. But Mary Francis admits that 'as a result of the huge concerns and grief that had appeared during that week, it was felt right that when the Queen came back from Balmoral, she should make a broadcast and very great care then was taken over getting that right'.

Just how to get it right, though, posed an even greater difficulty. As Elizabeth's cousin and fellow sovereign, Harald of Norway, observes, 'What are you supposed to say in a situation like that? I'm sure she was distraught herself and it's difficult to come and say what you feel in those circumstances.' But many people in the country were not so sure that Elizabeth was in any way distraught – quite the reverse, in fact. The challenge the Queen faced was how to make a sincere and convincing show of mourning for a woman who had been such a divisive and destructive figure in the Royal Family.

Speaking from the Chinese Dining Room at Buckingham Palace, with the crowds milling outside visible through the window behind her, Elizabeth did her best. 'We have all been trying in our different ways to cope,' she began. 'It is not easy to express a sense of loss, since the initial shock is often succeeded by a mixture of other feelings: disbelief, incomprehension, anger – and concern for those who remain. We have all felt those emotions in these last few days. So what I say to you now, as your Queen and as a grandmother, I say from my heart . . .'

Like all her live speeches, her delivery was wooden, and if people had hoped for a naked display of emotion in keeping with the spirit of the times they were disappointed. It was even claimed by some journalists that some of the more human phrases – like 'as a grandmother' – had been forced on the Palace by the Prime Minister's office. Nonetheless, Elizabeth did pay tribute to Diana, insisting that she had admired and respected her and that she shared the public's determination to cherish her memory. In an echo of the speech she had made five years earlier after the Windsor Fire she also acknowledged her own weakness, admitting that 'I for one believe there are lessons to be drawn from her life and from the extraordinary and moving reaction to her death' before ending on a note that was both hopeful and admonitory. 'I hope,' Elizabeth said, 'that tomorrow we can all, wherever we are, join in expressing our grief at Diana's loss, and gratitude for her all-too-short life. It is a chance to show to the whole world the British nation united in grief and respect.'

The next day, Saturday, Elizabeth waited outside the gates of the Palace to pay her own final respects to the Princess of Wales. Flanked by other members of her family, it was, as Barbara Castle remembers, an extraordinary scene. 'I think that one of the most revealing photos at her funeral was that unhappy little clutch of women at the gates of Buckingham Palace,' she says. 'And she stood there in her unhappy neat black mourning, not knowing what to register. That's a funny thing.'

The public reaction to Diana's death may have taken the Queen by surprise but she recognised that she had to make up the ground she had lost, and as the funeral cortège trundled past the Palace gates she bowed her head to the coffin in a unique gesture of submission. The last time Elizabeth had bowed to anyone was in 1952 as her father's coffin was carried off the train at Paddington Station on its way to lie in state at Westminster. Now, on a Saturday morning forty-five years later, she paid the same honour to the woman who had done more than any other to threaten the legacy Elizabeth's father had left her.

Just how much Diana had changed things was underlined during the funeral procession. Her coffin was carried on a gun-carriage to Westminster Abbey and walking behind it came her two sons, her brother, the Prince of Wales and Prince Philip. Behind them were representatives of the various charities Diana had patronised and as they made their way through the streets it was, as Cliff Richard recalls, 'really, really weird. It was like watching a movie. You know how when they try to make an effect on a movie they remove every-thing. The music stops and you know something's going to happen – it felt like that. It was surreal.' Just as they had for the Coronation and the 1981 Royal Wedding, many of the crowds lining the streets had slept there overnight but where before there had been cheering and happiness, now there was only silence, broken only by the clicking of cameras and the occasional low moan as the coffin went by. It was, by any lights, an unprecedented show of public grief and, as the funeral service itself made clear, Diana's death had become as much a political event as a private tragedy.

The people who had been invited to join the congregation inside Westminster Abbey had, inevitably, been chosen in great haste and the method of their selection was, to one mourner at least, surprising. ' "Apparently you've turned up in Diana's Christmas card list," ' Cliff

Richard was told, 'and of course she had sent me Christmas cards. But I didn't think that was going to be the criterion for being at Westminster Abbey.' Doubtless many of those in the Abbey, like the hundreds of thousands of people outside, did feel genuine grief, but those of Diana's friends and relatives who had suffered real loss – not least her sons – had only walk-on parts that Saturday. The day really belonged to the crowds outside and although the dominant emotion was one of mourning there was also strong anger – directed at the press who had hounded Diana and the family who had apparently rejected her.

The tone was set by Diana's brother, Charles Spencer, whose funeral oration included stinging attacks on the press and the Royal Family. Addressing the media, he confessed himself baffled by the relentless and unsympathetic coverage his sister had attracted and concluded that 'my own and only explanation is that genuine goodness is threatening to those at the opposite end of the moral spectrum. It is a point to remember that of all the ironies about Diana, perhaps the greatest was this – a girl given the name of the ancient goddess of hunting was, in the end, the most hunted person of the modern age.'

As Elizabeth sat stony-faced only a few feet away from him, Spencer then turned to the Royal Family, whose old-fashioned and straight-laced emotional world he contrasted unfavourably with that of his sister and whose undiluted impact on her sons he feared. 'We, your blood family,' he pledged her memory, 'will do all we can to continue the imaginative way in which you were steering these two exceptional young men so that their souls are not simply immersed by duty and tradition but can sing openly as you planned. We fully respect the heritage into which they have both been born and will always respect and encourage them in their royal role but we, like you, recognise the need for them to experience as many different aspects of life as possible to arm them spiritually and emotionally for the years ahead.'

In stark contrast to Elizabeth's own words the day before, Spencer's was an emotional, wholehearted and fulsome tribute that touched a deep chord with most of those inside and outside the Abbey. The full import of what he had done – implying in front of Princes William and Harry that their own family was incapable of bringing them up properly without the deft and helping hand of the Spencers – may have taken time to sink in. But if some of the details of his speech were lost, the message – broadcast on loudspeakers to the crowds outside – was clear and it was greeted with a swell of applause which began outside the Abbey and spread to the congregation until nearly everybody except the Queen joined in.

Diana's death brought Elizabeth to the lowest point of her reign. Never before had she been so roundly condemned in the press. Never before had she faced the prospect of openly hostile crowds on the street. 'It was a terrible trial for them in every sense,' says Elizabeth's cousin, the Queen of Denmark. 'It shocked me a lot that they had to go through such a hard time. Personally if I can speak out for once, they were very unfairly treated in many ways.' Nearly half a century earlier, speaking by radio on the day of her Coronation, Elizabeth had told the country that 'throughout this memorable day I have been uplifted and supported by the knowledge that your thoughts and prayers were with me . . . All of you, near or far, have been united in one purpose. It is hard for me to find words in which to tell you of the strength which this knowledge has given me.' The idea that there was a special link between the Queen and her people was a theme to which Elizabeth often returned in her public speeches throughout her reign. By September 1997, though, it seemed to be hanging by the most tenuous of threads and if Britain was united by any purpose, it appeared to be that of criticising Elizabeth and all she stood for.

Diana's strength, as Bill Deedes explains, was that 'she was seen to be fallible. That was one of the deepest bonds between Diana and the public.' Elizabeth's weakness was that she was not. She may have always made a point of referring gratefully to the support and strength she drew from public affection but it was not something that she ever openly sought and when she did acknowledge it – for all that it did make a real difference to her – there was a sense that she did so from on high. Diana, by contrast, engaged with the public at or beneath their own level. Her flaws were quite apparent and those who loved her did so all the more for them. As her brother reminded people in the speech he made at her funeral, 'Diana explained to me once that it was her innermost feelings of suffering that made it possible for her to connect with her constituency of the rejected.' The cult of suffering that the Princess of Wales encouraged may have seemed to some to be pernicious nonsense, but it did give her a clear advantage when it came to public support. She made it clear that she wanted to be loved by people, and repaid them with obvious gratitude. Elizabeth was both less needy and less demonstrative and it was very seldom that anyone saw how pleased she was when she was greeted by cheering and enthusiastic crowds. Whereas Diana would welcome displays of public support with open arms, Elizabeth usually did so as though she had just received another bunch of unsolicited flowers.

The task Elizabeth faced in the aftermath of Diana's funeral was how to bridge the gap and create a more modern and sympathetic monarchy. It was a problem which many of her fellow sovereigns recognised ('Maybe you shouldn't be in the forefront of change,' comments the Norwegian King, 'but I think you have to change with the society you're living in, otherwise you will be in trouble very quickly') but one which Elizabeth had avoided for many years. 'The Queen absolutely understands about change,' says her former Lord

Chamberlain, David Airlie. 'She entirely accepts that change is necessary from time to time. But I think that, very rightly, she doesn't like the idea of change for change's sake.' Rightly or wrongly, Elizabeth had done little to reform the public image of the monarchy since the 1970s and after the high point of her Silver Jubilee, in the opinion of one courtier, 'there were so many missed opportunities. In any business one is always looking over one's shoulder and in that decade nothing happened, it was just more of the same.'[144]

On the most basic level – of co-ordinating what the various members of the Royal Family did and making sure that their work was presented to the public in the best possible light – the monarchy barely functioned as a cohesive organisation at all. If it really had been a firm, as Prince Philip liked to call it, it would have gone out of business decades ago. Even at the end of the 1980s, as Kenneth Scott – one of Elizabeth's private secretaries – recalls, 'I remember being struck on a visit to the Netherlands with the Queen to discover that the Netherlands Royal Family sit round the table regularly and talk about their programme and allocate jobs to each other. And the idea of the British Royal Family actually doing that was very remote in those days.'

Elizabeth had made some changes before the crisis of Diana's death. Her private secretary, Robert Fellowes, acknowledges that for years the Court had been 'frozen into an Edwardian time-warp'[145] and under David Airlie as Lord Chamberlain, the internal workings and finances of the Royal Household were drastically overhauled. Around the same time the Way Ahead Group, consisting of the most senior members of the Royal Family and their advisers, was set up to co-ordinate their public engagements and make sure that there was some sort of strategic direction to what they were all doing.

By the time Mary Francis joined the Queen's private office in 1995, 'There was a lot of thinking about whether the Royal Family should perhaps do more engagements that recognised social issues, the style in which they did them and the amount of money they should spend doing them – all those questions were up in the air when I arrived.' As Francis admits though, 'undoubtedly it was the death of the Princess of Wales and the outpouring of public grief and attention to the way in which the Royal Family conducted its role that was a stimulus for change.'

'I think,' says Kenneth Scott, 'the Queen realised that Princess Diana had a gift for putting herself across to people and making people feel that she identified with them, and that partly because of her age, partly because she has been doing things the same way for a long time, it was not easy for her to do it in the same way, but that somehow one had to improve the general feeling and image of the family.' Elizabeth was never going to be able to achieve the rapport with individual members of the public that the Princess of Wales so effortlessly managed, but she did try to be more informal and to unbend slightly when she appeared in public.

Two months after Diana's funeral, when the Queen celebrated her fiftieth wedding anniversary, she suggested that instead of driving to the celebration lunch at Mansion House she should walk and show herself to the crowds along the way. Later on she made a speech in which she returned to the old theme of the bond between Queen and people, but this time offering ' "humble and hearty thanks" to all those in Britain and around the world who have welcomed us and sustained us and our family, in the good times and the bad, so unstintingly over many years. This has given us strength, most recently during the sad days after the tragedy of Diana's death. It is you, if I may now speak to all of you directly, who have seen us through and helped us to make our duty fun. We are deeply grateful to you, each and every one.' Of the whole country, it was perhaps only Elizabeth who could combine so earnestly and glumly the concepts of duty and pleasure – but if 'fun' was not a word that had often dropped from her lips, her message was clear: she had listened to the criticisms that had been made of her and even if the country's message was hard to read, 'obscured as it can be by deference, rhetoric or the conflicting currents of public opinion . . . read it we must'.

Throughout her reign, the Queen's story has been one of belated and cautious change. 'I shall always work as my father did,' she had promised in 1952 and for the next fifty years she has tried to do just that, responding to changes in the outside world and to family crises only when absolutely forced to do so. 'I think the Queen's conservatism is in her temperament,' says John Grigg. 'It's allied to her supreme virtues of steadiness and stability, so one must never forget that, but it's in her temperament and it's also been greatly reinforced throughout her life by parental influence and by the example of previous generations.'

For all its impact at the time, what is perhaps most striking about Diana's death five years on is how little it has really altered things. 'I think,' says Elizabeth's cousin, Margaret Rhodes, 'things have margin-ally changed. I think that the Queen has a wider circle of people working as private secretaries. And I think really the fact that she sees the public more has made everybody more aware of what ordinary people are doing and thinking. I think there's a greater awareness due to the new, more relaxed and less formal life in the Court.' But if there has been a softening of the Queen's style and her advisers now pay greater attention to how her public duties are presented, the duties themselves remain fundamentally the same – a reflection of the fact that Diana's genius lay not so much in what she did as the manner in which she did it.

'The media have tended to portray the Queen as having suddenly become much more open to the public – going to visit odd parts of the country, talking to humble people, visiting them in hospital and so on,' points out Kenneth Scott. 'She's been doing that for fifty years, but the press never reported it before.' At the same time, while Elizabeth had said that she was open to public criticism, she remains the conservative woman she always has been and it would be nothing short of miraculous if, as she heads into her late seventies, she were to tear up all the rules and protocols which had supported her as Queen for nearly fifty years. The characteristics of life in the Royal Family which Diana had found most oppressive and unbearable were exactly those which Elizabeth found most sustaining. 'If you live this sort of life – which people don't very much,' the Queen wryly observed in a documentary made to celebrate her fortieth year on the throne, 'you live very much by tradition and by continuity.'

'If you have an institution like the monarchy, of course it's going to be set in its ways,' points out Michael Shea. 'It's like the judiciary or the House of Lords or the senior ranks of the police. Anything in any society gets set in its ways.' There was, though, one pressing issue that Elizabeth faced at the end of the 1990s – the romantic life of her eldest son, which continued to dominate public interest in the Royal Family at the end of the decade just as it had at the beginning. In a way, the death of Diana had actually removed some of the Queen's problems – she was at least no longer a constant rival for the public's affections – but the relationship between Prince Charles and Camilla Parker Bowles was still very much alive and threatening immense damage to the monarchy.

Charles's own standing had never recovered from the multiple embarrassments of the 'Camilla-gate' tapes and his televised confession of adultery, and since Diana had voiced her own doubts on *Panorama* there had been open and constant discussion in the media about his fitness to be King. Mrs Parker Bowles herself was, for a time, one of the most publicly reviled and hated women in Britain – for no better reason, at heart, than the fact that she was alive and Diana was not. The added complication that the heir to the throne was in love with a divorcée was a distant echo, wearying and worrying, of Edward VIII and the Abdication Crisis. Prince Charles was a figure of public scorn, went the critics' argument: there was no possibility that the British people would accept Camilla as their future Queen if he married her and it would be equally unacceptable for him to keep her as his mistress. He should therefore take himself out of the running and allow William to succeed Elizabeth.

The idea that the country could pick and mix its sovereigns in advance was anathema to Elizabeth on every level but she was unsure how to handle the Charles and Camilla problem. 'Obviously she can't condone the relationship because she is Head of the Church,' points out one of her former advisers. 'Equally she won't condemn it because that would be to go against the family and the family is everything. No one is allowed to criticise the children even if she disapproves of something herself. The Queen doesn't really want to address the question – and in a way she doesn't have to because it only really comes to the fore once she is dead.'[146] Though her natural inclination was to let things lie, her sense of duty dictated that at her death she should hand the monarchy to her son in a healthy state – and it would clearly be to the Crown's advantage if some order had been restored to Charles's private life by the time he became King.

Typically, it was not Elizabeth who took the lead but the Prince of Wales's own officials, who since Charles's divorce had been hard at work rehabilitating their master's – and Camilla's – image. They were greatly assisted by the careful use of the prince's two sons, William and Harry, in whom the spirit of Diana was popularly supposed to rest. A year after his mother's death, sixteen-year-old William issued a public statement that in effect asked the country to allow the rest of the Royal Family to live their lives in peace. 'Prince William and Prince Harry have been enormously comforted by the public sympathy and support they have been given,' read an official statement from St James's Palace, which ended 'they believe their mother would want people now to move on – because she would have known that constant reminders of her death can create nothing but pain to those she left behind'.

Later on, photo-opportunities that showed a relaxed Prince Charles laughing and playing around with his sons helped to restore some notion that the Windsors were capable of an intimate and happy family life. It was even leaked to journalists that William had met Camilla and got on very well with her: she often stayed with the Wales household when they were in the country, it was said, where the four of them would enjoy happy family breakfasts together.

For most of this period, Elizabeth had indicated her disapproval of her son's choice of partner in the time-honoured way of refusing to meet her. In June 2000, though, perhaps recognising that as long as Charles stuck loyally to Camilla she really had no choice in the matter, Elizabeth further eased the country's acceptance of their relationship by agreeing to meet Camilla for the first time since the 1970s. According to some opinion polls, by August 2001 – for the first time – a sizeable proportion of the public backed the idea of Charles marrying Camilla. There were even press reports that the Queen herself had come round to the idea and that after celebrating her Golden Jubilee in 2002 she would give her blessing to their marriage.

On nearly every other front, though, the Queen has stood her ground. In 1999, when Prince Edward married Sophie Rhys-Jones, the new Countess of Wessex (as Rhys-Jones became) insisted that she would continue her career in public relations. There would, she argued, be no conflict of interest between her business career and her royal duties and from the Palace's point of view it seemed like a good idea for younger members of the Royal Family to earn their keep rather than rely on hand-outs from the Government or Elizabeth herself. According to Mary Francis, she had the Queen's support. But three years later the countess was caught in a tabloid sting when she admitted to a journalist disguised as an Arab businessman that her royal connections were indeed useful to her. She was also quoted making indiscreet comments about her in-laws and politicians. In the scandal that followed the Palace began a review of the rules governing what members of the Royal Family were allowed to do.

Many people – including the Prince of Wales, according to some reports – hoped that the Queen would draw a clear line between her relatives' private lives and public duties and create a much smaller Royal Family. As long as people like Sophie Wessex had a foot in both worlds – working for a living yet also carrying out public engagements that were reported in the Court Circular, or allowing themselves to be associated with any one of the innumerable charities that were desperate to secure some sort of royal patronage – they would be fair game for the press and sooner or later something embarrassing would come to light that would reflect unfavourably on the monarchy. For those working in the media – like Prince Edward whose television company employees were later accused of ignoring restrictions on filming Prince William at university – there were particular pitfalls. Other relations of the Queen, like Princess Margaret's children, had managed to create a private life for themselves and stick to it: now, the reformers argued, Elizabeth should insist that everyone else should do the same, leaving a slimmed-down version of the Royal Family that would consist only of its most senior members.

It was an opportunity for change that the Queen ducked. According to Mary Francis, 'One of the lessons that's been learned is that the focus needs to be on the Head of State and her immediate family and that people are less tolerant of there being a large Royal Family taking part in public life.' But Elizabeth shows little sign of having really taken the lesson to heart. Backed forcefully by the Duke of Edinburgh, she refused to clamp down on Sophie and Edward's business interests, or to tell them to give up their royal duties. It was a decision that, once again, revealed the soft spot she has always had for her children but one that can only store up trouble for the future. 'It's incumbent on those round her to be more careful than anybody else,' points out Michael Oswald. 'The person who draws the flak is almost inevitably the Queen. And sometimes that is very unfair.' But the more people there are around her who are also official members of the Royal Family, the more flak there is likely to be.

It has been the paradox of Elizabeth's reign that she has granted such latitude to her family, while allowing herself so little freedom. In the summer of 2001 the Queen Mother celebrated her one hundred and first birthday. If Elizabeth lives as long, she will face another twenty-five years on the throne, but as she approaches her Golden Jubilee there is no question in her mind but that she will carry on with the job. 'Abdication,' says her cousin Constantine, 'is something that is not in theory part of the process of being a sovereign. If you go down that line you might as well then just have a republic.'

Her friend, Lady Penn, recalls, 'Once, when she hadn't been Queen for all that long and she'd been very seasick on *Britannia* she did say jokingly, "Oh, I do feel so ill I thought I must abdicate." It's the only time I've ever heard her use the word.' In *Elizabeth R*, a television documentary that celebrated her fortieth year on the throne, Elizabeth herself made her position clear. 'In a way,' she said, 'I didn't have an apprenticeship. My father died much too young and so it was all a very sudden kind of taking on and making the best job you can. It's a question of maturing into something that one's got used to doing and accepting the fact that here you are and it's your fate. Because I think continuity is very important. It is a job for life.'

As everyone who has observed Elizabeth agrees, duty and tradition have been the watchwords of her reign. But underlying her attachment to both is her ability unquestioningly to accept the hand that life has dealt her. 'She believes in fate all right,' says John Taylor, one of her longest-serving members of staff. That belief has been both her strength and her weakness. 'She was brought up,' says Lady Mountbatten, 'to feel that if you were going to be on show and if you were going to do your job properly vis-à-vis the public, that you mustn't let your emotions get the better of you. Not that you should never show your emotions at all, but that you mustn't be over the top. And I think this is the way she copes with everything, by just keeping calm and still and not letting it get to her.'

Three-quarters of a century ago, calm acceptance and the ability to master one's emotions were qualities that anyone might admire and strive to emulate. But they have lost much of their appeal in the dawn of a new millennium and the very qualities that enabled Elizabeth to carry out a task that had, by the late 1990s, become thankless make her today appear stuffy and out of touch. At the same time, while most people agree that the monarchy should provide stability and a constant back-drop against which the country's ever-changing life can be played out, the Queen's understated personal style and her fatalistic approach to any crisis have provided critics of the monarchy with ample ammuni-tion. It is unfair to claim that after fifty years of Elizabeth's reign the monarchy has not changed. Her life is also far from over, and in another twenty-five years it may be that the unhappy events of the 1990s will not stand out so jaggedly. As the new century begins, though, it has been both the Queen's gift and her ultimate weakness to make such claims appear the truth.

POSTSCRIPT

Shortly after this book was written the Queen suffered the double blow of the death of her sister and her mother in a period of less than seven weeks. Princess Margaret died on 9 February followed by the Queen Mother on 30 March 2002. That this should have happened in her jubilee year was an added misfortune, clouding what should have been a time of great celebration.

The public and media reaction to the deaths of Princess Margaret and Queen Elizabeth the Queen Mother brought into focus once more the nature of an ancient institution in a society that has changed out of all recognition since the Queen ascended the throne. At a time when deference to the royal family has greatly diminished, the obituaries of Princess Margaret did not veil the less attractive traits of her complex personality; and many of the reports and features about the Queen Mother pointed to the end of an era. Yet at the same time, the many thousands who queued for hours to pay their last respects in Westminster Hall and file past the royal catafalque were a sign of the abiding place that the monarchy retains in the British consciousness.

Elizabeth's loss of her mother may well moderate her innate conservatism, and lead to more fundamental reforms that many think necessary if the institution is to survive. It was the Queen Mother's steely will that helped save the rocking throne in 1936, but contributed to its ossification in the turbulent 80s and 90s. Now the calls for change will be less easy to ignore, and the Queen can benefit from the great public sympathy for her, and move forward confident that change will have the support of her family and her people.

BIBLIOGRAPHY

E.C. Acland, *The Princess Elizabeth*, The John C. Winston Co Ltd, 1937.

Walter Bagehot, *The English Constitution*, reprinted from the 'Fortnightly Review' Chapman and Hall, 1867.

Sarah Bradford, *Elizabeth*, William Heinemann, 1996.

Sarah Bradford, *George VI*, Fontana, 1991.

Piers Brendon and Phillip Whitehead, *The Windsors: A Dynasty Revealed 1917–2000*, Pimlico, 2000.

J. Bryan III and Charles J.V. Murphy, *The Windsor Story*, Granada, 1979.

Barbara Castle, *The Castle Diaries 1964–1970*, Weidenfeld and Nicolson, 1984.

Peter Chippindale and Chris Horrie, *Stick It Up Your Punter*, William Heinemann, 1990.

Tim Clayton and Phil Craig, *Diana: Story of a Princess*, Hodder and Stoughton, 2001.

J. Colville, *The Fringes of Power: 10 Downing Street Diaries 1939–1955*, Hodder and Stoughton, 1985.

Noel Coward Diaries, Ed. Graham Payn and Sheridan Morley, Weidenfeld and Nicolson, 1982.

Marion Crawford, *The Little Princesses*, Cassell, 1957.

Nicholas Davies, *Elizabeth: Behind Palace Doors*, Mainstream, 2000.

Nigel Dempster, *H.R.H. The Princess Margaret: A Life Unfulfilled*, Quartet Books, 1981.

Jonathan Dimbleby, *The Prince of Wales: A Biography*, Little Brown, 1994.

Frances Donaldson, *Edward VIII, The Road to Abdication*, Weidenfeld, 1974.

J. Ellis (ed), *Thatched with Gold: The Memoir of Mabel, Countess of Airlie*, Hutchinson, 1962.

Phillip Hall, Royal Fortune – *Tax, Money and the Monarchy*, Bloomsbury, 1992.

Patrick Jephson, *Shadows of a Princess*, HarperCollins, 2000.

Dermot Morrah, *To Be a King*, Hutchinson, 1968.

Andrew Morton, *Diana: Her True Story*, Michael O'Mara Books, 1993 & 1998.

Adam Nicolson, *Restoration*, Penguin, 1997.

Harold Nicolson Diaries, William Collins Sons and Co, 1968.

Ben Pimlott, *The Queen: A Biography of Elizabeth II*, HarperCollins, 1997.

J. Pope-Hennessy, *Queen Mary*, George Allen and Unwin, 1959.

Penny Junor, *Charles: Victim or Villain*, HarperCollins, 1999.

Anne Ring, *The Story of Princess Elizabeth and Princess Margaret*, John Murray, 1930.

Robert Rhodes James, *A Spirit Undaunted: The Political Role of George VI*, Little, Brown, 1998.

Kenneth Rose, *King George V*, Weidenfeld and Nicolson, 1983.

Ingrid Seward, *The Queen and Di*, HarperCollins, 2000.

Peter Townsend, *Time and Chance*, William Collins and Sons, 1978.

Christopher Warwick, *Princess Margaret*, Weidenfeld and Nicolson, 1983.

John W. Wheeler Bennett, *King George VI: His Life and Reign*, Macmillan, 1958.

Philip Ziegler, *Crown and People*, Collins, 1978.

Philip Ziegler, *King Edward VIII: The Official Biography*, HarperCollins, 1990.

The Tongs and the Bones, The Memoirs of Lord Harewood, Weidenfeld and Nicolson, 1981.

NOTES

Chapter One

[1] Ingrid Seward, *The Queen and Di*, p. 78.

[2] J. Pope-Hennessy, *Queen Mary*, p. 272.

[3] Anne Ring, *The Story of Princess Elizabeth and Princess Margaret*, p. 24.

[4] Kenneth Rose, *King George V*, p. 389.

[5] Harold Macmillan, in conversation with Harold Nicolson, *Harold Nicolson Diaries*, 2.7.1930.

[6] Ben Pimlott, *The Queen: A Biography of Elizabeth II*, pp. 31–2.

[7] J. Bryan III and Charles J.V. Murphy, *The Windsor Story*, p. 69.

[8] Stanley Baldwin, House of Commons, 10.12.1926.

[9] Dermot Morrah, *To Be a King*, pp. 28–32.

Chapter Two

[10] Nicolson, op. cit., p. 301.

[11] Sarah Bradford, *George VI*, p. 280.

[12] Pimlott, op. cit., p. 46.

[13] Private interview.

[14] Piers Brendon and Phillip Whitehead, *The Windsors: A Dynasty Revealed 1917–2000*, p. 122.

[15] Martin Charteris in an interview for *The Windsors* (Channel 4).

[16] Barbara Castle, *The Castle Diaries 1964–1970*, pp. 24–5.

[17] Pimlott, op. cit., p. 52.

[18] Pope-Hennessy, op. cit., p. 594.

[19] Ibid., p. 594.

[20] Pimlott, op. cit., p. 75, from *The Times*, 5.3.1945.

Chapter Three

[21] Interviewed by Graham Turner, *Daily Telegraph*, 21.5.2001.

[22] Ibid.

[23] Bradford, *George VI*, p. 557.

[24] Ibid., p. 556.

[25] Ibid., p. 517, reported in *The Cape Times*.

[26] Pimlott, op. cit., p. 133, cited J. Ellis (ed), *Thatched with Gold: The Memoir of Mabel, Countess of Airlie*, p. 307.

[27] Bradford, *George VI*, p. 559.

[28] Ibid.

[29] Sarah Bradford, *Elizabeth*, p. 151.

[30] Pope-Hennessy, op. cit., p. 616.

[31] Edwina Mountbatten, quoted in Bradford, *Elizabeth*, p. 162.

[32] Private interview.

[33] Ibid.

[34] Bradford, *George VI*, p. 607.

[35] Ben Pimlott, op. cit., p. 175.

[36] Bradford, *Elizabeth*, p. 165.

[37] *The Times*, 9.2.1952.

Chapter Four

[38] *Daily Mail*, 31.2.1952.

[39] Bradford, *Elizabeth*, p. 169.

[40] *Elizabeth R*, BBC documentary, 1992.

[41] Pope-Hennessy, op. cit., p. 619.

[42] Bradford, *Elizabeth*, p. 168.

[43] Private interview.

[44] Ibid.

[45] Interviewed by Graham Turner, *Daily Telegraph*, 21.5.2001.

[46] Pimlott, op. cit., p. 184.

[47] Ibid., p. 206.

[48] BBC Home & Overseas broadcast, 2.6.1953, quoted in *The Times*, 3.6.1953.

[49] *The Times*, 23.11.1953.

[50] Private interview.

Chapter Five

[51] Bradford, *Elizabeth*, p. 196.

[52] Pimlott, op. cit., p. 200.

[53] Ibid., p. 201.

[54] Pimlott, op. cit., p. 237.

[55] Ibid., p. 219.

[56] Private interview.

[57] Ibid.

[58] *Daily Mirror*, 21.7.1953.

[59] Private interview.

[60] Telegram from R.A. Butler to Macmillan, quoted in Pimlott, op. cit., p. 297.

[61] Private interview.

[62] *Daily Mail*, 5.8.1957.

[63] Ibid., 8.8. 1957.

[64] Private interview.

Chapter Six

[65] Private interview.

[66] Ibid.

[67] Ibid.

[68] Ibid.

[69] Jonathan Dimbleby, *The Prince of Wales: A Biography*, p. 36, from Queen Victoria, *Leaves from the Journal of our Life in the Highlands*.

[70] Ibid., p. 167.

[71] *Nicolson Diaries*, op. cit., 7.8.1959.

[72] Ibid., 29.12.1960.

[73] Pimlott, op. cit., p. 291.

[74] Philip Ziegler, *Crown and People*, p. 134.

[75] Bradford, *Elizabeth*, p. 353.

Chapter Seven

[76] Private interview.

[77] Philip Ziegler, *King Edward VIII: The Official Biography*, p. 27.

[78] *The Times*, 2.7.1969.

[79] Private interview.

[80] Dimbleby, op. cit., p. 149, from BBC/ITV interview, 26.6.1969.

[81] Ibid., p. 160.

[82] Ibid., p. 163, from Prince Charles's Diary, 1.7.1969.

[83] *The Times*, 2.7.1969.

[84] Pimlott, op. cit., p. 391, from *Noel Coward Diaries*, 27.7.1969.

[85] *The Guardian*, 12.6.2000.

[86] Quoted Paul Johnson, *History of the English Speaking Peoples*, p. 401.

[87] Ziegler, *Crown* and *People*, p. 159.

[88] *Face the Press* (Tyne Tees Television), 20.3.1968.

[89] Pimlott, op. cit., p. 393.

[90] Ziegler, *Crown and People*, p. 141.

[91] Ibid., p. 142.

[92] Private interview.

[93] Quoted in Bradford, *Elizabeth*, p. 288.

[94] Ibid., p. 291.

[95] Interview with Lord Stockton.

[96] Willie Hamilton, quoted in Bradford, *Elizabeth*, p. 407.

[97] Ibid., p. 404.

[98] Ibid., p. 407.

[99] Ibid., p. 405.

[100] *Sun*, 19.3.1976.

[101] *Daily Mail*, 18.3.1976.

Chapter Eight

[102] Ziegler, *Crown and People*, p. 166.

[103] Mass Observation quotations from Ziegler, *Crown and People*, pp. 165–6.

[104] Ibid., p. 169.

[105] Rose, op. cit., p. 396.

[106] Pimlott, op. cit., p. 447.

[107] Private interview.

[108] Ibid.

[109] Quoted in Ziegler, *Crown and People*, p. 183.

[110] Private interview.

[111] *The Times*, 13.8.1977.

[112] Ziegler, *Crown and People*, p. 184.

[113] Rose, op. cit., p. 156.

[114] Dimbleby, op. cit., p. 314.

[115] Ibid., p. 248.

[116] Ibid., p. 316.

[117] Patty Palmer-Tomkinson, quoted in Dimbleby, op. cit., p. 338.

Chapter Nine

[118] Pimlott, op. cit., p. 491.

[119] Ibid., p. 491.

[120] *Daily Mail*, 7.2.1952.

[121] The only exception today is Mozambique, which joined the Commonwealth in 1995: it had been a Portuguese colony until 1975.

[122] Pimlott, op. cit., p. 511.

[123] Peter Chippindale and Chris Horrie, *Stick It Up Your Punter*, p. 123.

[124] Private interview.

[125] Ibid.

[126] *Elizabeth R*, BBC documentary, 1992.

[127] Private interview.

[128] Seward, op. cit., p. 48.

[129] Ibid., p. 46.

[130] Ibid., p. 7.

[131] Private interview.

[132] Ibid.

[133] Andrew Morton, *Diana: Her True Story*, p. 136.

[134] Ibid., p. 128.

[135] Seward, op. cit., p. 199.

[136] Marshall Smith, interviewed by Adam Nicolson in *Restoration*, p. 12.

Chapter Ten

[137] Jonathan Dimbleby, op. cit., p. 189.

[138] Seward, op. cit., p. 232.

[139] Patrick Jephson, *Shadows of a Princess*, p. 365.

[140] Quoted in Seward, op. cit., p. 235.

[141] Ibid., p. 14.

[142] Ibid., p. 25.

[143] Private interview.

[144] Ibid.

[145] Quoted in Brendon and Whitehead, op. cit., p. 253.

[146] Private interview.

INDEX